AKBAR'S INDIA:
Art from the Mughal City of Victory

AKBAR'S INDIA:

Art from the Mughal City of Victory

BY MICHAEL BRAND AND GLENN D. LOWRY

The Asia Society Galleries
New York

Akbar's India: Art from the Mughal City of Victory is the catalogue of an exhibition organized by The Asia Society in celebration of the Festival of India 1985-86.

The Asia Society Galleries, New York
OCTOBER 10, 1985 – JANUARY 5, 1986

Harvard University Art Museums (Arthur M. Sackler Museum),
Cambridge, Massachusetts
JANUARY 24 – MARCH 16, 1986

Museum of Fine Arts, Houston
APRIL 19 – JUNE 15, 1986

This project is supported by grants from the André and Bella Meyer Foundation, The Andrew W. Mellon Foundation, The Robert Lehman Foundation Inc., the Friends of The Asia Society Galleries, the National Endowment for the Arts, and the National Endowment for the Humanities, Washington, D.C., federal agencies, with the participation of the Indo-U.S. Subcommission for Education and Culture and Air India.

FRONTISPIECE:
Akbar Presiding over Discussions in the Ibadatkhana,
detail *(Akbarnama, ca. 1604).*

Published by The Asia Society Galleries
Cloth edition distributed by Sotheby Publications,
ISBN: 0-87848-061-7 (TASG paper)
ISBN: 0-87848-062-5 (TASG cloth)
ISBN: 0 85667 312 9 (SP cloth)
Copyright © 1985 The Asia Society Galleries

Library of Congress Catalogue Card Number: 85-071961

Printed in Japan

CONTENTS

LENDERS TO THE EXHIBITION

The American Numismatic Society, New York
The Archdiocese of Agra, India
The Art Museum, Princeton University
The Chester Beatty Library and Gallery of Oriental Art, Dublin
Catherine and Ralph Benkaim
Edwin Binney, 3rd
The British Library, Department of Oriental Manuscripts and Printed Books, London
The British Museum, Department of Oriental Antiquities, London
The Brooklyn Museum, New York
The Chrysler Museum, Norfolk, Virginia
The Cleveland Museum
The Fitzwilliam Museum, Cambridge, England
Harvard University Art Museums, Cambridge, Massachusetts
Howard Hodgkin
Houghton Library, Harvard University, Cambridge, Massachusetts
India Office Library, London
Los Angeles County Museum of Art
McGill University Libraries, Department of Rare Books and Special Collections, Montreal
The Metropolitan Museum of Art, New York
Museum für Ostasiatische Kunst, Cologne
Museum of Art, Rhode Island School of Design, Providence
Museum of Fine Arts, Boston
National Gallery of Art, Washington, D.C.
Royal Asiatic Society, London
Prince Sadruddin Aga Khan Collection
The St. Louis Art Museum
A. Soudavar Collection
Staatsbibliothek Preussischer Kulturbesitz, West Berlin
Victoria and Albert Museum, London
The Virginia Museum of Fine Art, Richmond
Williams College Museum of Art, Williamstown, Massachusetts
Private Collections

FOREWORD

THIS YEAR marks the twenty-fifth anniversary of The Asia Society Galleries. Among the many roles that the Galleries has played over this quarter century, one of the most important has been the encouragement of scholarly study of Asian art. This role is particularly evident in the area of Mughal painting, beginning with the 1964 exhibition *The Art of Mughal India,* organized by Stuart Cary Welch of Harvard University. Thanks to the work of such scholars and their exhibitions, the study of Asian art has matured in America.

This exhibition is a very special one, not only because of the spectacular beauty of the artworks, which have been lent by very generous and cooperative individuals and institutions both in this country and abroad, but also because it marks a new generation of scholarship and a strong conceptual approach to the making of an exhibition.

Our curators, Michael Brand of the Rhode Island School of Design, and Glenn D. Lowry of the Freer Gallery of Art, have been intensely involved in the comprehensive re-examination of Mughal art. The five years of research that they devoted to this task led to this exhibition and to their recent publication, *Fatehpur-Sikri: A Sourcebook,* in addition to the organization of an international conference to take place during the period of the exhibition.

This exhibition and book focus on a specific moment and place in the history of Mughal art, the brief period when Akbar's capital was the city of Fatehpur-Sikri. The treasures that have been gathered from that time and setting can bring Akbar's world vividly to our imagination. Visitors to the impressive and majestic buildings of Fatehpur-Sikri, so well-preserved after four hundred years, must wonder what the city was like when Akbar ruled.

This exhibition provides a detailed view of that remarkable place and time. Looking at the images gathered here, we can realize just how spectacular that court must have appeared. From the text, we can learn how exciting it must have been for artists and their patrons.

This research has a broader significance, for it also documents how the intelligence and personality of a powerful individual can direct the development of art forms. This is a key motivation in the creation of art and deserves close attention. This text also reveals the spiritual and philosophical depth of these beautiful images and Akbar's comprehensive, almost mystical view of the world.

We are very grateful to Michael Brand and Glenn D. Lowry for their work and cooperation, and to Stuart Cary Welch for his efforts on behalf of the exhibition. I also want to acknowledge the dedication and skill of the Galleries' staff most intimately involved with the project, Osa Brown, who produced the book, and Jean Mihich, who coordinated the loans.

This exhibition and book have been made possible through a splendid combination of private and public support. We are deeply grateful to the André and Bella Meyer Foundation, The Andrew W. Mellon Foundation, The Robert Lehman Foundation, Inc., the Friends of The Asia Society Galleries, the Indo-U.S. Subcommission for Education and Culture and Air India. We are also indebted to the National Endowment for the Arts and the National Endowment for the Humanities, Washington, D.C., both of which provided major grants for this project.

ANDREW PEKARIK
Director, The Asia Society Galleries

ACKNOWLEDGMENTS

THIS EXHIBITION would not have been possible without the enthusiastic support of Stuart Cary Welch, whom we have long been fortunate to have as a teacher and a friend. His pioneering work in the field of Mughal art has been a constant source of inspiration for our own studies. We hope our work also reflects the generosity of Oleg Grabar and Milo Beach in sharing their insights on Islamic and Indian art with us. At The Asia Society, Andrew Pekarik provided us with endless support and encouragement, while Osa Brown, and her assistant Oonagh Church, worked with great dedication on the production of the catalogue, and Jean Mihich deftly handled the considerable logistic problems for a show composed entirely of borrowed objects. Peter Oldenburg's skillful design of the catalogue gave outward form to our research and we are grateful for his sensitive interpretation of the material. We will always be extremely grateful to Allen Wardwell, the former Director of The Asia Society Galleries, for his initial support of this project. Special thanks are due to Edward Egan for his constructive editing of our book, and to the Freer Gallery's Pat Bragdon for her initial help in preparing the manuscript. Our research in the United States, Europe, and India was generously supported by grants from the Friends of The Asia Society Galleries and the Indo-U.S. Subcommission on Education and Culture. We are also very grateful for the assistance of Air India, and we are especially indebted to Pallavi Shah of the New York office.

Ted Tanen, American Executive Director of the Subcommission, and Niranjan Desai, Minister for Culture at the Indian Embassy in Washington, were tireless in their efforts on our behalf. This year's nationwide Festival of India is a tribute to their dedication. On the Indian side of the Festival, we are deeply appreciative of the courtesies extended to us by Pupul Jayakar, S. K. Misra, Martand Singh, Vijay Singh, and Kapila Vatsyayan. Our research in India was aided by the Archaeological Survey of India, especially by M. S. Nagaraja Rao, M. D. Khare and M. C. Joshi in Delhi, and H. K. Narain in Agra. Father John Correia-Afonso of the Heras Institute in Bombay provided us with many invaluable suggestions, and Archbishop Cecil D'sa of Agra graciously permitted us to borrow an extremely rare Akbari document in the possession of his archdiocesan archives.

Without the private collectors (including a number who wish to remain anonymous), the curators and trustees of the institutions who so willingly lent works from their collections, this exhibition could never have attained its desired form. Their generosity is especially appreciated in the context of the increased demands and frequently conflicting schedules occasioned by the Festival of India. Indeed, it is not possible to mention each instance separately, but we are sure that all those named below realize how much we appreciate their individual acts of assistance and hospitality.

In this country, we are especially grateful to Michael Bates of The American Numismatic Society; Edwin Binney, 3rd; J. Carter Brown, National Gallery of Art; Stanislaw Czuma, The Cleveland Museum of Art; Joseph M. Dye, The Virginia Museum of Fine Arts; Carolyn Kane and Marie Lukens Swietokowski, The Metropolitan Museum of Art; Thomas Krens, Williams College Museum of Art; Thomas Lentz, Edward Maeder, and Catherine McLean, Los Angeles County Museum of Art; Steven Owyoung, The Saint Louis Art Museum; Amy Poster, The Brooklyn Museum; Abolala Soudavar; Woodman Taylor, Harvard University Art Museums; Jean-Michel Tuchscherer, Museum of Fine Arts, Boston. As ever, special thanks are due to Annemarie Schimmel, Wheeler Thackston and Ali Asani at Harvard University for their help in deciphering and interpreting frequently complex Persian historical sources. In Canada, we owe a debt of gratitude to Elizabeth Lewis of the McLennan Library, McGill University.

In Europe, we would like to thank Simon Digby, Royal Asiatic Society, London; H. O. Fiestel and Dieter George, Staatsbibliothek Preussischer Kulturbesitz, West Berlin; Roger Goepper and Ulrich Wiesner, Museum für Ostasiatische Kunst, Cologne; Howard Hodgkin; David James, The Chester Beatty Library, Dublin; Jeremiah P. Losty and Yasin Safadi, The British Library, London; Clare Miles and Pauline Rohatgi, India Office Library, London; Michael Rogers, The British Museum, London; Prince Sadruddin Aga Khan; David Scrase, The Fitzwilliam Museum, Cambridge University; and Robert Skelton, The Victoria and Albert Museum, London. Ziauddin A. Shakeb kindly translated the Akbari *farman* for us. As ever, Attilio Petruccioli of the Islamic Environmental Design Research Centre in Rome, was extremely generous in allowing us to publish his magnificent plans of Fatehpur-Sikri.

Finally, we would like to thank Susan, Nicholas, and Alexis Lowry for putting up with lost weekends and endless late night telephone calls up and down the East Coast as we struggled to complete our work.

MICHAEL BRAND
Rhode Island School of Design

GLENN D. LOWRY
Freer Gallery of Art

AKBAR'S INDIA:
Art from the Mughal City of Victory

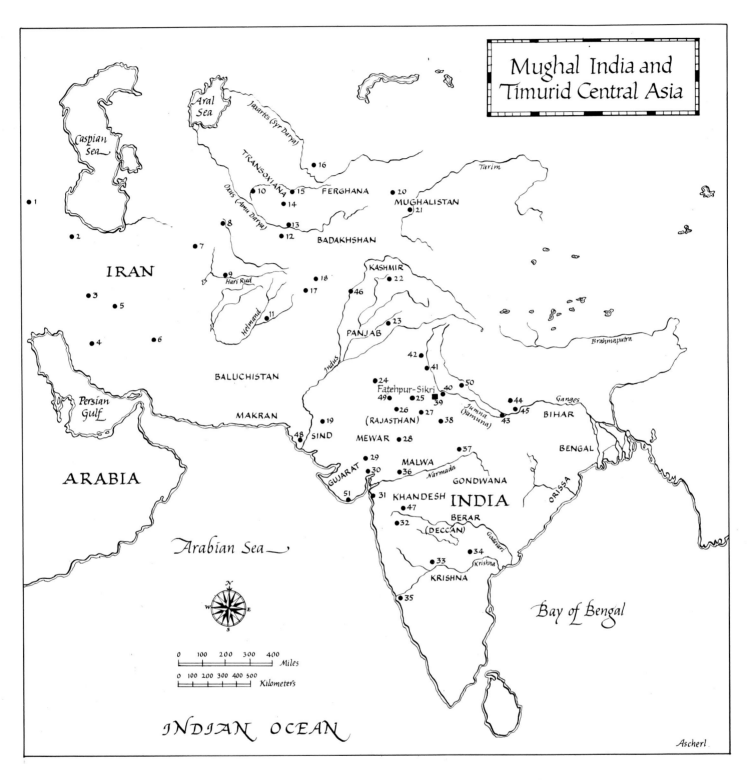

Mughal India and Timurid Central Asia

1 Tabriz	12 Balkh	22 Srinagar	32 Ahmadnagar	42 Panipat
2 Qazvin	13 Tirmiz	23 Lahore	33 Bijapur	43 Allahabad
3 Isfahan	14 Kesh/Shahr-i Sabz	24 Bikaner	34 Hyderabad	44 Jaunpur
5 Yazd	15 Samarqand	25 Amber (Jaipur)	35 Goa	45 Varanasi (Banaras)
6 Kirman	16 Tashkent	26 Ajmer	36 Mandu	46 Atak Banaras
7 Mashhad	17 Ghazni	27 Ranthambhor	37 Panna	47 Daulatabad
8 Marv	18 Kabul	28 Chittorgarh	38 Gwalior	48 Thatta
9 Herat	19 Umarkot	29 Ahmadabad	39 Fatehpur-Sikri	49 Nagaur
10 Bukhara	20 Kasghar	30 Cambay	40 Agra	50 Kanauj
11 Qandahar	21 Yarkhand	31 Surat	41 Delhi	51 Diu

INTRODUCTION

Although Fatehpur-Sikri, the Mughal City of Victory, served as Akbar's residence for only fourteen years – from 1571 until 1585 – it developed into one of the most extraordinary cities in all of India. Its red sandstone buildings with their bold façades and graceful lines were the setting for a court where the arts were as powerful and original as the politics were daring.

The aim of this exhibition and catalogue is to investigate Akbar's personality and the Mughal culture into which he was born by focusing on the critical years he spent at Fatehpur-Sikri. In doing so we have illustrated our ideas with paintings, textiles, manuscripts, woodwork, and metalware of the period. Throughout, our concern has been the relationship between the architectural and social environment created at Fatehpur-Sikri and the development of new artistic forms and images. Because of the rather broad nature of these we have not concerned ourselves with the attribution of paintings, or objects, to the hands of individual artists and only rarely have we ventured to suggest new dates for the material under consideration. It is only the extensive work of Stuart Cary Welch, Milo Cleveland Beach and Robert Skelton in these critical areas that has allowed us, however, the luxury of exploring an expanded range of cultural issues within a narrowly defined chronological framework.

While the exhibition and catalogue concentrate on Akbar's years at his new city, the objects we have selected are not limited to the 1570s and 1580s. Many of them have been chosen to show how themes initiated at Fatehpur-Sikri were interpreted and elaborated upon during the rest of the emperor's reign. In order to better understand the dynamics of these years we have tried to interpret the material according to the Mughals' own categories and terminology as found in contemporary Iranian and Mughal sources. This approach provides an exciting glimpse into the actual organization of artistic production at Fatehpur-Sikri and the intellectual criteria that guided the development of the visual arts under Akbar's patronage. The catalogue begins with a historical introduction to Akbar as a patron and statesman and then proceeds to a discussion of the topography and history of Fatehpur-Sikri, the formation and function of the emperor's library *(kitabkhana)*, both as a center of production and collection, and the imperial workshops *(karkhanas)*, and concludes with an analysis of Akbar's use of images.

Two key issues emerge from this examination of Akbar's response to his native Mughal culture and the new possibilities brought forth by the social and political experiments that were undertaken at Fatehpur-Sikri. The first is the emperor's great interest in his family's past. He traced his ancestry back to Chingiz Khan (Genghis Khan) as well as to Timur (Tamerlane) and was preoccupied with living up to the expectations of this dual legacy. The second is Akbar's adherence to traditional Islamic concepts of kingship despite his interest in Indian and European culture and religions. He was particularly concerned with the dichotomy between the realms of the physical or material world *(surat)* and the spiritual world of inner meaning *(manavi)* on both the practical and theoretical level. This polarity, we believe, provides the basis for understanding and approaching the emperor's character and his often grandiose ambitions. Just as Fatehpur-Sikri usurped to some degree the roles of both Agra (the old political capital) and Ajmer (the former spiritual center of the empire), Akbar sought to combine within himself political and spiritual authority.

It was at this new City of Victory that the emperor realized the full potential of focusing upon himself the sovereignty of the material and spiritual worlds. It was also there that Akbar sought to create a new artistic language of visual forms that would allow him to explore, and reveal, the finer distinctions of inner meaning. The exquisite illustrated manuscripts, bold carpets and dramatic objects created for Akbar are as dazzling to the eye as they are indicative of the emperor's struggle to define his – and ultimately the Mughals' – vision of the world.

CHAPTER I

AKBAR AND THE FORMATION OF MUGHAL ART

In 1571, Jalal ad-Din Akbar (r. 1556-1605), the third Mughal ruler of India, began the construction of Fatehpur-Sikri thirty-eight kilometers (twenty-four miles) to the west of Agra. When Akbar issued the order for work to commence at Fatehpur-Sikri, he was twenty-nine years old but had ruled the most important throne of northern India since the age of fourteen. By the time of his death in 1605, Akbar had extended his kingdom to include virtually all of the Indian subcontinent. The emperor's political and military feats, however, were matched by his patronage of the arts and his years at Fatehpur-Sikri were among the most productive in this respect. The buildings of Fatehpur-Sikri, and the various works of art that were created there between 1571 and 1585, reflect the emperor's vision of his world.

Akbar (whose name means "The Great") was a man of tremendous energy and power. According to Father Monserrate, a member of the Jesuit mission that resided at the Mughal court during the early 1580s, the emperor was,

…of good stature, sturdy body, arms and legs, broad-shouldered. The configuration of his face is ordinary, and does not reflect the grandeur and dignity of the person because, besides being Chinese-like as the Mughals usually are, it is lean, sparse of beard, wrinkled and not very fair. The eyes are small but extremely vivid and when he looks at you it seems as if they hurt you with their brightness, and thus nothing escapes his notice, be it a person or something trivial, and they also reveal sharpness of mind and keenness of intellect. And so he is very much feared by his subjects. To his people he displays a certain amount of cheerfulness which in no way detracts from his imperial bearing. He dresses plainly.[1]

Akbar inherited an empire in 1556 that was fragmented and unstable. Against incredible odds he expanded his territory and brought the Hindu and Muslim factions at his court into a strong and lasting union. Through a series of social and administrative reforms he also changed the very structure of Indian life. It is this combination of dynamism and political skill that makes Akbar such a fascinating figure.

The emperor was born on October 15, 1542 at Umarkot, a small desert town in western India (now Pakistan). At that time the Mughal empire existed in name only. Akbar's father, Nasir ad-Din Muhammad Humayun (r. 1530-1540; 1555-56), was in the process of fleeing India for the safety of Qazwin, the capital of Safavid Iran. Although intellectually gifted, Humayun was militarily inept. He was unable to consolidate the fragile kingdom left to him by his father, Zahir ad-Din Babur (r. 1526-30), the founder of the dynasty. By 1537, Gujarat on the western coast of India had become independent and Bengal on the opposite side of the subcontinent was in revolt. With brilliant tactics, Sher Shah Sur, a Muslim of Afghan descent, succeeded in defeating Humayun in a series of battles. Finally, in 1540, after a disastrous encounter at Kanauj, Sher Shah forced Humayun to abandon the imperial cities of Agra and Delhi for Lahore in the north. Several attempts at peace failed and Sher Shah continued to pursue Humayun, who retreated first down the Indus to Sind and then back to Rajasthan, in the hope of mustering new forces. When these never materialized, Humayun and his ever diminishing group of followers were compelled to seek asylum outside of India. Akbar was left behind with several servants in

A Carved Sandstone Column in the Palace Complex (Plan: 54)

the care of his uncle, while Humayun went to Iran in search of aid.

In Iran the emperor's fortunes began to improve. Shah Tahmasp, the Safavid ruler (r. 1524-76), greeted him warmly and eventually gave him an army of twelve thousand horsemen that enabled him to regain his kingdom. By 1545, Qandahar and Kabul had been taken and the emperor was reunited with his son. Ten years later, Humayun, aided by the rapid disintegration of the dynasty founded by Sher Shah, recovered India. His victory over Sher Shah's descendants, though, was short-lived. On January 20, 1556, the emperor slipped on the stairs of his library as he tried to bow his head in response to the muezzin's call to prayer. He suffered severe head injuries in the ensuing fall and four days later he was dead.

While it is easy to imagine the hardships that Humayun must have endured as he sought safety for his family and the alliances necessary to rebuild his forces, it is more difficult to gauge the impact these years had on Akbar. According to several of the emperor's biographers, Akbar spent a great deal of time at his father's side as the latter tried to expand his base of operations from Kabul. He also visited several major Central Asian cities such as Balkh and Ghazni, where he saw many of the great architectural monuments of the preceding centuries. Much of his time, though, was spent hunting and playing. A miniature in the *Akbarnama* (The History of Akbar) depicts the young prince wrestling with his slightly older cousin, Ibrahim Mirza, outside Kabul in 1545 (NO. 1). Akbar's surprising victory was seen as an omen of Humayun's rising fortunes.

At the age of four, Akbar began his formal education under the tutelage of Mulla Asam ad-Din Ibrahim and Mawlana Bayazid.[2] Although he never learned to read or write, Akbar developed a keen interest in classical Persian and Indian literature.[3] A painting by Abd as-Samad, an Iranian artist who joined Humayun's court in Kabul in 1549, depicts another aspect of the young prince's education: the development of an artistic awareness.[4] Akbar is shown presenting a miniature painting to his father. The emperor and his son are seated in an elaborate garden pavilion surrounded by servants and musicians. One senses immediately the refinement of Humayun's court and the pride the emperor would have felt in his son's developing awareness of the arts. For Humayun, despite the ardors of incessant campaigns, remained an extremely cultured man who was interested in literature and the arts as well as astrology and metaphysics, and who imparted all of these concerns to his young son. In his

love for literature Humayun resembled his father, who was not only a skilled poet but a man of great artistic sensibility and refinement and an accomplished writer, whose memoirs, known as the *Baburnama* (The History of Babur), are as entertaining as they are informative.

In art as well as in politics Babur, Humayun and Akbar saw themselves first and foremost as princes of the house of Timur (1336-1405), who conquered vast tracts of territory in Central Asia and even sacked Delhi in 1398. The Mughals, however, traced their ancestry even further back to the Mongol warrior Chingiz (Genghis) Khan (1167-1227). Upon the death of Chingiz Khan, his empire was divided among his four sons, a crucial event later illustrated by Akbar's artists (NO. 35). Mughalistan (including the western Tarim Basin and Kashgar) and Transoxiana were bestowed on his second son Chaghatay Khan (d. 1242). When these two wings of the dominion were split up late in the thirteenth century, Transoxiana in the west became the scene of mass conversion to Islam and a great deal of intermarriage with Turkic tribespeople before it eventually fell to Timur, a Barlas Turk. Though not a Mongol himself, Timur sought to enhance the legitimacy of his rule by assuming the mantle of the line of Chaghatay Khan, with whom he claimed kinship. He did this by adopting the title of *Gurkan* (son-in-law) in reference to his marriage to Tukul Khanum, whose father was directly related to Chaghatay Khan. Timur's descendants ruled Transoxiana until they succumbed to the forces of the Shaybanid Uzbeks in 1508-09.

The most revealing source of Akbar's ancestry is the official history of his reign written by his close companion, Abul Fazl. The opening chapters of the *Akbarnama,* though riddled with inconsistencies and exaggerated claims, delineate the emperor's family history as he wanted it to be seen. Abul Fazl traces Akbar's lineage back to the semi-mythical Mongol queen Alanquva (NO. 2) who, after having been widowed, "was reposing on her bed one night when a glorious light cast a ray into the tent and entered the mouth and throat of that fount of spiritual knowledge and glory. The cupola of chastity became pregnant by that light in the same way as did her Majesty...Miryam [the Virgin Mary]."[5] It was this divine light that is said to have initiated the line of rulers whose glory passed through Chingiz Khan and Timur to Akbar:

1. *The Infant Akbar Wrestling with Ibrahim Mirza (Akbarnama, ca. 1604.)*

That day (*viz*, of Alanquwa's conception) was the beginning of the manifestation of his Majesty, the king of kings [Akbar], who after passing through divers stages was revealed to the world from the holy womb of her Majesty Miryam-makani for the accomplishment of things visible and invisible.[6]

It is no coincidence that Alanquva also figures prominently in the genealogy of Timur given on the jade sarcophagus of his tomb in Samarqand, where he is claimed to be a descendent of Ali (and thus a Shiite Muslim). Describing Timur's last paternal ancestor, the inscription says: "And no father was known to this glorious (man), but his mother (was) Alanquva. It is said that her character was righteous and chaste, and that she was not an adultress. She conceived him through a light which came into her from an upper part of a door and assumed for her the likeness of a perfect man (Koran 19:17)."[7] Since the reference to the Koran concerning the story of the Virgin Mary suggests an early Christian influence on Timurid ideology,[8] an extra dimension is added to Akbar's fascination with Alanquva and the Virgin Mary, after whose name he devised titles for both his mother (Maryam Makani), and wife (Maryam az-Zamani).

Babur's father, Umar Shaykh, was the ruler of Ferghana, one of the petty Timurid courts of the Chaghatay Khanate in Transoxiana, while his mother, Qutlag Nigar Khanum, was the daughter of Yunus Khan, also a direct descendant of Chaghatay Khan. In these courts, Persian literature was patronized alongside work in the native Chaghatay Turkish, the language in which Babur wrote his memoirs. Chaghatay Turkish was, in fact, the mother tongue of Babur and Humayun as well as Akbar, but it was superseded during the second half of the sixteenth century in India by Persian.

Akbar was thus brought up at the very moment when Persian was replacing Chaghatay Turkish as the Mughals' preferred language. Nevertheless, Abul Fazl firmly states that because of the connection through Timur to Chaghatay Khan, Akbar's "noble line" came to be named "Chaghatay."[9] "Mughal" (a Persian variation of the word "Mongol") is therefore somewhat of a misnomer for Babur's dynasty, although the term was commonly used by the Mughals to distinguish themselves racially from other Muslims in India such as the Afghans. More importantly, Babur did not see himself as the founder of an entirely new dynasty in India. Instead he viewed himself as the prince who

2. *Alanquva and Her Three Sons* (Chingiznama, ca. 1596).

finally revived the Timurid cause and procured a throne for the illustrious and ancient ruling house that had lost power. He explained his position in a moving speech to the members of his council shortly before setting off to conquer India:

Strangers and ancient foes, such as Shaibaq [Shaybani] Khan and the Auzbegs, are in possession of all the countries once held by Timur Beg's descendants; even where Turks and Chaghatais survive in corners and border-lands, they have all joined the Auzbeg, willingly or with aversion; one remains, I myself, in Kabul, the foe mightily strong, I very weak, with no means of making terms, no strength to oppose; that, in the presence of such power and potency, we had to think of some place for ourselves and, at this crisis and in the crack of time there was, to put a wider space between us and the strong foeman; that choice lay between Badakhshan and Hindustan [India] and that decision must now be made.[10]

The importance of Babur for the revival of Timurid fortunes was even recognized by the great calligrapher Mir Ali, who honored him with the following verse:

My head is the dust of the door of the Lord of the kingdom of letters,
The pride of the kings of kingdoms, the honor of Timur's family
The sovereign of the virtuous, the sea of generosity, the mine of kindness,
The leader of the talents, Shah Muhammad Babur.[11]

For the Mughals, because of their family background, Timurid art and architecture represented the epitome of civilization and culture. Herat and Samarqand, Timur's capital, were particularly revered and both Babur and Humayun spent a great deal of time admiring the monuments that inspired their own buildings. Timurid objects, whether lavishly illustrated manuscripts or small jade vessels, were also greatly revered. Many of these objects found their way into the collections of Babur and Humayun, such as the copy of Firdausi's *Shahnama* (Book of Kings) made for Timur's grandson Muhammad Juki (ca. 1440). In addition to bearing the seals of all of the Mughal emperors through Aurangzeb (r. 1658-1707), this manuscript also has autograph inscriptions by Jahangir (r. 1605-27) and Shah Jahan (r. 1627-58), Akbar's son and grandson, suggesting that it was among the Mughal's most prized dynastic possessions (see below, p. 23 and fig. 10).

Akbar too saw himself as a Timurid. His response to his heritage, however, differed from that of Babur and Humayun. Unlike either of them, he was born in India and clearly thought of the subcontinent as his home (even while he was in exile in Kabul with his father).

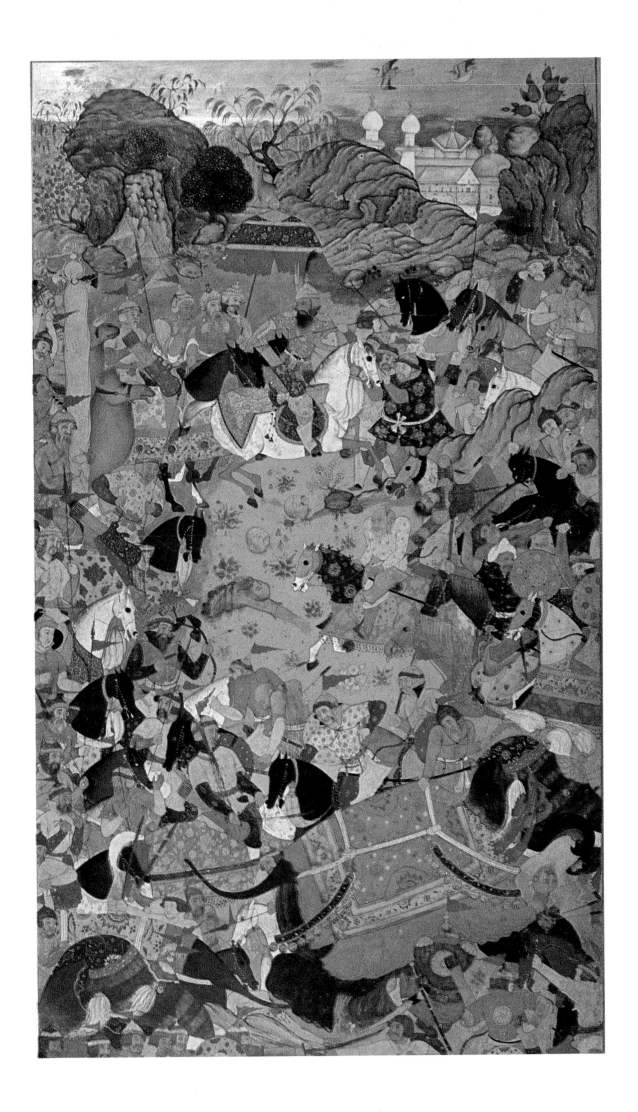

Where Babur found fault with everything from the climate and the people of Hindustan[12] to the poor quality of Indian mosques,[13] Akbar remained unbothered by these "defects." Indeed he admired them. This vital change in attitude is evident in the way Abul Fazl, who arrived at court in 1564, describes India and its inhabitants:

Shall I portray the beauty that charms the heart or sing of purity unstained? Shall I tell of heroic valour or weave romances of their vivacity of intellect and their lore? The inhabitants of this land are religious, affectionate, hospitable, genial and frank. They are fond of scientific pursuits, inclined to austerity of life, seekers after justice, contented, industrious, capable in affairs, loyal, truthful and constant...

The soil [of India] is for the most part arable and of such productive power that the same land is sown each year and in many places three harvests and more are taken in a single twelve-month and the vine bears fruit in its first year.[14]

Under Bayram Khan, who had been appointed Akbar's guardian by Humayun shortly before his death, the Mughal armies moved quickly to consolidate their power (NO. 3). Thus when Akbar succeeded his father to the throne in 1556, he did not see his nascent empire as inferior to Timurid Iran and Central Asia – as his ancestor had – but as equal to them. On November 5, 1556, Hemu, a Hindu who had seized Delhi from the Mughals, was defeated at Panipat, the site of Babur's victory over Sultan Ibrahim Lodi of Delhi thirty years earlier. After retaking Delhi, Akbar moved to the Panjab in order to subdue Sikandar Shah, one of the last of the Surs with any claim to power. In 1557, he too was defeated in battle. Shortly after that, Adil Shah, another rival, was killed fighting in Bengal. The result of this was that, within a year and a half of assuming power, Akbar had transformed his fragile inheritance into a relatively secure kingdom.

Bayram Khan played a crucial role in shaping these early victories. Nonetheless, Akbar began to distance himself from his guardian. By 1560 he no longer felt the need for Bayram Khan's services and dismissed him from his post as chief minister. Now fully independent, Akbar quickly demonstrated his abilities as a soldier by annexing Malwa (in central India) in 1561,[15] Gondwana (in eastern India) in 1564 and the Rajput centers of Chittorgarh and Ranthambhor (to the southwest of Delhi) in 1567-8 and 1569. The siege of Chittorgarh was a particularly savage affair. The fortress, located on top of a plateau protected by steep cliffs, was defended by Jaimal, a young Rajput warrior who easily resisted Akbar's initial advances. After

3. *Battle Scene (unidentified ms., ca. 1590).*

much debate, the emperor decided to mine the hill but some of the explosives were accidentally detonated and several hundred Mughals and Rajputs lost their lives in the subsequent disaster. In a miniature from the *Akbarnama* depicting this event, bodies fly skyward in an explosive burst suggesting both the intensity of the battle and the horrors of the fighting (NO. 4). When the fort finally succumbed to the Mughals, no mercy was shown to the defenders:

There were 8,000 fighting Rajputs collected in the fortress, but there were more than 40,000 peasants who took part in watching and serving. When the standards entered the fort some of the garrison squeezed themselves into the temples, thinking that they were holy places and that the idols would help them, and awaited the sacrificing of their lives. Others waited their doom in their own houses...

From early dawn till midday the bodies of those ill-starred men were consumed by the majesty of the great warrior. Nearly 30,000 men were killed.[16]

While such conquests secured the flanks of the empire and significantly enriched Akbar's treasuries, they were also a means of keeping the vast imperial armies occupied. The risks of an idle force – restlessness, disenchantment, even rebellion – were many. Akbar expressed his own thoughts on this subject bluntly: "A monarch should be ever intent on conquest, otherwise his neighbours rise in arms against him. The army should be exercised in warfare, lest from want of training they become self-indulgent."[17]

The strength of Akbar's empire, however, did not rest on his military achievements alone. In 1562 he married the daughter of the Raja of Amber, head of one of the most powerful Rajput clans. He gave her the name Maryam az-Zamani (Mary of the Age). The marriage at once sealed an important political alliance and brought the benefits of Rajput military skill, administrative abilities, and prestige to the Mughal court. Akbar's union with a Hindu princess also signaled his emerging policy of religious tolerance. Two years after his marriage to Maryam az-Zamani (who eventually provided Akbar with his first son and heir), Akbar revoked the *jizya,* a discriminatory poll tax imposed on those outside the Islamic faith. In doing so he incurred the enmity of orthodox Muslims at his court and laid the seeds of a rift between conservative and liberal Muslims that became an intrinsic part of the political climate of the Mughal empire. At the same time, though, the abolition of the *jizya* created a feeling of conciliation among the Hindus and encouraged Hindu artists, musicians and civil servants to enter the imperial service. In a paradoxical statement attributed to Akbar by Abul Fazl, the emperor clearly shows his willingness to regulate in favor of his Hindu subjects and even intentionally provoke his Muslim courtiers: "Formerly I persecuted men into conformity with faith and deemed it Islam. As I grew in knowledge, I was overwhelmed with shame. Not being a Muslim myself, it was unmeet to force others to become such. What constancy is to be expected from proselytes on compulsion?"[18]

Akbar's quest for religious understanding and interest in defining the range and limitations of his own personality led to the foundation of a House of Worship[19] in 1575 at Fatehpur-Sikri and a Declaration of Infallibility in 1579. Akbar so enjoyed exploring the kinds of religious, metaphysical, and philosophical issues that were examined at the House of Worship that he complained: "Discourses on philosophy have such a charm for me that they distract me from all else, and I forcibly restrain myself from listening to them, lest the necessary duties of the hour should be neglected."[20]

The *ulama* (a group of religous scholars often appointed to judiciary positions) was upset both by the Declaration of Infallibility, which gave the emperor the authority to decide religious as well as political questions, and by the unorthodox nature of the conversations that occurred at the House of Worship. Abd al-Qadir Badauni, another of Akbar's biographers and an orthodox Muslim, gives a sense of the *ulama*'s dismay at the emperor's usurping its rights, and his religious openness:

No sooner had His Majesty obtained this legal document, than the road of deciding any religious question was open; the superiority of the intellect of the Iman was established, and opposition was rendered impossible. All orders regarding things which our law allows or disallows were abolished, and the superiority of the intellect of the Iman became law. They called Islam a travesty.[21]

With the promulgation of the Declaration of Infallibility, Akbar gained full control over the temporal as well as the spiritual realms of his empire. Although the powers he now held were unprecedented, they were in keeping with the Timurid concepts of kingship that the emperor inherited from his father and grandfather. This involved a strong centrally controlled bureaucracy, a large army that served at the personal command of the emperor, powerful but subordinate provincial governments, and frequent intervention in religious affairs.[22] Under Timur, control of the *ulama* was accomplished through the *sadr,* a scholar appointed by the ruler to oversee land grants and gifts to the *ulama* and other religious groups.[23] Akbar's decision to transfer that power to himself, and thus centralize his authority over the *ulama,* can therefore be seen as an innovation to enhance his absolute control over all aspects of his domains. "A monarch," in Akbar's own words, "is a pre-eminent cause of good. Upon his conduct depends the efficiency of any course of action. His gratitude to his Lord, therefore, should be shown in just government and due recognition of merit; that of his people, in obedience and praise."[24] Akbar's reforms (many of which were based on ideas developed by Sher Shah and earlier Muslim rulers in India) were not limited to religious matters. Efforts were made to regulate gambling, ban child marriages, restrict prostitution to carefully controlled quarters and to do away with *sati* or the self-immolation of Hindu widows on their husbands' funeral pyres. Akbar's thoughts on *sati* are particularly revealing:

It is an ancient custom in Hindustan for a woman to burn herself however unwilling she may be, on her husband's death, and to give her priceless life with a cheerful countenance, conceiving it to be a means of her husband's salvation. It is a strange commentary on the magnanimity of men that they should seek their deliverance through the self-sacrifice of their wives.[25]

In addition to the various administrative, social, and political reforms of the 1560s and 1570s, Akbar also undertook a series of major architectural projects. Besides the creation of Fatehpur-Sikri, the three most important of these were the construction of Humayan's tomb at Delhi in 1562-63, the building of a fort at Agra in 1565, and the repairing and enlarging of the fort at Ajmer in 1570. Akbar's decision to build in Delhi, Agra and Ajmer—the three principal cities of the Mughal empire—was part of his overall attempt to construct his empire in stone as well as statute. Muhammad Arif Qandahari, another of the emperor's chroniclers, indicates the importance of architecture in establishing imperial power:

It will not be hidden from the mind of the perfect incomparable architects of blessed monuments and clever unequalled artisans of sweet works that a good name for kings is achieved [by means of] lofty buildings, just as they have said, "the builder is long-lived" ... In other words the name of kings lasts long on account of their works—From this ..., it is clear that the advantages of building cannot be expressed.[26]

The third volume of the *Akbarnama,* known as the *Ain-i Akbari* (The Institutes of Akbar), records in detail the emperor's regulations for governing his vast kingdom. There are chapters on such diverse topics as the arsenal and the imperial stables as well as the royal

4. *Akbar Attacking the Fortress at Chittorgarh* (Akbarnama, *ca. 1590).*

fruitery, building regulations, the imperial harem and the rules for mounting guard. Abul Fazl's enumeration of Akbar's institutions and administrative policies, though, is much more than just an account of courtly life. It is also a detailed description of civilization as it should be fostered by an ideal ruler.[27] Seen in conjunction with the first two volumes of the *Akbarnama,* which record past deeds as they "ought to have happened," the *Ain-i Akbari* provides us with a portrait of Akbar as both the ideal worldly king and symbol of God. Almost every action of the emperor's is invested with a divine quality, as can be seen in Abul Fazl's description of the emperor's taming of a wild elephant:

On the day that he halted at the stage of Karoha he calmly mounted the elephant Ran Sangar, whom experienced men would not approach on account of his being violently *mast* [aroused]. That riotous one submitted to the might of his majesty's fortune, and the spectators were filled with astonishment... but the farsighted and clear of heart rejoiced in accordance with their knowledge. Some learnt one of the thousand laudable qualities of H.M., and some emerged from the ravine of denial and entered the rose-garden of devotion. Wonderful acts were always oozing forth from that great man.[28]

Although this passage can be interpreted simply as standard praise for a bold king, it also suggests that in the eyes of his followers the emperor had superhuman qualities. That Akbar was graced by divine power is made clear in the *Ain-i Akbari* where Abul Fazl, in a deft reference to the radiance of Alanquva's divine impregnation, writes that:

Royalty is a light emanating from God, and a ray from the sun, the illuminator of the universe, the argument of the book of perfection, the receptacle of all virtues. Modern language calls this light *farr-i izidi* (the divine light) and the tongue of antiquity called it *kiyan khura* (the sublime halo). It is communicated by God to kings without the intermediate assistance of anyone, and men in the presence of it bend the forehead of praise towards the ground of submission.[29]

Akbar himself states that "The very sight of kings has been held to be a part of divine worship. They have been styled conventionally the shadow of God, and indeed to behold them is a means of calling to mind the Creator, and suggests the protection of the Almighty."[30] In order to demonstrate the emperor's unique spiritual powers, Abul Fazl presents him as the "perfect man" around whom the world revolves. The extent to which Akbar was thought to have divine powers can be seen in his teaching of disciples – an act usually reserved for holy men and spiritual guides:

At the above mentioned time of everlasing auspiciousness, the novice with his turban in his hands, puts his head on the feet of his majesty... His majesty the chosen one of God, then stretches out his hand of favour, raises the suppliant, and replaces the turban on his head, meaning by these symbolical actions that he has raised up a man of pure intention... who has now entered into real life.[31]

Fayzi, Abul Fazl's brother and one of Akbar's greatest poets, is even more explicit about the emperor's divinity. He states that, "If you wish to see the path of guidance as I have done, you will never see it without seeing the king." In an even bolder statement he writes "Thy old fashioned prostration is of no advantage to thee – see Akbar and you see God."[32]

By emphasizing Akbar's divinity, Abul Fazl and Fayzi articulate the emperor's attempts to focus upon himself all the forces of his empire. Badauni, who saw this happening, noted with some disdain that:

In this year [1579] the Emperor was anxious to unite in his person the spiritual as well as the secular headships, for he held it to be an insufferable burden to be subordinate to anyone, as he had heard that the Prophet (God be gracious to him, and give him peace!) and his lawful successors, and some of the most powerful kings, as Amir Timur Cahibqiran and Mirza Ulugh Beg-i-Gurgan, and several others had themselves read the *khutba* [the Friday sermon], he resolved to do the same, apparently in order to imitate their example.[33]

While it is difficult to know the degree to which Akbar was truly perceived as divine by all of his followers, the attention given this question by his principal biographers indicates that it was a major issue at his court. Moreover, by even raising the question of the emperor's sanctity, Abul Fazl (and by extension Akbar himself) makes an extremely important political point. He suggests that Akbar, and Akbar alone, is the rightful ruler of India, for only he possesses unique spiritual powers. In so doing he immediately distinguishes the emperor from all possible rivals and places him above any worldly scrutiny.

Metaphysics and philosophy were not abstract questions at Akbar's court, but very real pursuits that were examined and discussed in detail. The emperor seems to have been particularly interested in the relationship between inward and outward form or, more precisely, between the spiritual and material worlds. Given Akbar's vision of himself as the bridge between these two realms – he is even called in the *Akbarnama* "Lord of the world, depicter of the external, revealer of the internal,"[34] – this is not surprising. The manifestation of form posed a critical question for the emperor and he was preoccupied with trying to understand the role of the imagination in apprehending "that which is without form." It is because of this fascination with the meaning of form that Akbar was so devoted to painting. The making of images represented for him a way of exploring both the external or physical qualities of an object and its inner or hidden meaning.

Akbar's interest in painting can be traced back to his youth. A portrait by Abd as-Samad dated 1551 (when the prince was nine years old) depicts him seated in a garden in the act of painting.[35] To his right a musician plays a stringed instrument. It is tempting to think that the miniature discussed earlier of "Akbar Presenting a Painting to His Father," and which comes from the same album as this portrait, is its complement and represents the prince offering this work to the emperor. An incident recorded in the *Akbarnama* that occurred in 1555-6, shortly after the Mughals' return to India, further describes Akbar's artistic abilities:

> The skillful artists such as Mir Sayyid Ali and Khwaja Abdul-Samad Shirinqalam, who were among the matchless ones in this art, were in his service [Akbar's] and were instructing him. One day this cyclopedia of Divine things was in the library of H. M. Jahanbani [Humayun] and in order to sharpen his mind was employing himself in drawing. He drew with inspired pencil the figure of a man with all his limbs separated...[36]

Both Mir Sayyid Ali and Abd as-Samad were among the Iranian artists who entered Akbar's service upon Humayun's death. They had been recruited by Humayun during his brief stay at Shah Tahmasp's court and had resided in Kabul prior to coming to India with the emperor. At least four other Iranian artists also worked for Humayun: Dust Muhammad, Mawlana Darvish Muhammad, Mawlana Yusuf, and Mir Musavvir (Mir Sayyid Ali's father).[37] Humayun, however, had established an atelier of painters even before he acquired the talents of these artists. Jawhar Aftabchi records that shortly before Akbar's birth in 1542, while Humayun was in the process of fleeing India:

> The king undressed, and ordered his clothes to be washed, and in the meanwhile he wore his dressing gown; while thus sitting, a beautiful bird flew into the tent, the doors of which were immediately closed, and the bird caught; His Majesty then took a pair of scissors and cut some of the feathers off of the animal; he then sent for a painter, and had a picture taken of the bird, and afterwards ordered it to be released.[38]

Unfortunately no paintings survive from this period, nor do we know if Humayun's father had time to establish a workshop in India prior to his death in 1530. Babur, however, did collect books, many of which were profusely illustrated, such as the Muhammad Juki *Shahnama* (fig. 10) and the 1467-68 *Zafarnama* (NO. 57).[39] The paintings in both of these manuscripts with their fine lines, keen characterizations and exquisite colors, are of extraordinary quality and represent the finest achievements of Timurid Iran. The balanced compositions, minute details and subtle palette of these miniatures contrast sharply with contemporary Indian paintings which rely, for their effect, on simple, compartmentalized scenes, large flat areas of strong color, and a small repertoire of stylized figures.

The Iranian masters who came to India brought with them the ideals of Shah Tahmasp's court where most of them had been trained. There exists, fortunately, a large enough body of material – either signed and dated or attributable to the 1550s – to give us a good idea about what painting was like under Humayun. Among the most important of these works of art are:

"A Young Musician and Painter in a Garden," from the Gulshan Album, by Abd as-Samad, dated 1551.[40]
"Akbar Presenting a Miniature to his Father," from the Gulshan Album, by Abd as-Samad, ca 1550-55.[41]
"A Youth and a Musician," (NO. 5) ca. 1550-1555.
"A Young Scribe," (NO. 6) by Mir Sayyid Ali, ca. 1550-55.
"The Court of Humayun," attributable to Dust Muhammad, ca. 1550-1555.[42]
"Two Figures," now in the Fitzwilliam Museum, Cambridge, ca. 1550-1555.[43]
"A Prince Hunting," (NO. 7), now in the Fitzwilliam Museum, Cambridge, ca. 1555-60.
"A Feast in a Garden Pavilion," (also known as the "House of Timur"), ca. 1550-1555.[44]
"A *Khamsa* of Nizami," now in the Lalbhai collection, ca. 1550-1555.[45]
"Shah Abu al-Maali", (NO. 81)[46] by Dust Muhammad, ca. 1556-60.
"A Horse and Groom," from the Gulshan Album by Abd as-Samad, dated 1557.[47]

These miniatures share, for the most part, many characteristics. They are all executed in a manner closely resembling mid-sixteenth-century Persian painting, their colors tend to be bright and bold, though the quality of the pigments is often poor, and many of the figures wear an elaborate, high-peaked turban generally associated with Humayun. The miniature of "A Youth and a Musician" (NO. 5), is typical of these paintings. Its attenuated bodies, long necks, minuscule hands and narrow almond-shaped eyes are almost identical to the work of such Safavid artists as Mirza Ali. Indeed, except for the painting's thin, sketchy pigments and the carefully observed interaction between the figures, it could be mistaken for a product of Shah Tahmasp's court.

The two most important artists to join Humayun's court were Mir Sayyid Ali and Abd as-Samad. In 1552, in a letter to Rashid Khan, the ruler of Kashgar, that accompanied a gift of assorted works of art, Humayun describes their brilliance:

From among those matchless artists who had presented themselves before me in Iraq and Khurasan and were generously rewarded, a group came and joined my service in Shawwal A. H. 959 [September-October 1552]. One of them is the painter Mir Sayyid Ali, the *nadir al-Asr,* who is matchless in painting (*taswir*). He has painted on a grain of rice a polo scene—two horsemen stand within the field, a third comes galloping from one corner, while a fourth horseman stands at one end receiving a mallet from a footman; at each end of the field are two goal posts...

Another is the painter Maulana Abd al-Samad, the unique one of the time (*farid al-dahr*), the *shirin-qalam,* who has surpassed his contemporaries. He has made on a grain of rice a large field on which a group is playing polo.[48]

Although both artists were obviously extremely talented and technically accomplished, Mir Sayyid Ali was the more innovative of the two. His title, "Rarity of the Realm," reflects Humayun's interest in his work. In such paintings as "Nomadic Encampment" from a *Khamsa* of Nizami made for Shah Tahmasp between 1539 and 1543, one can immediately see what attracted the emperor to Mir Sayyid Ali's paintings.[49] Each figure is rendered with extraordinary accuracy. Textiles, trees, cooking utensils, and animals are scrutinized for their every form and texture. The precision with which Mir Sayyid Ali depicts each object in his paintings shows the same kind of concern for nature expressed by Humayun in his examination of the bird that flew into his tent.

"A Young Scribe" (NO. 6), painted sometime between Mir Sayyid Ali's arrival in Kabul in 1549[50] and Humayun's death in 1556, elaborates on the themes of the paintings from the *Khamsa* of Nizami. Seated on a boldly patterned carpet, the scribe leans forward contemplating his work. A finely detailed bookstand rests to his left and several sheets of paper and an inkpot and pen lie on the ground to his right. The careful study of the scribe's face and gestures—the tilt of his head and the twist of his hands, for instance, and the sensitive drawing of the wildflowers that surround his carpet—suggest that this is a portrait of a very real person possibly done from life. Only the gold of the sky and the slightly skewed perspective of the bookstand are at variance with the naturalism of the scene.

Mir Sayyid Ali's work, despite its heightened sense of observation and interest in nature, still operates within the established norms of Safavid painting. His miniatures share the same vocabulary of forms and handling of space as the more conservative paintings of the other Iranian artists who worked for Humayun. The lack of depth in the miniature of the "Young Scribe" as well as the figure's shadowless (and consequently volumeless) body are identical to the shallow space and almost weightless figures of Abd as-Samad's "Akbar Presenting a Miniature to His Father" or Dust Muhammad's "Court of Humayun."

A noticeable shift away from the standard conventions and interests of sixteenth-century Persian painting can, however, be detected in some of the works painted for Humayun. In "A Feast in a Garden Pavilion" or in several of the miniatures in the Lalbhai *Khamsa* of Nizami, there is an emphasis on the naturalism of the setting and the interaction of the

5. *A Youth and a Musician (ca. 1550-60).*

24

6. *A Young Scribe (ca. 1550).*

figures that differs markedly from the more stylized compositions of Safavid Iran. Moreover the diversity of the Lalbhai manuscript's illustrations – some are done in a Persian manner resembling Bukharan work of the 1520-50s, others are executed in the imperial tradition of Shah Tahmasp's court, and a last group are clearly painted in the provincial manner of several of the Islamic courts of India[51] – reflect a lack of visual unity that is antithetical to Persian ideals and anticipates the eclectic nature of the *Tutinama* (Tales of a Parrot), one of the first manuscripts illustrated for Akbar.

The most remarkable of these early paintings is the Fitzwilliam's "A Prince Hunting" (NO. 7). It almost certainly depicts the young Akbar and is thus one of only three portraits that we have of the prince prior to his assumption of power. However, unlike the other two portraits discussed earlier (both of which are by Abd as-Samad), this one may depict a historical event of 1555 that was later recorded in the *Akbarnama*:

> On this day and while on the march His Majesty the Shahinshah struck a *nilagao* [an antelope]...with his sword and took it as a prey so that the huntsmen were surprised, while the acute obtained a sign of his capturing the booty of sublime intention and were made glad.[52]

Many aspects of "A Prince Hunting" are awkward, such as the way Akbar rides his horse, and the thickness of the paint; however, the artist has made a real effort to create a plausible landscape and to infuse the prince with a sense of vitality and action. The extent to which the artist has altered his palette, articulated Akbar's limbs, and emphasized the fullness of the rocks behind him distinguishes this painting immediately from similar Persian miniatures.

It is against the conventions and background of "A Prince Hunting" and the work of artists like Mir Sayyid Ali and Abd as-Samad, that Akbar's impact on Indian art must be seen. During his reign the artistic tendencies that first evolved under Humayun coalesced into a coherent, consistent, and dynamic mode of representation. Four manuscripts made within a decade of Akbar's ascension to power show how radically painting under Akbar departed from earlier norms. These are the *Tutinama*, ca. 1560-65; the *Hamzanama*, ca. 1562-1577; the *Tilasm and Zodiac*, ca. 1565; and the *Ashiqa* of Amir Khusrau Dihlavi of 1567-68 (also known as the *Duval Rani Khizr Khan*), the earliest dated Mughal manuscript, made within a decade of Akbar's accession to power.

The *Tutinama* (NOS. 8, 9, 10) is to a large extent a summation of pre-Akbari Indian painting. At least four different kinds of miniatures can be observed in the manuscript: those based on what can be called the Caurapancasika and the Candayana styles (both derived from fifteenth-century western Indian painting), those related to various fifteenth- and sixteenth-century Islamic schools of Indian painting, and those in an altogether new idiom. Two aspects of this manuscript are especially fascinating. The first is the fact that so many different traditions are mixed together. While the varied nature of the Lalbhai *Khamsa* of Nizami provides a formal precedent for this, the *Tutinama* differs from that manuscript in that Islamic as well as Hindu traditions are represented. One senses immediately in this mingling of forms the diversity of the artists – both Hindu and Muslim – who were at Akbar's court. The second aspect is that in several instances the integrity of the individual artists' traditions has been violated so that it is difficult to determine in which tradition they had originally been

8. *The Parrot Mother Cautions Her Young (*Tutinama, ca. 1560-65)*.

7. *A Prince Hunting (ca. 1550-55)*.

جامہ شیر کر پیوند خر   اوهمان خربود زد شیر غزین

9. *A Donkey in a Tiger's Skin* (Tutinama, *ca. 1560-65*).

trained. One can see, in the flat colors of some backgrounds and in the profiles of some faces, suggestions of western Indian painting, while in the articulation of other areas there is a more naturalistic and expressive quality that reflects an attempt to come to grips with the new standards of Mughal painting.

In the most exciting of the *Tutinama's* miniatures, such as "The Parrot Mother Cautions Her Young" (NO. 8), "A Donkey in a Tiger's Skin" (NO. 9), and "A Storm at Sea" (NO. 10), there is a completely new manner of representation that is distinct from both its Indian and Persian sources. The main features of this novel style are its full-bodied figures, well developed three-dimensional landscape, carefully observed trees and vegetation, bold and thickly applied colors, and highly animated forms that are charged with an intensity of action that is almost electric.

The most startling aspect of these paintings is the way in which figures and personalities come alive. Each person in "A Storm at Sea," for example, is a

study in terror. Eyes bulge and mouths gape as passengers grab desperately for one another. The artist's treatment of the figures as individuals (as opposed to standard types) and his emphasis on their relationship to each other (through their gestures as well as facial expressions) heighten the drama of the scene.

What makes these images so exciting is not their inherent action but the fact that the artists have infused them with a sense of drama. The degree to which these paintings depart from their Indian and Persian antecedents is evident when one compares the turbulent waves of "A Storm at Sea" with the staid and stylized forms of such Iranian paintings as those in the *Shahnama* (fig. 10). Despite the success of several of the *Tutinama's* miniatures, it is nevertheless a somewhat awkward manuscript. The various manners of representation that coexist are often incompatible and prevent the manuscript from appearing visually coherent. Also, even the finest paintings in the manuscript have a rough quality to them that suggests that Akbar was less interested in their finish than he was in their attempt to articulate his ideas about art.

The two paintings of the *Ashiqa* of Amir Khusrau and the numerous illustrations in the *Tilasm and Zodiac* manuscript (fig. 1) are far more unified than those in the *Tutinama*. While they share the same basic

FIG. 1. "Plowing Ox Brought for Drinking Water," detail from *Tilasm and Zodiac*, ca. 1565-70: Raza Library, Rampur, India (Acc. No. 1352, f. 8b).

approach to painting found in the most experimental works of the *Tutinama,* their compositions are generally more complex and sophisticated. "A Prince Enthroned" from the *Ashiqa,* for instance, is made up of a series of interrelated events in both the foreground and background, as opposed to the paintings of the *Tutinama,* which invariably focus on a single event and plane of action. What distinctions do exist in the miniatures of the *Ashiqa* and *Tilasm and Zodiac* are due more to the skill and personality of the individual artists than to their original training.

The speed at which the innovations of the *Tutinama* were assimilated into a well developed manner of representation is remarkable, for less than a decade separates it from the *Tilasm and Zodiac* and the *Ashiqa* of Amir Khusrau of 1567-1568. The rapidity of this transformation is a direct product of Akbar's dynamism and ability to move quickly on a number of fronts – military, political and artistic, among others. The excitement about the arts that must have permeated Akbar's court can be sensed in one of the most famous passages of the *Ain-i-Akbari:*

> Drawing the likeness (*sabih*) of anything is called *taswir* (painting, pictorializing). Since it is an excellent source, both of study and entertainment, His Majesty, from the time he came to an awareness of things (i.e. his childhood), has taken a deep interest in painting and sought its spread and development. Consequently this magical art has gained in beauty. A very large number of painters has been set to work. Each week the several *darogahs* and *bitikchis* submit before the king the work done by each artist, and His Majesty gives a reward and increases the monthly salaries according to the excellence displayed.[53]

Akbar's involvement with the production of paintings, as Abul Fazl clearly indicates, was intense and personal. By reviewing the work of the various artists in the *kitabkhana* (the imperial library discussed at length in Chapter III) on a regular basis and by promoting those artists who responded to his ideas, the emperor was able to directly influence both the formation and development of a Mughal idiom.

Akbar's impact on Mughal painting was not limited to his "control" of the various artists who worked for him but extended to his selection of manuscripts to be illustrated. Thus in choosing the *Tutinama, Ashiqa* of Amir Khusrau, *Tilasm and Zodiac* and *Hamzanama* as some of the first works to be illustrated by his artists, Akbar made an extremely pointed decision, for at least three of these manuscripts have specifically Indian connections. The *Tutinama* is a loose Persian translation of a Sanskrit classic, the *Ashiqa* of Amir Khusrau was written by one of India's greatest Muslim poets, and the recension used for the *Hamzanama* was

freshly composed at the Mughal court.[54] At the same time none of the four manuscripts (including the *Tilasm and Zodiac*) had lengthy traditions of illustration. The implications of this are twofold. On the one hand, Akbar affirmed his interest in Indian culture – both Hindu and Islamic – and the richness of Indian history. On the other hand, by choosing manuscripts for which there was no clearly established tradition of illustration the emperor freed his artists from the rigid iconographic conventions connected with such standard works as the *Khamsa* of Nizami. In doing so he allowed his artists to experiment with new manners of representation without being hindered by models that imposed predetermined responses.

Of all of these manuscripts, the *Hamzanama* (The Story of Hamza) is undoubtedly the most extraordinary (NOS. 11, 12). It originally consisted of fourteen volumes, each having one hundred large illustrations (approximately 67 by 51 cms., 27 by 20.5 in.) on cloth, of which only about a tenth have survived. According to Badauni, it took fifteen years to complete the manuscript,[55] and recent scholarship has shown that its production probably lasted from 1562 to 1577.[56] By 1564 enough of the manuscript's text existed that Akbar could be entertained by its recitation:

> When the world warming sun had sate on the throne of the horizons, H. M. the Shahinshah with the desired prey in his net and the cup of success at his lip sate on that auspicious throne and graciously ordered his courtiers to be seated. Then for the sake of delight and pleasure he listened for some time to Darbar Khan's recital of the story of Amir Hamza.[57]

Mir Sayyid Ali was in charge of organizing the illustration of the manuscript until his departure in 1572 for Mecca, after which Abd as-Samad took over its supervision. Mir Ala ad-Dawla, who was at Akbar's court during the 1560s, has left us with a vivid account of the making of the *Hamzanama:*

> It is now seven years that the Mir [Sayyid Ali] has been busy in the royal bureau of books (*kitab khana-i ali*), as commanded by His Majesty (*hazrat-i ala*), in the decoration and painting of the large compositions (*taswir-i majalis*), of the story of Amir Hamza (*qissa-i amir hamza*), and strives to finish that wondrous book which is one of the astonishing novelties that His Majesty has conceived of... The amazing descriptions and the strange events of that story are being drawn on the sheets for illustrations in minuscule detail and not the subtlest requirement of the art of painting goes unfulfilled... Opposite each illustration, the events and incidents relative to it, put into contemporary language, have

11. *Amr and a Fallen Stranger outside the Castle of Fulad* (*Hamzanama, ca. 1562-77*).

been written down in a delightful style. The composition of these tales, which are full of delight and whet your fancy, is being accomplished by Khwaja Ataullah, the master prose stylist (*munshi*) from Qazwin.[58]

While the *Hamzanama*'s paintings share many formal features with those of the *Tutinama* and the *Ashiqa* of Amir Khusrau, they differ in several important ways. In the first place, because of their large size and dramatic subject matter – the adventurous and often wild tales of Hamza, the Prophet Muhammad's uncle – they are for the most part far more daring and innovative. In the second place, many of the *Hamzanama*'s images, particularly those that have been preserved in Volumes X and XI (when the manuscript was under Abd as-Samad's direction), are more refined: lines are crisper and cleaner, pigments finer, and details are rendered with greater precision. The boldly modelled figures in "Muzmahil Treating the Sorcerers" (NO. 12), with their expressive gestures and lively faces, are typical of the manuscript's best miniatures.

Through their immediate impact and engaging stories, the *Hamzanama*'s paintings are meant to be both visually arresting and self-explanatory. They reflect an attempt to establish an imagery that can be quickly perceived and understood without having to be explained by elaborate textual references. The dynamic action of these miniatures provide an almost exact visual metaphor for Akbar's tremendous energy during the years when he was defining the scope of his empire.[59] The directness of the *Hamzanama*'s stories reflects the emperor's youthful enthusiasm and it is easy to see why he would have liked them. To the more sophisticated and traditional tastes of someone like Babur, these stories were not only repugnant but "one long, far-fetched lie, opposed to sense and nature."[60]

In many ways these paintings represent the culmination of the experiments begun in the *Tutinama*. The conventions established in the earlier manuscript have become the norm and are used consistently and with ease. They represent a new visual language. To a large extent the formal history of Mughal painting for the remainder of the sixteenth century and throughout the seventeenth century can be seen as an exploration of the elasticity and range of this idiom as artists sought to express in ever more subtle ways the ideas and interests of their imperial patrons.

The *Hamzanama* also represents a crucial turning point in the history of Akbar's reign. It was begun at a time when the empire was fragile. When the manuscript was completed fifteen years later, Akbar's lands were politically as well as militarily secure and the capital had been moved to Fatehpur-Sikri. The move to the new capital occured almost exactly in the middle of the making of the *Hamzanama*. Thus both in its subject matter and mode of presentation the *Hamzanama* straddles the moment when the directions of the first years of Akbar's rule gave way to the innovations and developments of his years at Fatehpur-Sikri.

12. *Muzmahil Treating the Sorcerers* (Hamzanama, ca. 1562-77).

CHAPTER II

FATEHPUR-SIKRI: AKBAR'S CITY OF VICTORY

*In an auspicious moment the unique pearl
of the caliphate emerged from the shell
of the womb, and arrived at the shore
of existence in the city of Fathpur.* [1]

ON AUGUST 30, 1569 Akbar's longest standing wish was fulfilled when Prince Muhammad Salim Mirza was born at the residence of an elderly Sufi mystic outside a little town named Sikri that nestled beneath a sandstone ridge not far from Agra. Several children, including twin sons, had previously been born to Akbar, but all had soon succumbed to illness and thus in 1569 Akbar still lacked a male heir to whom he could eventually pass on his ever expanding Indian kingdom. It was the arrival of Prince Salim that sparked in Akbar the desire "to give outward splendour to this spot which possessed spiritual grandeur," [2] a desire that led to the transformation of the barren ridge above Sikri into a spectacular new city overlooking the cooling vista of what was then a broad and expansive lake.

As concern mounted over the sad fate of the emperor's first children, a number of courtiers suggested that Akbar seek the blessings of Shaykh Salim ad-Din Chishti (1479-1572) in Sikri. Little persuasion was needed before Akbar set off to visit this Shaykh, who belonged to the esteemed Chishti order that had been established in India at the end of the twelfth century by Khwaja Muin ad-Din Chishti (d. 1236). In 1562, Akbar began a number of pilgrimages to the grave of Khwaja Muin ad-Din at Ajmer in Rajasthan (NO. 13 and NO. 32) and was thus well acquainted with the teachings of this relatively orthodox order that had originally shunned close ties with worldly rulers. Shaykh Salim, however, graciously received Akbar and, in addition, foretold that he would be blessed

with three sons. Thus when Maryam az-Zamani became pregnant in 1569, she was conveyed to the Shaykh's monastery [3] in Sikri and it was there that she gave birth to Prince Salim, the future emperor Jahangir.

A miniature from the Victoria and Albert Museum *Akbarnama* (NO. 14) designed by Kesu the Elder and painted by Dharm Das vividly records this joyous event. Since the manuscript was illustrated around 1590, artistic liberties have been taken, and the scene has been transposed to the completed Fatehpur-Sikri, with Maryam az-Zamani reclining in an open pavilion high in the palace complex overlooking the lake. As the new-born prince is bathed by maidservants with water from a golden ewer, crowds gather outside the red sandstone walls of the palace awaiting the disbursement of alms that traditionally follows such an auspicious event. Here the motley crowd, which includes an ash-daubed Hindu ascetic, is rewarded with a shower of coins, as the vibrant sounds of horns and drums surge from an inner whitewashed courtyard.

Akbar was in Agra when the birth took place, but as soon as the good news reached him he ordered the preparation of celebrations lasting seven days. Alms were distributed to the public and many prisoners were also released as part of the general festivities. At any such celebration it was customary for the court poets to vie with one another in recording their praises, often in the form of a pithy Persian chronogram, where the date of the event would be given by the combined numeric value of the letters used to

The Gateway to the Jami Masjid (Plan: 17)

express the appropriate sentiment. On this occasion, Khwaja Husayn of Merv (a city in Central Asia between Herat and Bukhara) excelled himself, and presumably all his competitors, by composing an ode in which the first line of each couplet gave the date of Akbar's accession to the throne, and the second one the date of Prince Salim's birth. The Khwaja was rewarded with the staggering sum of 200,000 silver coins for his brilliantly devised ode, which began:

Praise to God for the pomp and grandeur of the Shah,
A pearl of greatness to the shore of the sea of justice has come.[4]

Another, anonymous, chronogram was composed in the form of a bold restatement of the Prince's heritage: "The king of the House of Timur."[5]

Salim's birth left Akbar in a newly optimistic, if not ecstatic, frame of mind. Following his great military and political successes of the 1560s, this joyous personal event instilled in Akbar a mood for action that revitalized the very basis of his aspirations in India. It

13. *Akbar Praying at a Tomb* (**unidentified ms.,** *ca. 1600*).

14. *The Birth of Prince Salim* (**Akbarnama**, *ca. 1590*).

is in the dramatic events of this period that the daring originality of Akbar's personality left one of its most telling marks: the foundation of Fatehpur-Sikri, a new city that served as the Mughal capital until 1585.

According to one Akbari historian, Muhammad Arif Qandahari, the order to start work on the construction of Fatehpur-Sikri was not actually issued by Akbar until August-September, 1571, upon his return to Agra from a visit to Shaykh Salim that coincided with the second anniversary of Prince Salim's birth.[6] While other writers imply a date closer to 1569, it is reasonable to assume that some delay was in order until everyone was sure that the young prince would survive. Trust in Shaykh Salim continued to rise in court circles when a second healthy prince, Murad, was born at his residence in Sikri on June 7, 1570 (fig. 2). The new city at Sikri was at first named Fathabad (City of Victory),[7] but through popular usage it eventually became known as Fathpur (with the same meaning) or Fathpur Sikri, hence the modern form Fatehpur-Sikri.

The sandstone quarries at Fatehpur-Sikri were already busy sending out countless cartloads of red stone blocks for the work on the fort in Agra, so, once the order for the construction of the new city was issued, progress must have been almost immediate. Residents of the Chishti quarter, at the far western end of the ridge, must have been rather alarmed by all the new activity. A miniature from the ca. 1590 *Akbarnama* designed by Tulsi the Elder and painted by Bhavani depicts the construction at Fatehpur-Sikri at a fairly advanced stage (NO. 15). A crowd of stonemasons and laborers is shown at work between the southern shore of the lake and the Elephant Gate.[8] The arch of the gateway is still supported by a heavy wooden framework but the waterworks at the left are in full working order. The logistics of such an ambitious project might have seemed nightmarish but, according to Monserrate, Akbar had at least one practical means of coping with the situation: "In order to prevent himself being deafened by the noise of the tools with which stones are shaped and beams and other timber cut, he had everything cleverly fashioned elsewhere, in accordance with the exact plan of the building, and then brought to the spot, and there fitted and fastened together."[9]

Qandahari gives the most detailed description of the construction of Fatehpur-Sikri, as well as some insights into the actual design process. Presumably

36

15. *The Construction of Fatehpur-Sikri* (Akbarnama, ca. 1590).

LEFT: *Detail of Elephant Gate, 1984*

through first hand observation, though perhaps embellished with a touch of flattery, he assigns Akbar a major role in the planning of his new City of Victory:

> When the engineer of sound judgement [Akbar] drew the line of its foundation on the paper of fancy, he ordered it to have a circumference of approximately four to six miles on the face of the earth, and for houses to be built on the top of the hill and that they should lay out orchards and gardens at its periphery and center.[10]

Qandahari then continues with a description of the radical transformation the work entailed for the environs of Shaykh Salim's monastery:

> The lands which were desolate like the hearts of lovers and lifeless like the work of artisans attained freshness, purity, splendor and value like the cheeks of the beautiful and the tulip-faced ones. Trees were grown in the environs which had formerly been the habitat of rabbits and jackals, and mosques, bazaars, baths, caravanserais and other fine buildings were constructed in the city.[11]

Rising above the caravanserai and the main gate near the banks of the lake, two distinct structures began to take shape. To the east was the main palace complex (p. 43), comprised of a series of stone pavilions, courtyards and gardens, while to the west, towards the old Chishti quarter, lay the massive Jami Masjid or congregational mosque (Plan: 17). Construction of the city was carried on from 1571 until at least 1576 but it is not known in what order this activity proceeded. There may be a good deal of truth in Monserrate's remark that Akbar first "ordered a country-house – small but of royal magnificence – to be erected as swiftly as possible" and that "this was shortly afterwards enlarged into a palace."[12]

As late as 1576-77, Akbar ordered the construction of a long bazaar running down from the main palace complex on the top of the hill to the Agra Gate and a four-sided marketplace termed the Chahar Suq. Qandahari states that while he was writing his history, around the year 1580, only three of the four arched sandstone gateways leading into this Chahar Suq (Plan: 75, 77, 76) had been completed.[13] Unfortu-

LEFT:

FIG. 2. "The Birth of Prince Murad," *Akbarnama,* ca. 1590: Victoria and Albert Museum, London (I.S. 2-1896 80/117).

nately none of the sources mention the planners and architects who devised the city of Fatehpur-Sikri and its individual structures.[14] The histories are equally unhelpful regarding the question of who administered the burgeoning city until Shaykh Ibrahim, a nephew of Shaykh Salim and one of Akbar's leading soldiers and courtiers, was appointed its governor in 1578.

It is impossible to underestimate Akbar's keen interest in architecture and his awareness of its recent history. In the space of roughly six years he ordered the construction of a pleasure palace at Nagarchin, the reconstruction of the fort at Agra and then the creation of a whole new city at Sikri, no doubt in full awareness of the popular sentiment that "the standard of measure of men is assessed by the worth of [their] building."[15] Throughout the 1560s he had also visited (and in most cases added to his dominion) some of the most impressive cities in India, such as the Muslim centers of Lahore, Ahmadabad, Mandu and Jaunpur, and the magnificent Rajput strongholds of Chittorgarh and Ranthambhor. Akbar's childhood memories of Kabul, Qandahar, Ghazni, and Balkh, and Babur's descriptions of the great Timurid cities of Herat and Samarqand must have further whetted his appetite for construction.

The practical bent of the early Mughal emperors is just as clear as their love of building. It is amusing that in Babur's description of the wonders of Samarqand one of the first things he did upon setting out for sightseeing was to have someone pace out the exact measurement of the city ramparts. In a similar vein, Monserrate, whose somewhat anecdotal account of his stay in Fatehpur-Sikri acts as a perfect complement to the more formal style of the Mughal historians, adds the curious insight that Akbar "is so devoted to building that he sometimes quarries stone himself, along with the other workmen."[16] Furthermore, there is the visual evidence of Akbar's involvement in the building process afforded by another miniature in the *Akbarnama* designed by Tulsi the Elder, painted this time by Bandi with portraits added by Madhu the Younger (NO. 16). Here Akbar stands at the site of construction, presumably in the area between the Jami Masjid on the right and the main palace complex, and gestures to one of his stone-masons as the imperial entourage looks on. At the very least he wanted to live up to his symbolic epithet as "the architect of the spiritual and material world,"[17] both in real life, and, for posterity, in the painted version of the event. Most telling, however, is a walk through the interconnected courtyards of Akbar's palace itself, where it is hard not to feel the vibrant presence of his will to create a perfect stage for the full range of his imperial activities.

The decision to build a new city at Sikri was neither pure whimsy nor the rash action of an ecstatic young father. Apart from being the home of Shaykh Salim since the end of the fifteenth century, Sikri had a long connection with the Mughals themselves. In 1527, Babur won a crucial victory against Rana Sangram Singh of Chittorgarh (Mewar) at Khanva, just sixteen kilometers (ten miles) to the west of Sikri where he had set up camp for his army by the banks of the lake. Later that year he commissioned a "Garden of Victory" to be laid out there in addition to a number of other structures. One of these was an octagonal platform built in the middle of the lake where, in his own words, "we went over by boat, had an awning set up on it and elected for *majun* [an opium confection]."[18] For many years Sikri served as a pleasure retreat from Agra and, even in the unfortunate circumstances of 1540, Humayun halted there briefly in his father's garden while fleeing from Agra towards temporary exile in Iran.

It was an enticing site physically as well as spiritually, with its lake providing the pleasant breezes that the palaces were designed to catch. Although it is a little hard to imagine today, with the lake now completely dried up, Fatehpur-Sikri was as much a waterfront city as the other great Mughal centers of Delhi and Agra, which both lie on the banks of the River Jumna. More importantly, Fatehpur-Sikri was also part of a "royal corridor" stretching from Agra to Ajmer. It was along this route that Akbar used to make an annual pilgrimage on foot from Agra, still the great metropolitan center of the time as well as a bustling river port, to the tomb of Khwaja Muin ad-Din Chishti in Ajmer (NOS. 13 and 32), from where the road continued on to Ahmadabad in Gujarat and the great seaports of Cambay and Surat. Fatehpur-Sikri can thus be seen as an almost perfect symbolic and formal point of connection between the older spiritual and political axes of Ajmer and Agra.

For Akbar, who once travelled from Fatehpur-Sikri to Gujarat in just nine marches, the thirty-eight kilometers (twenty-four miles) separating Agra from the new capital was a comfortable day's journey. He could have made the trip in a matter of hours, if necessary, in spite of the frequently heavy traffic on

16. *Akbar Inspecting the Construction of Fatehpur-Sikri* (Akbarnama, *ca. 1590).*

١٧٣

٩٤

PLAN OF FATEHPUR-SIKRI

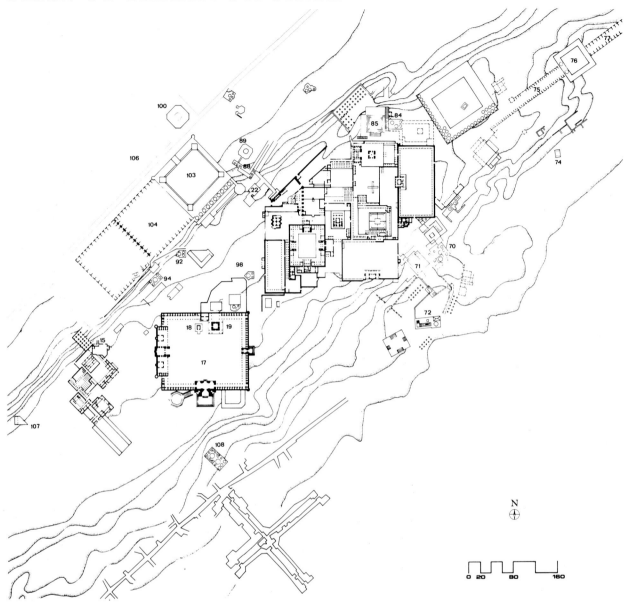

N
⊕

KEY TO PLANS

Many apocryphal names have been given to the buildings of Fatehpur-Sikri, causing much confusion. The plans reproduced here have the same numbering system that appears in our *Fatehpur-Sikri: A Sourcebook,* where only structures whose names are known from contemporary descriptions, or whose functions are easily identifiable, were included in the key. Here, however, we have added a number of buildings mentioned in our text that have yet to be conclusively identified. We have also substituted English translations for some Persian names.

Surveyed and drawn by Attilio Petruccioli.

15 Mosque known as the Stonecutters' Mosque
17 Jami Masjid
18 Tomb of Shaykh Salim ad-Din Chishti
19 Tomb of Nawab Islam Khan
22 Elephant Gate with House of the Kettledrum
25 Unidentified gate
30 Mosque known as the Nagina Masjid
31 Unidentified gate
33 Unidentified gate
36 Unidentified pavilion ["Panch Mahal"]
37 Unidentified gate
38 Unidentified pavilion ["Maryam's House"]
40 Unidentified garden
43 Unidentified viaduct
46 Harem(?)

THE IMPERIAL PALACE COMPLEX

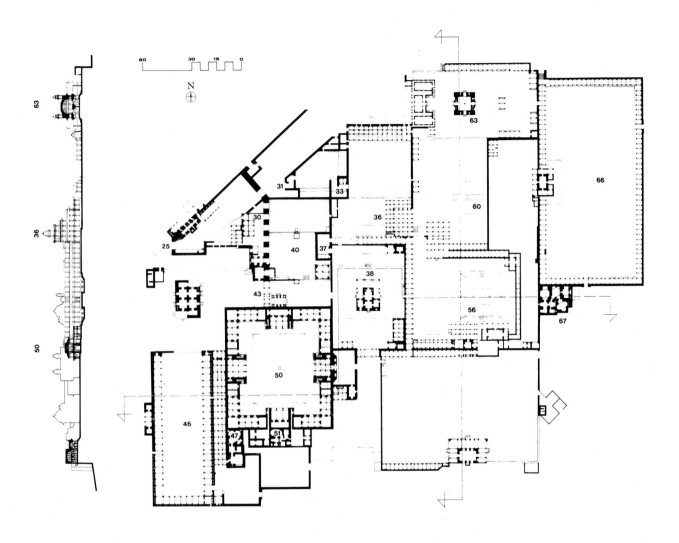

47 Baths attached to No. 46
50 Akbar's Private Palace(?) ["Jodh Bai's Palace"]
51 Baths attached to No. 50
56 Anup Talau tank
60 *Chawpar* game board
63 Unidentified pavilion ["Divan-i Khass"]
66 State Hall
67 Baths attached to No. 65
70 Unidentified baths
71 Unidentified tank
72 Unidentified step-well
74 Unidentified gate
75 Bazaar
76 Chahar Suq marketplace
77 Bazaar

84 Unidentified baths
85 Unidentified tank
88 Waterworks adjacent to Elephant Gate
89 Well attached to waterworks
92 Unidentified baths
94 Unidentified baths
98 Unidentified baths
100 Unidentified tower ["Hiran Minar"]
103 Caravanserai
104 Unidentified garden
106 Maydan(?)
107 Mosque known as Nawab Ibrahim's Mosque
108 Unidentified baths

this main trade route. According to the English merchant Ralph Fitch, who visited Fatehpur-Sikri in 1584, this road was virtually one long bazaar.[19] The first thing to catch the attention of a Sikri-bound traveller would have been the strange mileposts along the side of the road; from each one of these, according to contemporary accounts, projected a profusion of deer antlers, allegedly all taken from animals hunted by Akbar himself. The few squat towers that still remain have been stripped of their decoration but originally they would have appeared as fine visual puns to the many literati who travelled this road to the emperor's court, for their very description, "antler tower" (mil-i shakh), is also a chronogram for the date of their construction in 1573-74 (A.H. 981).

Akbar ordered one of these towers to be built at intervals of one kuroh (approximately three kilometers or two miles) along the entire three-hundred-sixty-five-kilometer (two-hundred-twenty-eight-mile) distance from Agra to Ajmer. After every thirty-two kilometers (twenty miles) a resthouse was added, partly to lessen the need for Akbar to take along his full tent camp every time he made the pilgrimage to the tomb of Khwaja Muin ad-Din Chishti.[20] The rest-houses would have been equally appreciated by many other travellers, but the quirky spiked towers were apparently too much for some courtiers. True to form, the irascible Badauni lamented, "Would that instead of these he had ordered gardens and caravanserais to be made!"[21]

Also along the route from Agra was the garden built by Akbar's mother Maryam Makani at Bustan-saray, near the modern town of Kiraoli, about sixteen kilometers (ten miles) from Fatehpur-Sikri. In some respects Bustan-saray marked the true ceremonial boundary of Fatehpur-Sikri. It was here, for example, that Akbar came for New Year celebrations in 1584, and it was probably also one of the staging posts sixteen kilometers (ten miles) outside the city where Akbar officially welcomed important guests in true Timurid fashion. When Mirza Sulayman, the elderly Timurid ruler of Badakhshan, arrived in 1583 to seek aid from Akbar, the population of Fatehpur-Sikri witnessed one of the grandest displays of Mughal pomp and etiquette of Akbar's entire reign.

On that day, as Akbar and his assembled nobles rode out the socially prescribed four or five kurohs to meet the Mirza, according to Badauni,

5,000 elephants, some with housings of European velvet, and some with Turkish cloth of gold, and some with chains of gold and silver, and with black and white fringes hung on their heads and necks, were drawn up in a line on both sides [of the road]: also Arabian and Persian horses with golden saddles of like splendour. And between each pair of elephants they placed a car of cheetahs with golden collars, and coverings of velvet and fine linen, and an oxen-car with fillets of embroidered gold. And the whole face of the wilderness, in this manner, became like a vision of Spring, and the desert and hill-country like the reflection of a tulip-bed.[22]

Akbar then dismounted from his horse to embrace the Mirza, absolved him from performing the customary forms of salutation, and accorded him the added privilege of riding alongside him into the city proper, where another round of celebrations began. During the visit, Akbar tried to impress his honored guest by reviving an old Chaghatay custom and spreading the royal tables in one of the audience halls so that the high nobles and generals could eat together. "But," Badauni noted sarcastically, "when the Mirza departed, all these (revised customs) departed too."[23]

Upon reaching the outer walls of Fatehpur-Sikri (see plan, p. 42), which stretch for eleven kilometers (seven miles) around all sides of the city except the northwest, where the lakeshore once extended, a traveller was faced with a choice of massive red sandstone gateways. Continuing straight ahead, the road through the Agra Gate (now the main entrance for all motor traffic) leads up to the rear of the palace complex and the enclosed plain to the southeast of the ridge, but it appears that the main route originally branched off to the right shortly before the Agra Gate. This road, past a particularly impressive stretch of wall leading up and over the eastern end of the ridge, heads towards two gates into the old town of Sikri: the Red Gate and the Delhi Gate farther on around the northern corner of the city wall.

Leaving Sikri, with its modest mosques and graves dating back to the fourteenth and fifteenth centuries, the traveller soon found himself proceeding towards the southwest, with the ridge on his left and the lake with Babur's platform, which still existed up until at least the 1580s, on his right. It is along this route that the spectacular skyline of Fatehpur-Sikri first becomes apparent. It was surely this view, commencing with the chatris (small cupolas raised on four columns), domes, and tiled roofs of the palace complex and concluding with the extraordinary silhouette of the great Jami Masjid, that inspired Qandahari to compare Fatehpur-Sikri with "Paradise on the brink of the precipice."[24]

Slightly more than four hundred and fifty-five meters (five hundred yards) from the village of Sikri stands a curious tower popularly known as the "Hiran Minar" (Deer Tower; Plan: 100).[25] Over eighteen meters (sixty feet) high, its round body bristles with stone spikes that suggest elephant tusks but also bring to mind the mileposts along the road from Agra. From here the sixteenth-century traveller proceeded to the adjacent caravanserai (Plan: 103) whose entrance faces across the main road towards the lake. Within this huge structure, whose open central courtyard is almost seventy-three meters (eighty yards) square, was housed a wide variety of people and goods. The Jesuit fathers, among others, were lodged there upon their arrival at Fatehpur-Sikri, until they complained to Akbar about the excessive noise.

Nearby the caravanserai was also the *maydan* (Plan: 106), a huge open space where Akbar engaged in a number of public, or semi-public, activities. On one such occasion events took a tragic turn when upwards of one hundred thousand poor and needy citizens gathered for a distribution of alms; in the ensuing crush eighty people were trampled to death.[26] First and foremost among the uses of the *maydan*, however, was for the playing of polo, which Akbar had elevated in status beyond the mere pursuit of amusement. As Abul Fazl noted, "men of more exalted views see in it a means of learning promptitude and decision. It tests the value of a man, and strengthens bonds of friendship.... Hence His Majesty is very fond of this game. Externally, the game adds to the splendour of the Court; but viewed from a higher point, it reveals concealed talents."[27] True to his character, Akbar was also partial to playing polo at night, an added pleasure made possible by an ingenious illuminated ball that had been devised in the mid-1560s.[28]

Apart from elephant fights and gladiatorial battles which continued, accompanied by the rhythms of four pairs of drums, until death befell one of the combatants, the *maydan* was also used for displaying the brilliance, both in acrobatics and plumage, of the imperial pigeons. In this sport, where the birds turn somersaults together in the air and perform various other stunts at the sound of a whistle, Akbar prided himself on possessing trained pigeons that put to shame those of his great-grandfather Umar Shaykh Mirza, who had died in an accident while tending to his birds.[29] A recent survey has also revealed the possible existence of a chain of gardens in the area adjoining the southwestern wall of the caravanserai (Plan: 104, 105),[30] and it may be that one of these is Babur's original "Garden of Victory."

Farther to the southwest of these gardens, the road continues on by the lake up to the Ajmeri Gate from which, as the name implies, the road leads to Ajmer, the rest of Rajasthan, and eventually Gujarat. It was along this road that Akbar returned home after his conquest of Gujarat in 1573. A double-page miniature

from the ca. 1590 *Akbarnama* depicting the emperor's arrival in Fatehpur-Sikri also gives a remarkably accurate view of this public area between the city and the lake (fig. 3). Designed by Kesu the Elder, with the right and left halves painted by Nar Singh and Jagjivan respectively, the scene is viewed from a location near the lakeshore. In the right half, Akbar, still on horseback, is welcomed by his three young sons (the third prince, Daniyal, had been born in 1572), who have approached him on foot. High above to the right towers a dome at the western end of the Jami Masjid while at the very left of the page can be seen the "Hiran Minar." The left half of the composition offers a wonderful vista of the Elephant Gate (Plan: 22) as seen from the vicinity of the tower. At the very right of the page a man disappears through the main entrance of the caravanserai, while merchants sell *pan* (betel leaves wrapped around condiments) by the side of the paved ramp that rises dramatically to the gateway along the northeastern wall of the caravanserai. On the left of this rampway, Kesu has shown the same waterworks that appeared in Tulsi the Elder's design for the miniature illustrating the construction of Fatehpur-Sikri (NO. 15).

The Elephant Gate is the first barrier between the great public space by the edge of the lake, and the zone of the city restricted to the royal family and the nobility. Its name is derived from the two huge, but now much damaged, figures of elephants that stand on either side of the outer face of the gate. The use of such figures outside the gate of a palace or fortress appears to be a genuinely Indian architectural device that Babur first noticed during his visit to Gwalior; it was first used by Akbar during his reconstruction of the fort in Agra, where riders—said to represent Jaimal and Patta, the two Rajput heroes of the battle of Chittorgarh—were added on the elephant's backs (see below, p. 19).

Located above the gate was the House of the Kettledrum,[31] where a boisterous orchestra went through an elaborate multi-part performance at key times during the day and night. The sound of the band, which included about twenty pairs of kettledrums as well as a variety of horns and reed instruments, ranged in mood from the frenetic to the soulful, and provided an essential part of Fatehpur-Sikri's atmosphere.

Behind the Elephant Gate two important paths converge in an open area with a number of pavilions (Plan: 26-29) that probably housed such administrative departments as the Office of Administration,[32] where city passes were processed, royal supplies monitored, and official documents affixed with the

45

imperial seal. These paths lead to elite ridge-top residential areas. The first one, where a number of houses and public baths still stand, is located in the triangle of land overlooking the caravanserai and bordered by the palace and the northern wall of the Jami Masjid. To reach the second area, which stretches along the northern end of the ridge almost up to the Agra Gate, one first has to pass through a high plastered archway (Plan: 25) directly behind the Elephant Gate and then underneath a viaduct that comes down from the main palace enclosure. Internal divisions must have been complex in these residential areas for there were at least three major Muslim factions at Akbar's court as

well as members of the newly allied Rajput Hindu aristocracy. The main Muslim groups were the Turanis (Chaghatay Turkish speakers from Central Asia), the Iranis (Persian speakers from Iran and present-day western Afghanistan and eastern Iraq), and the Indian-born Muslims. The Turanis, who were in the ascendancy under Babur and Humayun, and the Indians were Sunni Muslims, but many of the Iranis were Shias, another possible source of tension.[33]

It was in a house in one of these areas that Prince Salim was married to the daughter of Raja Bhagvan Das of Amber in 1585. On this occasion Akbar honored the Raja by visiting his mansion, scattering gold, pearls, and gems among the onlookers along the way from the imperial palace. In return, the Raja gave as his daughter's dowry "several strings of horses, and a hundred elephants, and boys and girls of Abyssinia, India, and Circassia, and all sorts of golden vessels set with jewels, and jewels, and utensils of gold, and vessels of silver, and all sorts of stuffs, the quantity of

FIG. 3. "Akbar Welcomed Back to Fatehpur-Sikri," *Akbar-nama,* ca. 1590: Victoria and Albert Museum, London (double-page).

 a) I.S. 2-1896 110/117 (left)
 b) I.S. 2-1896 111/117 (right)

which is beyond all computation."[34] Other residents of these elite suburbs were the Safavid artist Abd as-Samad and the Hindu courtier Raja Birbar, who started out as a humble minstrel but later rose to a position of such prominence that in 1583 he too was granted the honor of hosting a feast for Akbar in his mansion.

Between the above-mentioned archway and the viaduct is a small open junction. Moving on from here, and passing under the viaduct, one immediately reaches an inconspicuous, but easily defendable, gateway (Plan: 31; now blocked up with modern masonry) that marks the barrier between the semi-public areas of Fatehpur-Sikri and the private zones of the imperial palace. From here Akbar's route into the palace proper took him up through a series of three more small gates to the very top of the ridge. Here the emperor would emerge at the northwest corner of the small courtyard containing the exquisitely proportioned stone pavilion popularly known as "Maryam's House" or the *Sunahra Makan* (Plan: 38). Standing before this compact building, which might be the "country-house" that Monserrate described as the first imperial structure built in Fatehpur-Sikri, Akbar would be in the true center of his palace complex.

The abandoned structures, studded with the remains of gardens, that are described today as monuments of the "streetless ghost town" of Fatehpur-Sikri are actually only the remains of Akbar's central palace enclosure. Measuring approximately three hundred and forty meters (three hundred and seventy yards) across from east to west and two hundred and seventy-five meters (three hundred yards) from north to south, the complex spreads back across the full width of the ridge from the Elephant Gate. The buildings, exquisitely fashioned out of the rich, red Sikri sandstone, stand in almost pristine condition. Although they lack occupants, furnishings, and, more importantly, the sounds and smells of the 1570s, no other site in India evokes so vividly the architectural and social nuances of the Mughal court. Richly tactile tones of red dominate one's first impressions, uniting variegated forms such as *chatri*, dome, pavilion, and verandah into a series of expansive courtyards. At this level the effect is extraordinarily bold, especially the skilfully massed red roofline, sharply silhouetted against the blue sky at the edge of the ridge. Upon closer inspection one is also dazzled by the brilliance of the surface treatment. Carved vegetal and geometric ornament excites the beholder with both its bold qualities of form and its razor-sharp technique. Inside, the faded remains of extensive wall paintings hint at an additional hidden brilliance.

The many fanciful names that later became attached to the palace buildings of Fatehpur-Sikri, mostly during the first half of the nineteenth century,[35] make the study and discussion of the imperial enclosure difficult. The exact name and function of a number of these buildings remain unknown. Nevertheless, a careful reading of the contemporary accounts of the city reveals a clear picture of the main divisions of function and access that were intended during the planning of Fatehpur-Sikri when Akbar "drew the line of its foundation on the paper of fancy." The same sources give an equally lively account of Akbar's court in action at Fatehpur-Sikri.

Monserrate divides the complex into four major palaces. In his account—perhaps the best contemporary overview of the imperial enclosure—he writes that its wall "easily embraces four great royal dwellings, of which the King's own palace is the largest and the finest. The second palace belongs to the queens, and the third to the royal princes, whilst the fourth is used as a store house and magazine."[36] The main functional division, however, was between private and public areas; the delineation of boundaries that determined who was able to view Akbar, and who was able to interact with him. The court etiquette was extremely strict, and complex, in these matters, for, according to Monserrate, Akbar "always took the greatest pains to imitate, even in the minutest details, the traditional system of Temurus [Timur]."[37]

The emperor granted two audiences daily, one open to the general public and another closed to all but his leading nobles. The first took place as soon as Akbar had finished his morning devotions and fulfilled what Abul Fazl considered to be a function crucial to the well-being of the state, "it is a pledge that the three branches of the government are properly looked after, and enables subjects personally to apply for redress of their grievances. Admittance to the ruler of the land is for the success of his government what irrigation is for a flower-bed; it is the field, on which the hopes of the nation ripen into fruit."[38]

This first occasion of the day was not, however, so much a meeting with the general public as an opportunity for Akbar to show himself, at a safe distance, to the general public standing outside the palace walls. The similarity of this practice to certain Hindu forms of worship was not lost on Abul Fazl, who actually goes on to describe this performance by the Hindi word *darshan,* meaning the viewing or worship of a sacred image.[39] Furthermore, Badauni uses the Hindi word *jharokha* to describe the window in which Akbar made these appearances. Fayzi's assertion to the effect that "see Akbar and you see God" takes on an added signficance when viewed against these ritualized performances. Badauni also implies that Akbar's devotions included a form of sun-worship,[40] a ritual that Monserrate describes as being performed in "a wooden building of ingenious workmanship" that had been added on the roof of his palace.[41]

The exact location of this *jharokha* window has yet to be conclusively identified, but if we are correct in believing that the largest building in the compound, popularly known as "Jodh Bai's Palace" (Plan: 50), was Akbar's main private residence, then either of the two balconied windows on its southeast corner seems to be a logical choice, especially considering their proximity to the palace wall. If Akbar did indeed worship the sun, and one does need to keep in mind Badauni's personal vendetta against Akbar's alleged heterodoxy when reading such accusations, the window on the palace's eastern façade further suggests itself as a perfect place from which to view the rising sun.

The second, more exclusive, audience was generally held in the morning but according to circumstances it could be delayed until the evening or later in the night. The location of these meetings remains hard to identify, and they may in fact have occurred in a number of places depending upon who the participants were. In all probability, a good deal of this activity, along with other important large-scale events, was consigned to the State Hall (Plan: 66), a large open quadrangle measuring approximately one hundred meters (one hundred and ten yards) long and fifty meters (fifty-five yards) wide at the eastern extremity of the palace. Abul Fazl described the courtyard, with its many bays and an elevated pavilion set into the center of the western wall, as the *dawlatkhana* (also translatable as the "Abode of Fortune"). It appears, however, that different terms employed by other Mughal historians, such as Badauni's *divankhana,* also refer to the same structure.[42] Today one may also enter the State Hall through gates cut into its south and east walls at a later date but the original entrance leads into the very northwest corner of the quadrangle.

The State Hall was the main theatre of public interaction within the palace, and as such witness to a wide range of events, not always entirely orthodox. Badauni, for example, mentions in passing that the Friday congregational prayers were frequently said there rather than in the mosque.[43] This in itself is not surprising, for it is a conveniently located space large enough to hold a sizeable assembly and, more importantly, is aligned facing west towards Mecca just like the mosque itself. However, when the State Hall is viewed as a surrogate mosque, some intriguing questions arise. Could it be a pure coincidence that directly in the middle of the western wall of the courtyard, towards which the assembly would pray, is the pavilion in which Akbar would have been seated? With his citizens prostrated towards him in prayer, Akbar must have revelled in the ironical pun of their repeated chant "Allahu akbar": meaning "God is great," but also construable as "Akbar is God."

Another curious event in the State Hall is illustrated in the *Akbarnama* by a miniature designed by the great master Basawan and painted by Mansur (NO. 17). In 1573 Ibrahim Husayn Mirza, a descendant of Timur who had settled in India, continued to instigate anti-government activities and was joined in rebellion by his younger brother Masud Husayn Mirza. Eventually the latter was captured in the Panjab and brought to Fatehpur-Sikri by Husayn Quli Khan, the governor of Lahore, shortly after the emperor arrived back from his conquest of Gujarat. The miniature shows Masud Husayn and a large group of co-conspirators, wrapped in animal skins by way of punishment and humiliation, being presented in the State Hall by Husayn Quli Khan. The passage in the *Akbarnama* illustrated here describes the prisoners as being wrapped in cowhides but Basawan apparently decided to draw instead from his own, fuller, memory of the event, which excited great amusement at court, and depicted the sad rebels in a far more splendid array of skins.[44]

The large courtyard behind and to the west of the State Hall is one of the most fascinating areas in Fatehpur-Sikri, although perhaps also the hardest to interpret. Presumably it was originally semi-private and pleasure-oriented in nature, but many of the internal barriers and connectors that might give further clues to its original use have since collapsed or been altered in subsequent repair work. Within this area one finds, among other structures, a unique single-pillared pavilion,[45] the man-sized game board on which Akbar and his courtiers played the game of *chawpar* (similar to pachisi), and the small pond or tank known as the Anup Talau, which Akbar had filled with gold, silver and copper coins during a fit of extravagance in 1579-80 (Plan: 63, 60, 56). Adjacent to the western wall of the courtyard stands the magnificent four-story structure topped by a domed *chatri* now known as the *"Panch Mahal"* (The Palace of Five Levels; Plan: 36). As a group, the buildings in and around this courtyard form a passage of architecture unique in Islamic India, and display perfectly the ex-

17. *Masud Husayn and Co-conspirators Presented to Akbar by Husayn Quli Khan (*Akbarnama, *ca. 1590).*

perimentation and yearning for new forms that characterize Akbar's personality during the Fatehpur-Sikri years.

Impressive as these stone structures are, they do not give the complete picture of the palace as Akbar lived in it. Apart from their inner furnishings, virtually every building at Fatehpur-Sikri had some form of temporary exterior appendage such as an awning to provide shade from the sun, or a screen to give added privacy or help define the all-important zones of access.[46] In the center of the large courtyards it is likely that whole tents and open pavilions were set up, something that must have been very comforting to the Mughal courtiers who still spent a large part of the year on the road in their magnificently organized tented camps.

Temporary decoration was particularly in evidence during the great festivals, the most extravagantly celebrated of which was the Persian New Year. For this festival, Nizam ad-Din Ahmad wrote,

The walls and pillars of the halls of the public and private palaces were distributed among the amirs, and being draped in rich fabrics, and painted curtains, were beautifully adorned; and were decorated in such a way that the spectators on seeing them were filled with wonder and admiration. The courtyards of the palaces were adorned with pavilions, and awnings of fabrics of gold embroidery and gold tissue; and a golden throne inlaid with emeralds and rubies was placed under them; and they became the object of envy of the higher paradise . . .

These beautiful mansions remained decorated for a period of eighteen days; and they were adorned during the nights by many coloured shades. His Majesty went there once or twice every day and night, and enjoyed social pleasure; and musicians of Persia and India were in attendance.[47]

On the anniversary of Akbar's accession to power another grand feast was held and as part of the festivities a special bazaar selling goods from all over the known world was assembled, which the women of the harem were invited to attend first. According to Abul Fazl, Akbar also used such days "to select any articles he wishes to buy, or to fix the price of things and thus add to his knowledge. The secrets of the empire, the character of the people, the good and bad qualities of each office and workshop, will then appear."[48] Afterwards, similar bazaars were opened for the male courtiers.

In his semi-public activities at court, Akbar was always surrounded by a large number of people. Twenty or so bodyguards were constantly in attendance, even though the emperor himself was well armed, and an equal number of courtiers would have been at his side. The prescribed court etiquette also called for the presence of entertainers such as wrestlers, musicians, jugglers and acrobats. All accounts agree that the court was constantly thronged with a vast crowd. Akbar, however, was always the focus of attention, whether seated cross-legged on his low rug-draped throne or promenading in a unique assortment of clothing that was often quite outlandish, and at least partially self-designed. Monserrate wrote that in contempt of earlier traditions Akbar, "wears garments of silk, beautifully embroidered in gold. His military cloak comes down only as far as the knee, according to the Christian fashion; and his boots cover his ankles completely. Moreover, he himself designed the fashion and shape of these boots. He wears gold ornaments, pearls and jewellery."[49] Badauni adds that at Fatehpur-Sikri Akbar took to choosing the color of his clothes according to the symbolic color of the day's regent planet, the revival of a practice initiated by Humayun.[50]

Little is known about Akbar's private life except that it was spent between a number of secluded apartments, not necessarily housed in the same building, and the harem, which can be identified with the long open structure adjoining Akbar's main palace at the southwest corner of the palace compound (Plan: 46). This building, with its numerous private cells and baths, was zealously guarded on the inside by eunuchs and on the outside by loyal Rajput soldiers and nobles such as Raisal Darbari (NO. 54). In general, Akbar spent the late evening hosting discussions and the early morning in private contemplation, after he had been awakened well before dawn by special musical performances. At which times he visited the harem is unclear, as is the location of his actual bedchamber. During the night Hindu and Muslim mystics were occasionally hoisted up to this room on a small cot (charpai) in order to talk with Akbar while suspended outside his window.[51] As was the tradition in other parts of the Muslim world, Akbar passed many relaxing hours in the baths behind his private residence and may also have joined his senior courtiers in the baths that adjoin the southwest corner of the State Hall (Plan: 51, 67). Akbar usually ate alone, his food having been sealed and secured against poison by the cook and then conveyed to his apartment by a chain of attendants. On certain days his diet was entirely vegetarian. His drinking water was always brought from the Ganges, the most sacred river of the Hindus.

Immediately to the west of the palace complex, on the highest part of the hill, is Akbar's enormous Jami Masjid (Plan: 17). Its monumental gateway, which

50

rises about thirty-four meters (one hundred and fifteen feet) above the level of the mosque, and forty-five meters (one hundred fifty feet) above the road below, faces neither the palace nor the path from the Elephant Gate but punctuates instead the southern wall of the mosque, looming up above the plains where Akbar intended the city's new population to settle. Passing through this gateway popularly called the *"Buland Darvaza"* (The Lofty Gateway), one enters a huge courtyard measuring approximately ninety-five meters (one hundred and five yards) by one hundred and eighteen meters (one hundred and thirty yards) and paved in the same red sandstone from which the mosque is built. Nestled within this vast expanse of earthy red is the pearl-like white marble tomb of Shaykh Salim, who died in 1572 (Plan: 18). Even today traditional songs in praise of the Shaykh are performed by singers seated on the white marble apron that extends in front of the tomb with its single dome and exquisite lattice-work screens.

It was in the Jami Masjid in 1579 that Akbar decided to read the Friday sermon (*khutba*) out of his desire to be seen to follow the example of Timur and other illustrious sultans. Badauni, who thoroughly disapproved of the whole performance, claims that Akbar was barely able to stammer his way through three verses of a poem composed for the occasion by Fayzi before he gave up, but this is not mentioned in other accounts of the event. All writers do, however, agree as to the content of those verses, which ended with the favorite court pun:

Almighty God, that on me the kingship conferred,
A mind of wisdom, and an arm of strength conferred,
To justice and equity, He did me guide;
Expelled all but justice from my thought.
His attributes beyond all comprehension soar,
Exalted is His Majesty, Allahu-Akbar (Almighty God).[52]

Akbar's spiritual endeavors were not exclusively confined to the Jami Masjid, nor were they restricted to the routine performance of the five required daily prayers. Upon his return to Fatehpur-Sikri in 1575 from his annual pilgrimage to Ajmer, Akbar ordered the construction of the House of Worship (exact location unknown), and it is fair to say that intellectual life in the capital was never quite the same again. No other building or part of the court routine at Fatehpur-Sikri is discussed at such great length by Akbari historians. Together with the formulation of a new code of religious behavior known as the *din-i ilahi*, often misinterpreted as an attempt to found a new religion,[53] this move caused a great deal of concern and bitterness among the orthodox. In both cases one notices the erosion of the status and power of orthodox Islam at the Mughal court in Fatehpur-Sikri and the concomitant strengthening of Akbar's position. The boundaries between politics and the "material world," on one hand and religion and the "spiritual world" on the other, gradually begin to blur.

The House of Worship was completed within a year. A general proclamation was then issued for "all orders and sects of mankind–those who searched after spiritual and physical truth, and those of the common public who sought for an awakening, and the inquirers of every sect–" to assemble there weekly on the designated "night of illumination."[54] The various participants were divided and seated, according to their affiliations, on the four sides of the building. Akbar adjudicated the frequent disputes as he moved around from one group to another. For about the first three years the discussions, which generally lasted the whole of Friday night, appear to have been restricted to members of the Muslim community, including orthodox mullas, Sufi mystics, jurists, and philosophers. But later a number of non-Muslim theologians, including Hindus, Jains, Christians, Jews and Zoroastrians, joined them in the House of Worship.

One of the evenings described at some length by Abul Fazl is illustrated in the *Akbarnama* of ca. 1604 by the artist Nar Singh, who sets the scene in an open courtyard under a full moon (NO. 18). The painting depicts the point in the narrative where Father Acquaviva, seated in the upper left corner with another member of the Jesuit mission, has just aroused a particularly hostile response from his Muslim opponents, who are shown seated around the lower edge of the carpet, during an argument over what constitutes the true word of God. Akbar presides from under a small canopy, looking out over a battlefield strewn with holy books. Eventually Father Acquaviva suggested that both the Gospels and the Koran be subjected to a test of fire and "the escape of any one will be a sign of his truthfulness," but according to Abul Fazl, the Muslim theologians backed down, thereby losing that round of the interminable struggle to the Jesuits, and also incurring the acute displeasure of Akbar.[55]

The main events of the early 1570s, during which the construction of Fatehpur-Sikri was in full swing, were centered around Akbar's growing family and the resolution of his initial territorial ambitions. The emperor's three young sons were circumcised in 1573 amidst great festivities that were perhaps also intended to formally signal the safe arrival of the next generation of Mughal rulers. Akbar's conquest of Gujarat in the same year was equally significant and assured the Mughals for the first time free access to seaport facilities and thus a share of the lucrative Indian Ocean trade. This led to greater contact with Europeans, whom Akbar had met for the first time during his campaign in Gujarat the previous year. In a further attempt to increase state revenue, which was always a priority in view of Akbar's massive spending on such costly projects as the construction of Fatehpur-Sikri and a general court taste for luxury, the cultivation of crops was rationalized in 1574-75 to encourage higher yields.

In 1576 Bengal was finally added to the Mughal dominions, but the years preceding this event were marked by indications that Akbar had yet to fully articulate the future direction of his newly stabilized empire. He appeared to waver between reform and tradition. On the one hand, land reform strengthened his position over *jagirdars* (holders of non-hereditary land grants) and the initiation of debates in the House of Worship in 1575 undermined the orthodox Turani establishment, whose political strength was clearly waning, along with their Chaghatay customs. However, Akbar re-imposed the *jizya* tax on non-Muslims in 1575[56] and the following year he briefly considered making the pilgrimage to Mecca, both moves that would have appealed to the more orthodox members of his court.

Towards the end of the 1570s, a more consistent policy emerged, the more radical and unorthodox approach having won the day. The new direction chosen by Akbar was not at all popular in many circles and it almost resulted in his being overthrown and replaced by a more conservative and pliable monarch. An event that appears to have played an important role in setting Akbar on this risky course of action is a mystical experience he had while hunting in the Panjab in 1578. Just as the hunt reached its climax, and the slaughter of the animals in the temporary corral was about to begin, a "sublime joy took possession of his bodily frame. The attraction (*jazaba*) of cognition of God cast its ray."[57] Akbar ordered the animals set free and by all accounts he came out of his experience a changed man.

In June the following year, Akbar read the Friday sermon in the Jami Masjid and just two months later the Decree of Infallibility was issued. This document granted Akbar the right to make binding decisions on religious matters should there be an irresolvable difference of opinion among the members of the *ulama*. In September, Akbar made his final pilgrimage to Ajmer, although he had actually wanted to give up the practice that year and only changed his mind in order

to assuage the growing public uncertainty and anxiety over his religious actions. During the course of the year, Akbar also re-revoked the *jizya* tax, the favorite political football of the day.

Feeling was already running too high, however, and open rebellion broke out in January, 1580 in the eastern provinces of Bihar and Bengal. Akbar's predicament was made even more awkward when the religious judge of Jaunpur declared revolt against Akbar lawful, due to the alleged gravity of his unorthodox activities. The aim of the rebels was to replace Akbar with his half-brother Mirza Hakim Muhammad, who was then the governor of Kabul.

Consequently Akbar marched on Kabul with Prince Salim in February, 1581 and eventually achieved a decisive victory, but not before the very foundation of his rule in India had reached the point of crumbling. After visiting the tomb of Babur in Kabul, Akbar set off for Fatehpur-Sikri where he arrived to a spectacular series of welcoming ceremonies:

On this day of joy the great officers, the loyal servants, and others were drawn up in two sides of the way for a distance of four *kos* from the city. The mountain-like elephants stood there in their majesty. . . . The noise of the drums and the melodies of the magician-like musicians gave forth news of joy. Crowds of men were gathered in astonishment on the roofs and at the doors. At the end of the day he sate in the lofty hall *(daulatkhana)* on the throne of sovereignty. He dispensed justice by rewarding the loyal and punishing the hostile.[58]

The point would not have been lost on Akbar that he had retained his throne only through the strong support of the Indian-born Muslims and his new Rajput allies, the Irani and Turani nobles having remained divided in loyalty during the course of the rebellion.[59]

After the suppression of this highly threatening rebellion, life at Fatehpur-Sikri returned to a more subdued pace and Akbar continued with the liberal policies of conciliation and consolidation that characterize the years he spent in his new capital. One such move was a thorough overhaul in 1583 of the administrative system so that, in the words of Abul Fazl, "In a short time the outer world attained an excellent management and the spiritual world a new development. . . . The wicked descended into the hollow of ignominy, and the good were exalted."[60] The three princes and loyal courtiers, including Abd as-Samad, were placed in key positions of power.

During the years in which Akbar resided at Fatehpur-Sikri the arts flourished consistently under his generous patronage. In music, Tansen (NO. 55) continued to reign supreme and worked in a manner that was to profoundly influence the subsequent development of Indian classical music. Similar developments were taking place in the field of dance, and a profusion of poets worked under Akbar's patronage, although many of them had actually been inherited by Akbar from such previous patrons as his father Humayun, his uncle Hindal and even his former regent Bayram Khan. The Translation Bureau[61] began the translation of many Indian texts into Persian for the first time and Akbar also started to take an interest in the writing of Mughal and world history. Artistic production at Fatehpur-Sikri was divided between the *kitabkhana* (library), the *karkhanas* (workshops), the Mint,[62] and even the Office of Administration, all of which were lavishly financed and lovingly supervised by Akbar.

Akbar's great experiment at Fatehpur-Sikri came to an end in September, 1585, less than fifteen years after the city was founded. In response to the death of the troublesome Mirza Hakim Muhammad, and the series of vital political options and problems that this event opened up in the northwest, Akbar set off with his army for Lahore and almost never visited Fatehpur-Sikri again.[63] No conscious decision to abandon Fatehpur-Sikri was ever made, and Akbar's followers were genuinely surprised when he did not return there after the completion of his initial campaign in the Panjab.[64]

After Akbar left Fatehpur-Sikri, military activity replaced social and administrative reform as his major concern. From 1586 onwards, operating from his new northern base in Lahore, Akbar once more harbored great ambitions for increasing his territory and replenishing his treasury, through renewed conquest. Although his success continued, his victories in Kashmir in the north (1586), Orissa in the east (1590), Sind, Makran and Baluchistan in the west (1592-94), and then the recapture of Qandahar (1595), were neither as decisive nor as strategically important as the ones he had gained earlier in his reign. After these successes he still dreamt of expanding the frontiers of his empire northwards into Central Asia and southwards beyond the Narmada River into the Deccan, or central plateau of peninsular India. His aims were kept in check, however, by fears of an Uzbek invasion from the north, by the growing Portuguese presence along the western coast of India, and by almost constant problems with his sons, who were all showing signs of various stages of alcoholism.

Almost no progress was ever made towards recapturing the Central Asian homelands beyond Qandahar and therefore most later military activity was

18. *Akbar Presiding over Discussions in the Ibadatkhana* (Akbarnama, *ca. 1604).*

directed toward the Deccan, a situation that prompted Akbar to move his capital back to Agra in 1598. Mughal forces had actually been deployed in the south under the command of Prince Murad since 1593 and Berar was captured in 1596. Murad's grasp of affairs was failing, however, and shortly before Abul Fazl arrived to take him back to Agra in 1599 he died of alcohol-induced *delirium tremens* near Daulatabad. Nevertheless, Abul Fazl managed to lead the imperial forces to victory in Ahmadnagar the following year and Akbar personally led the forces that succeeded in reducing Khandesh in early 1601 after a taxing nine-month siege, thus creating the third new southern province.

Akbar spent most of the last five years of his life facing a revolt by his son Salim, who even set up his own court in Allahabad, where he felt secure and settled enough to establish a separate atelier of painters. In 1602, Akbar only just managed to dissuade him from continuing with a threatening march on Agra itself, but in the same year Salim did succeed in arranging the assassination of Abul Fazl on his way back from the Deccan, a move that caused Akbar untold grief. Although a brief rapprochement between father and son was arranged in 1603 by some of the leading women of the family, it was only after Prince Daniyal finally succumbed to alcohol in April, 1604 that Akbar was fully reconciled to Salim becoming his official heir. On October 15, 1605, Akbar passed away on his sixty-third solar birthday after a protracted bout of dysentery. Despite a brief challenge from proponents of his own son, Khusrau, the Sikri-born Prince Salim succeeded his father on the Mughal throne. With a reference to the Mughals' supposedly divine origin, he noted in one of the first decisions he made that, "inasmuch as the business of kings is the controlling of the world, I should give myself the name of Jahangir (World-seizer) and make my title of honour *(laqab)* Nuru-d-din [Light of the Faith], inasmuch as my sitting on the throne coincided with rising of the great light."[65]

Despite Akbar's absence during the last twenty years of his reign, Fatehpur-Sikri did not die and even during the reigns of Jahangir (1605-27) and Shah Jahan (1627-58) the city continued to be an important dynastic center. Akbar's mother, Maryam Makani, appears to have spent much of the remaining two and a half decades of her life there, and, in 1619, Jahangir spent a number of months there with Prince Khurram, the future Shah Jahan, who by all accounts had been Akbar's favorite grandson. During that stay Khurram's birthday was celebrated with the traditional weighing ceremonies in what was to become an annual event there.[66] Throughout his reign Shah Jahan made many other visits to Fatehpur-Sikri both to hunt tigers in the surrounding forests and waterfowl on the lake, and to visit the tomb of Shaykh Salim. It was only during the reign of Aurangzeb (r. 1658-1707) that Fatehpur-Sikri lost its status as a living imperial center.

View of the northwest corner of the Palace Complex

CHAPTER III

THE KITABKHANA: THE IMPERIAL LIBRARY

THE CENTER OF manuscript production and painting at Fatehpur-Sikri was the imperial *kitabkhana* (library). Although *kitabkhana* can be translated as library, in reality it was a much more complicated institution made up of several units devoted to a variety of functions. Some of its components were in private areas, such as the interior of the emperor's palace, others were in more public places. Furthermore, its functions were not limited to a single city so that it was possible for the emperor to maintain branches simultaneously in other cities such as Agra and Lahore. The library of the celebrated Safavid bibliophile Sultan Ibrahim – Shah Tahmasp's nephew and son-in-law – operated in this way and had branches in at least three cities: Mashhad, Qazvin and Herat. Portions of manuscripts written in one city were sent to another in order to be collated and gathered into a single text.[1]

The precise location of the various parts of Akbar's library at Fatehpur-Sikri remains a mystery. A brief remark by Monserrate complaining of the noise of the scribes, who were near the Jesuits' new quarters suggests that at least some writing may have taken place adjacent to the part of the palace where the Jesuits were housed.[2] According to Abul Fazl, who has left us with a vivid account of Akbar's library, another part of it was located in the harem:

His majesty's library is divided into several parts; some of the books are kept within and some without the Harem. Each part of the library is subdivided, according to the value of the books and the estimation in which the sciences are held of which the books treat. Prose books, poetical works, Hindi, Persian, Greek, Kashmirian, Arabic, are all sepa-

rately placed. In this order they are also inspected. Experienced people bring them daily and read them before His Majesty, who hears every book from the beginning to the end...Among the books of renown there are few that are not read in His Majesty's assembly hall; and there are no historical facts of the past ages, or curiosities of science, or interesting points of philosophy, with which His Majesty, a leader of impartial sages, is unacquainted. He does not get tired of hearing a book over again, but listens to the reading of it with more interest.[3]

In addition to storing books in the harem, the emperor also kept important manuscripts in the royal treasury.[4] The use of the treasury as an extension of the imperial library suggests that it may have been the equivalent of a rare book room.

Libraries as separate entities first appeared in the Muslim world during the tenth century.[5] By the twelfth century they were found throughout Iran, Iraq and Egypt. The books in these libraries were kept in various rooms and stacked one above the other in small compartments.[6] Some libraries, such as that of the Persian ruler Azud ad-Dawla (949-983), were extremely large complexes composed of several buildings surrounded by gardens and lakes. Catalogues were kept of individual libraries – many of which had thousands of manuscripts – classifying their contents according to various branches of knowledge.[7] Often numerous copies of a single manuscript were present in a library so that scholars could read corrupt passages in one manuscript by referring to another.[8] The library of the Fatimids (909-1171) in Cairo had thirty copies of Khalil's *Kitab al-Ain* and twenty copies of at-Tabari's renowned *Universal History*.[9] Manuscripts were acquired either by purchase or by "in-house"

View West from the Palace Complex

production. Consequently library staffs usually included a director, at least one librarian, several attendants, and a group of professional copyists.[10] According to Qazi Ahmad, a sixteenth-century Persian artist, Sultan Ibrahim employed in his library "excellent calligraphers, painters, artists, gilders and bookbinders."[11]

Akbar's library — like many earlier Muslim libraries — served two related but separate functions. It was where imperial manuscripts were kept and it was also where many of them were produced. The creation of a Mughal manuscript involved a number of people performing a variety of tasks. Paper-makers were needed to prepare the folios of the manuscript, calligraphers to copy the text, gilders to illuminate the

FIG. 4. Artisans from the *kitabkhana,* border of page from a Jahangir album, ca. 1600: Freer Gallery, Washington, D.C. (54.116 recto).

pages, painters to illustrate selected stories, and bookbinders to gather the individual folios of the manuscript and set them within protective covers. The range of these activities and the artists who undertook them can easily be seen in a series of drawings from an album page made for Jahangir ca. 1600 (fig. 4).[12] In the upper right of the page a paper-maker is busily burnishing a sheet of newly laid paper with a highly polished stone. Opposite him a bookbinder, seated before a low table strewn with the tools of his trade, is energetically stamping the cover of a manuscript, while below him an artisan files the edges of a bound book held tight by a wooden clamp. Below this figure another man works away with a saw to make an elaborate bookstand. An adze and other tools lie by his feet. At the bottom of the page a smelter blows with a long rod into a fire contained in an open pot. Next to him is a bar of gold to be melted down and used in gilding the pages of a manuscript. To his right a scribe sits cross-legged in front of his table, pen in hand, ready to write in a bound book.

A page from an illustrated manuscript of the *Akhlaq-i Nasiri* (Nasirean Ethics), a philosophical and ethical discourse written by Nasir ad-Din Tusi (1201-1274) in 1235 and copied for Akbar ca. 1590, shows the kind of environment in which these artists worked. The miniature (NO. 19) depicts a scriptorium composed of a large building surrounded by a verandah set in the midst of a garden divided into four parts by cross-axial canals. Seated on the sumptuous carpets that cover the library's floor are a master dictating to a scribe, two painters, a paper-maker and a second scribe. Attendants stand to either side of the artists ready to serve them drinks from vessels resting on a low table at the edge of the porch. The sense of ease and luxury suggested by this scene, with its tranquil garden and fine appointments, represents the ideal setting for the creation of lavishly illustrated manuscripts and reflects the social status of the artisans.

Because Akbar, like his great ancestor Timur, was illiterate, his books were read out to him by professional reciters such as Naqib Khan, his brother Mir Sharif,[13] and Darbar Khan, whose father was Shah Tahmasp's reader.[14] A simple system of accounting was used to keep track of what had been read to the emperor: "At whatever page the readers daily stop, His Majesty makes with his own pen a sign, according to the number of pages; and rewards the readers with presents of cash, either in gold or silver, according to the number of leaves read out by them."[15]

19. *Manuscript Atelier* (Akhlaq-i Nasiri, *ca. 1590-95*).

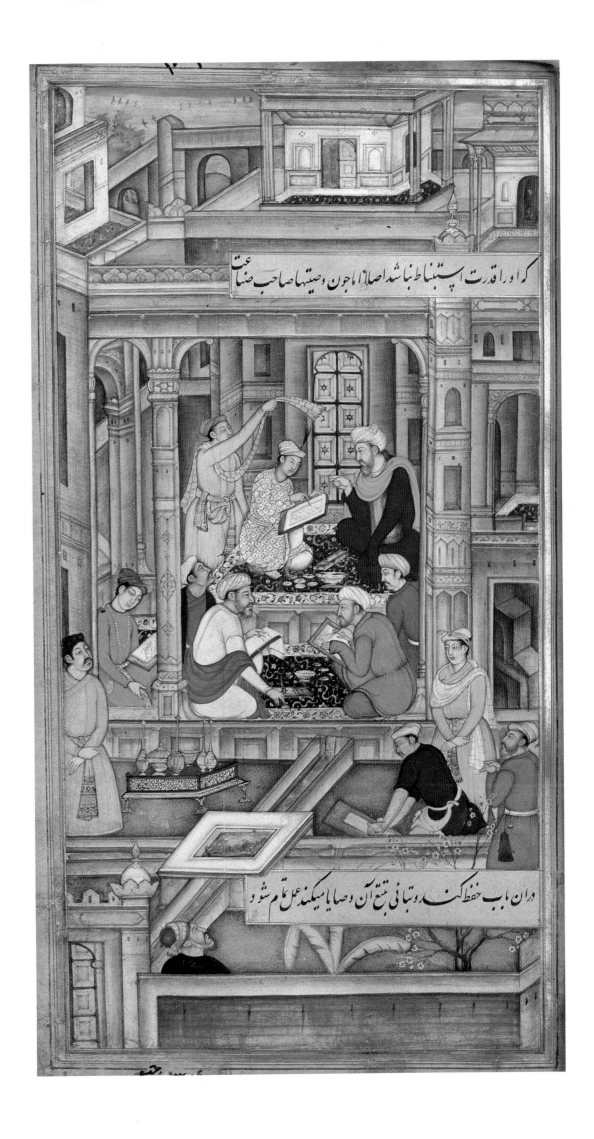

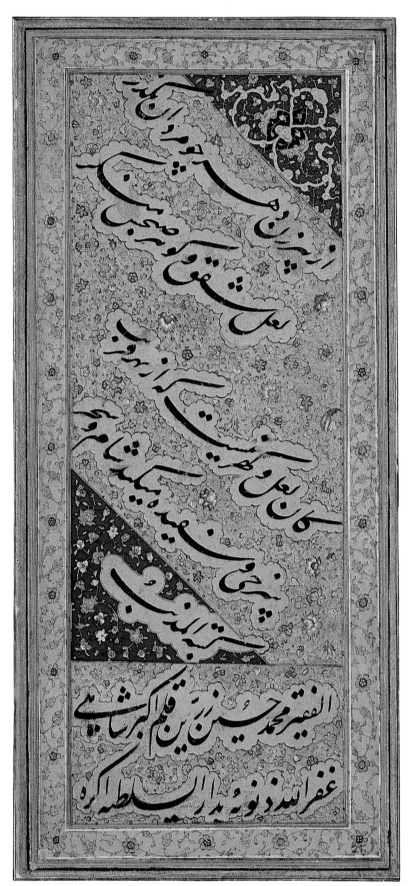

20. *Illuminated Calligraphic Folio (ca. 1575-1605).*

While little is known about the paper-makers and gilders at Akbar's court, Abul Fazl has left us with detailed descriptions of the emperor's most important calligraphers and painters. Calligraphers held the highest social standing as the art of writing was considered more important than painting.[16] A letter when properly written symbolized for the Mughals—as it did for all Muslims—a divine form containing magical powers.[17] The carefully formed letters of the Arabic alphabet (in which Persian is written) thus represented "the portrait painter of wisdom; a rough sketch from the realm of ideas; a dark night ushering in day; a black cloud pregnant with knowledge; the wand for the treasures of insight; speaking though dumb; stationary, yet travelling; stretched on the sheet, and yet soaring upward."[18] Akbar was extremely interested in the various scripts used by Muslim calligraphers and appears to have been especially fond of *nastaliq,* a manner of writing developed by Mir Ali at-Tabrizi at the beginning of the fifteenth century. The emperor's finest calligrapher was Muhammad Husayn of Kashmir (NOS. 20, 25). Contemporary critics considered Muhammad Husayn, who was honored with the title *Zarin Qalam* (Golden Pen), the rival of Mir Ali of Herat.[19] According to Abul Fazl the extensions and curvatures of his letters were perfectly proportioned. Other calligraphers of note, all of whom were Muslims with strong ties to Iran, included Mawlana Baqir (the son of Mir Ali), Abd ar-Rahim who was given the title *Anbarin Qalam* (Ambergris Pen) in the seventeenth century, Abd as-Samad, who was known as the *Shirin Qalam* (Sweet Pen) for his graceful writing, Mawlana Dawri, also known as Sultan Bayazid, Abd al-Hay, and Nurullah Qasim Arsalan.

Akbar's painters—unlike his calligraphers—were of Hindu as well as Muslim origin and came from all over India and Iran. By the end of the sixteenth century, Abul Fazl was able to write of them:

More than one hundred persons have reached the status of master and gained fame; and they are numerous who are near to reaching that state or are half-way there. What can I say of India! People had not even conceived of such glories; indeed, few nations in the world display them (such glories).[20]

In addition to Mir Sayyid Ali and Abd as-Samad—the Iranian masters responsible for supervising the production of the *Hamzanama* and the education of the emperor's artists—Abul Fazl singles out fifteen painters for their superior abilities. The two most celebrated of these were Daswanth, the son of a palanquin-bearer, and Basawan. The former used to draw images and designs on walls.[21] He received his formal training under Abd as-Samad. Unfortunately "the darkness of insanity enshrouded the brilliance of his mind" and in 1584 he committed suicide. Basawan, who was preferred by some critics to Daswanth, "excelled at designing *(tarrahi)*, painting faces *(chihra kusha'i)*, coloring *(rang-amezi)*, portrait painting *(manind nigari)*, and other aspects of this art."[22] Among the other artists mentioned by Abul Fazl are Kesu, Lal, Miskin, Farrukh the Qalmaq, Madhu, and Khem Karan.

By working in teams these painters were able to produce extensively illustrated manuscripts in a relatively short time. Between 1570 and 1580, for instance, at least eight manuscripts, with more than five hundred and thirty images, were made in the imperial atelier. For each miniature one man was responsible for its design while another – usually the designer's assistant – painted it. Sometimes a third person, either a colorist or a specialist in portraiture, would also collaborate on a painting. This assembly-line approach, developed during Akbar's years at Fatehpur-Sikri, was gradually abandoned in the 1590s as the emperor demanded more refined and consistent miniatures that reflected the individual skills of his artists.[23]

The emperor's interest in the creation of his manuscripts was intense and personal: he was the one who selected which scenes were to be illustrated[24] and presumably suggested who was to paint them. In

21. *Koran (1573-74).*

22. *Murder Scene* (Berlin Jahangir album) *ca. 1575-80.*

addition to librarians such as Inayatullah,[25] superintendents and clerks were charged with insuring that the emperor's demands were properly executed. They were also responsible for maintaining the library's organization and keeping its studios[26] well supplied. A royal decree issued by the founder of the Safavid dynasty, Shah Ismail, in 1522, appointing the renowned Persian artist Bihzad director of his library, gives some insight into the specific obligations of the various members of an imperial studio:

All enlightened Amirs and incomparable Wazirs and the secretaries of our world-protecting threshold and the envoys of our heaven-like court and the functionaries of royal business and the officials of our ministries, – in general – and the staff of the Royal Library and the persons mentioned above – in particular – must recognize the above mentioned Master as the director and superintendent. They must submit to his control and administration all activities of the library, and pay due consideration to all his administrative measures authorized by his seal and signature. There must be no disobedience or neglect of any orders or regulations he may make for the control and conduct of the Royal Library... He, for his part, must draw and depict upon the tablet of his heart and the page of his enlightened conscience the image of integrity and the form of uprightness.[27]

Akbar's literary interests were wide-ranging and numerous individual paintings (NOS. 22, 23, 24) and manuscripts – from Korans (NO. 21), to poetic collections, ethical texts, and astrological treatises – were made for him. In addition to previously discussed works such as the *Tutinama,* the *Ashiqa* of Amir Khusrau Dihlavi, the *Hamzanama,* and the *Akhlaq-i Nasiri,* at least twenty-eight other major manuscripts were illustrated for Akbar during his reign. These can be divided into three broad categories: belles-lettres (including literary and poetical texts as well as calligraphic tours de force), general and dynastic histories, and translations from Sanskrit and other languages. The majority of these manuscripts fall under the category of belles-lettres. Nine of them can be safely attributed to the years during which Akbar was at Fatehpur-Sikri or shortly thereafter. These include:

A copy of the *Anvar-i Suhayli* (Lights of Canopus), dated 1570, now in the School of Oriental and African Studies, London (fig. 5).[28]

A second, fragmentary, copy of the *Anvar-i Suhayli* ca. 1575, in the Prince of Wales Museum, Bombay.

A *Darabnama* (Story of Darab), ca. 1580, in the British Library (fig. 6).[29]

A *Divan* (Poetic Collection) of Hafiz copied by Abd as-Samad and dated 1582, now in the Chester Beatty Library.[30]

A *Gulistan* (Rose Garden) of Sadi copied by Muhammad Husayn Zarin Qalam and dated 1582-83, now in the collection of the Royal Asiatic Society of Great Britain (NO. 25).[31]

A *Khamsa* of Nizami copied by Ali ibn Mubarak al-Fahraji in Yazd between 1502-1506, with 35 Mughal miniatures added ca. 1585, in the Keir Collection.[32]

23. *Boat and Landscape (unidentified ms., ca. 1580-85).*

A second copy of the *Tutinama* ca. 1585, now in the Chester Beatty Library.[33]

A *Divan* of Anvari dated 1588 in the Fogg Art Museum, Harvard University (NOS. 26, 27).

A second *Divan* of Hafiz, ca. 1588 in the Raza Library, Rampur.

Often several copies of the same manuscript were made over a period of years, such as the *Anvar-i Suhayli* which was illustrated at least three times for the emperor. Both the 1570 *Anvar-i Suhayli* and the *Darabnama* have miniatures executed in a slightly more refined manner than the paintings of the *Hamzanama*. The former is a fifteenth-century Persian revision of the Arabic *Kalila wa Dimna* prepared by Husayn Vaiz al-Kashifi for the Timurid ruler Sultan Husayn Mirza Bayqara (1470-1506). Written on brown-flecked paper, the manuscript has small panels of text with margins ruled in blue, green, and gold and

twenty-seven miniatures. Although none of the illustrations is signed, they are all of fine quality. One of the most exciting aspects of the manuscript is the way the artists who worked on it extended their paintings beyond the margins of the text by adding an L-shaped border around the sides of their miniatures. In doing so they established a way of extending an image's space that remained the norm until the end of the sixteenth century.[34]

The *Darabnama* (fig. 6), the story of Darab, the son of Zal and the grandfather of Alexander the Great, was written by Abu Tahir Tarasusi, whose origins remain unknown. The manuscript, which is fragmentary, contains one hundred and fifty-seven miniatures on creamy brown paper many of which are attributed by marginal notation to Akbar's most important artists such as Basawan, Kesu, Madhu, Jagan, Mahesh, Tara, and Sanvalah, as well as Nanha, Miskin, and

24. *Prince Riding an Elephant (ca. 1575-80)*.

Dharmdas. The system of marginal inscriptions developed in this manuscript to indicate who worked on each miniature reflects Akbar's desire to know the individual manners of his artists. It provided as well a convenient way to keep track of how many paintings an artist made for a manuscript so that he could be properly rewarded.

The *Gulistan* (NO. 25), a collection of moral tales, was written by the great Persian poet Muslih ad-Din Sadi (1189-1291). The Royal Asiatic Society's manuscript was copied at Fatehpur-Sikri for Akbar by Muhammad Husayn Zarin Qalam. Each of the manuscript's one hundred and thirty folios is written in an elegant *nastaliq* on a cream-colored paper flecked with gold. Extremely fine studies of birds and other animals are scattered throughout the manuscript's pages. At the beginning of the book these studies are carefully organized and restrained, consisting usually of three or four per page. By the end of the text, however, whole flocks of birds are presented on a single page in swirling masses of brightly colored feathers that are as visually exciting as any image in Mughal painting. On the second-to-last folio of the manuscript is a miniature by Manohar, Basawan's son, depicting the artist and the scribe (p. 128).

During the second half of the 1580s, Akbar's tastes became increasingly refined. The relatively large and bold images of such manuscripts as the *Ashiqa* and *Darabnama* were replaced in poetic manuscripts by more sensitive and delicate paintings often executed in a minute scale. The Keir *Khamsa* of Nizami and the 1588 *Divan* of Anvari (NOS. 26, 27) are typical of this new trend. Both are extremely small manuscripts—literally pocket-books—illustrated by the emperor's leading artists. The fifteen miniatures of the *Divan* of Anvari, though not inscribed, can be attributed to Basawan, Shiv Das, Manohar, Mahesh, Abd as-Samad, Khem Karan, Nanha, and Miskin. The *Divan*'s poems, written by the twelfth-century Persian panegyrist Awhad ad-Din Anvari, are copied on marbleized paper in a fine hand that is consistent with the jewel-like quality of the miniatures.

FIG. 6. "Darab Left by Zahhak to Face the Dragon," *Darabnama,* ca. 1580-85: British Library, London (Or. 4615, f. 16a).

25a. *Manuscript of the* Gulistan *of Sadi (1582-83).*

While Akbar was at Fatehpur-Sikri, two developments occurred that had a profound effect on the types of manuscripts produced for the emperor: the creation of a bureau for the translation of works into Persian and the evolution of a new attitude towards history. The Translation Bureau, which was in operation by 1574, had its antecedents in the great libraries of the classical Muslim world. Through the efforts of the many people who worked in this department, a whole new group of manuscripts was produced for the emperor. Abul Fazl has left us with an excellent description of some of these:

At the command of His Majesty, Mukammal Khan of Gujarat translated into Persian the *Tajak*, a well-known work on Astronomy. The *Memoirs of Babar* [*Baburnama*], the Conqueror of the world, which may be called a code of practical wisdom, have been translated from Turkish [Turki] into Persian by Mirza Abdu-r-Rahim Khan, the present Khan Khanan (Commander in Chief). The *History of Kashmir,* which extends over the last four thousand years, has been translated from Kashmirian into Persian by Mawlana Shah Muhammad of Shahabad. The *Mujam-ul-Buldan,* an excellent work on towns and countries, has been translated from Arabic into Persian by several Arabic scholars, as Mulla Ahmad of Thattah, Qasim Beg, Shaykh Munawwar and others.[35]

In all, at least fifteen works were translated into Persian for Akbar, often by his leading courtiers, such as Abd ar-Rahim, the Khan Khanan (Army Minister) and son of Bayram Khan, and Abul Fazl (who prepared a new rendition of the great Arabic fable *Kalila wa Dimna* which he called the *Iyar-i Danish*). Four of these translations from Sanskrit are either dated, or

66

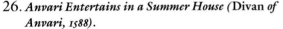

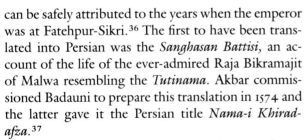

26. *Anvari Entertains in a Summer House* (Divan of Anvari, 1588).

27. *It's the Day for the Garden* (Divan of Anvari, 1588).

can be safely attributed to the years when the emperor was at Fatehpur-Sikri.[36] The first to have been translated into Persian was the *Sanghasan Battisi,* an account of the life of the ever-admired Raja Bikramajit of Malwa resembling the *Tutinama.* Akbar commissioned Badauni to prepare this translation in 1574 and the latter gave it the Persian title *Nama-i Khirad-afza.*[37]

In 1582 Badauni was again ordered to translate a work from Sanskrit to Persian. This time he was assigned the great Indian epic *Mahabharata* which became known in Persian as the *Razmnama* (Book of Wars). The project was completed in 1584 after which Badauni immediately undertook the translation of the *Ramayana,* Hinduism's other great literary epic. Illustrations by the imperial studio's best artists accom-

panied both the *Razmnama* (fig. 7) and the *Ramayana.* During Akbar's last year at Fatehpur-Sikri Mawlana Shiri began a translation of the *Harivamsa* (NOS. 28, 29) a genealogy of Hari, the Hindu god Vishnu, that focuses on the life of Krishna. Only twenty-eight miniatures appear to have survived from this copy of the manuscript, though originally there would have been many more. Translation of the manuscript must have been relatively quick as Mawlana Shiri died in a battle in Kashmir in 1586. Among the other works translated into Persian from Sanskrit for Akbar were the *Nal Damayan* (by Fayzi) and the *Jog Bashisht* (NO. 30). Farmuli's translation of the *Jog Bashisht* (the story of Rama and the Yoga-teaching of Vasishta) which was illustrated in 1602, and the forty-seven miniatures in this manuscript represent some of the finest late-

28. *Krishna and Balarama Arrive in Brindaban*
(Harivamsa, *ca. 1585*).

sixteenth-century Mughal paintings produced by Akbar's artists.

The process of translating manuscripts into Persian involved several people. Specialists in the relevant languages would make direct translations, usually under the supervision of one person. After these were completed another person, generally a poet of distinction, was commissioned to prepare a final version in flowing verse. Badauni has left us with an excellent description of how this was done for the *Mahabharata*:

After this Mulla Sheri and Naqib Khan together accomplished a portion, and another was completed by Sultan Haji of Thanessar by himself. Shaikh Faizi was then directed to convert the rough translation into sections. The Haji aforesaid revised these two sections, and as for the omissions which had taken place in his first edition, those defects he put right, and comparing it word for word with the original, one hundred sheets were written out closely, and the work was brought to such a point of perfection that not a fly-mark of the original was omitted.[38]

Akbar used the translation department both as a means of increasing his knowledge and awareness of the world and as a way of educating (and perhaps chastising) various members of his court. Badauni, for example, who as an extremely orthodox Muslim was constantly provoked by being ordered to translate

29. *Krishna and Balarama Fight Jarasandha's Army*
(Harivamsa, *ca. 1585*).

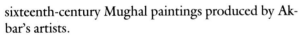

69

30. *Manuscript of the* Jog Bashisht *(1602).*

Sanskrit works such as the *Mahabharata* and *Sanghasan Battisi* into Persian. His lengthy comments on the translation of the *Mahabharata* reveal both Akbar's attitude towards Indian literature and the author's mixed feelings about his work:

Among the remarkable events of this year [1582] is the translation of the *Mahabharata,* which is the most famous of Hindu books, and contains all sorts of stories and moral reflections, and advice... The following considerations disposed the emperor to the work. When he had the *Shahnama* and the story of Amir Hamzah, in seventeen volumes transcribed in fifteen years, and had spent much gold in illuminating it... it suddenly came into his mind that these books were nothing but poetry and fiction; but that since they were related in a lucky hour, and when their star was in the act of passing over the sky, they obtained great fame. But now he ordered that those Hindu books, which holy and staid sages had written, and were all clear and convincing proofs... be translated into Persian. Accordingly he became interested in the work, and having assembled some learned

Hindus, he gave directions to write an explanation of the *Mahabharata,* and for several nights devoted his attention to explaining the meaning to Naqib Khan, so that the Khan might sketch out the gist of it in Persian. On the third night the emperor sent for me, and desired me to translate the *Mahabharata,* in conjunction with Naqib Khan. The consequence was that in three or four months I translated two out of the eighteen sections, as the puerile absurdities of which the eighteen thousand creations may well be amazed...But such is my fate to be employed on such works.[39]

At the same time that the *Mahabharata, Harivamsa,* and *Ramayana* were being translated for the imperial *kitabkhana,* Akbar ordered the compilation, copying, and illustration of a series of historical manuscripts. These included the *Tarikh-i Alfi* (The History of One Thousand Years), the *Tarikh-i Khandan-i Timuriyya* (The History of the House of Timur), the *Chingiznama* (The History of Chingiz Khan), the *Baburnama,* and the *Akbarnama.* The first of these projects undertaken was the *Tarikh-i Alfi.* In 1581-2 the emperor asked his courtiers to prepare a new history of the Muslim world in anticipation of the millennium of the hijra calendar, which was approaching in 1591-2. Seven people were ordered to begin work on the *Tarikh-i Alfi,* as it came to be called, compiling information from "the date of the death of the last of the Prophets [Muhammad] (the blessing of God be upon him and may he give him peace!) up to the present day, and to mention therein the events of the whole world."[40] According to Badauni, Akbar:

assigned the first year to Naqib Khan, the second to Shah Fathullah and so on to Hakim Humam, Hakim Ali, Haji Ibrahim Sarhindi (who had just then arrived from Gujarat), Mirza Nizam-ud-din Ahmad, and myself. And after that another seven years, and in this way the distribution of 35 years was provided for.[41]

Progress on the manuscript, which was given an introduction by Abul Fazl,[42] was not as rapid as anticipated and consequently, at the recommendation of Hakim Abul Fath, the project from the thirty-sixth year on was turned over to Mulla Ahmad of Thatta. The completion of the *Tarikh-i Alfi* was then entrusted to Asaf Khan Jafar Beg. After Asaf Khan had prepared the rest of the manuscript Badauni was ordered to "proceed to Lahor, to revise the composition, compare it with other histories, and arrange the dates in their proper sequence."[43] Badauni managed to edit two of the three volumes in one year and presented his completed work to Akbar at Lahore in 1593-94, almost exactly twelve years to the date after the manuscript was begun. Only twenty-six illustrated pages appear to have survived from the *Tarikh-i Alfi*—all from episodes between the reigns of the Caliphs Harun ar-Rashid (786-806) and al-Mutazz (866-69) – suggesting that originally the manuscript must have contained as many as three hundred paintings.[44] Three features distinguish these miniatures: the large size of the folios they are painted on (47 by 25 cm.), the occasional illustration of several scenes on the same page, and the relationship of the images to the text. A page from the *Tarikh-i Alfi*, now in the Cleveland Museum of Art, (NO. 31) is typical of the manuscript. It is divided into four horizontal registers on one side and two on the other. On the first side three scenes are depicted, while on the second there are two. As one image leads into another a somewhat confusing kaleidoscopic effect is created. The miniatures, though, are not meant to be seen as individual paintings but as specific illustrations to the text which forms the focal point of the page. In later manuscripts, such as the *Chingiznama* and the *Akbarnama*, this relationship is reversed and the images become paintings that can be understood independently from textual references as opposed to simple illustrations.

The history of the Muslim world described in the *Tarikh-i Alfi* provided Akbar with a broad background against which to measure his own accomplishments. The emperor's interest in history, however, went beyond a desire to simply know the past. Through the commissioning of a series of manuscripts tracing the deeds of his most illustrious ancestors as well as his immediate forebears, Akbar attempted to define the historical significance of his own dynasty. The first of these dynastic histories to have been written was the *Tarikh-i Khandan-i Timuriyya* (fig. 8) whose first miniature was painted by Daswanth, who committed suicide in 1584. The work is a history of Timur and his descendants through Babur, Humayun and Akbar: its more popular name *Timurnama* (The History of Timur) is therefore misleading. Indeed, a third of the manuscript, from folios 238 through 335, is devoted to a detailed account of the early Mughals.

Over forty folios describe the first nineteen years of Akbar's reign and provide us with a great deal of information not included in other manuscripts. The author, for instance, states that both Mir Sayyid Ali and Abd as-Samad taught Humayun how to paint, affirming the emperor's direct interest in the arts.[45] Unfortunately the copy of the manuscript that has survived is not complete and we know neither the name of its author nor the sources upon which it was based though the author does refer to the *Zafarnama* in the introduction and the *Baburnama* towards the end of the book. We do know, however, that it must

have been considered a major project by the emperor, on the scale of the translation of the *Razmnama,* for a number of Akbar's most important artists such as Basawan, Daswanth, Nanha, Miskin and Madhu the Elder, worked on the one hundred and thirty-seven extant illustrations. These miniatures, unlike those of the *Tarikh-i Alfi,* dominate their pages. They are intended to be dramatic portrayals of crucial events in the life of the Timurid dynasty that can be comprehended independently of any written record. The

31. *Three Events during the Reign of the Caliph al-Mutawwakil* (Tarikh-i Alfi, *ca. 1592-94*).

FIG. 8. "The Child Timur Playing as a King," *Tarikhi-i Khandan-i Timuriyya*, ca. 1584: Khudabakhsh Library, Patna, India (Acc. No. 107).

design and execution of its paintings exude a sense of confidence and accomplishment that sets the standard for Akbar's historical manuscripts.

The *Tarikh-i Khandan-i Timuriyya*'s many illustrations make explicit the Mughals' Timurid connections and establish them, at least on a visual level, as the legitimate heirs to the great empire of the Timurids and as the just rulers of India. The focus of the manuscript, however, is clearly on Timur and his immediate descendants. During the years at Fatehpur-Sikri, Akbar's need to define himself and his empire in relationship to Timur changed to such a point that he ordered, in the late 1580s and 1590s, the writing of his own history and commissioned works on his father's and grandfather's lives. Abul Fazl was entrusted with the task of preparing the emperor's official biography, the *Akbarnama* and began writing it in 1590,[46] though other authors, such as Nizam ad-Din Ahmad, Qandahari, Mir Ala ad-Dawla Qazvini and

Badauni had already started chronicles of Akbar's reign. It was Abul Fazl's intention to,

write in four volumes a record of the transactions of the royal house during one hundred and twenty years, which are four generations, that it may stand as a memorial for those who seek knowledge in justice, and with the Institutions of His Majesty [*Ain-i Akbari*] as the concluding book, purposed the completion of the *Akbarnamah* in these five volumes.[47]

Abul Fazl's goals, which were ambitious and predicated on Akbar living for an unlikely number of years (four cycles of thirty years each), were never fully realized. What was accomplished, however, remains a lasting memorial to the greatness of Akbar's reign and the most important text of the period. By 1602, when Abul Fazl was assassinated by Rajput horsemen acting on Prince Salim's orders, only two of the proposed five volumes had been written. The first volume, comprised of a brief description of Akbar's ancestry and an account of the first thirty years of the emperor's reign (to September 1572) was presented to Akbar in 1596.[48]

In a miniature by Govardhan recording this momentous event, Abul Fazl kneels before Akbar in anticipation of the emperor's praise, a copy of his manuscript held delicately in his hands.[49] Two years later a second volume was presented to the emperor, bringing the narrative of his rule to the forty-second year (1597) and including a detailed record of his rules and regulations.[50] This account, known today as the *Ain-i Akbari*, and never illustrated, is usually treated as a third volume to the manuscript. The magnitude of the author's accomplishment is suggested by the following lines from the *Ain-i Akbari*: "Firdausi [the author of the *Shahnama*] took thirty years of labour to secure eternal execration, while I have borne with seven years of toil for the sake of everlasting glory. He fused his worth into the cast of verse which is a matrix of determinate shape, and I have strung into writing, gems of the purest water through the infinite expanse of prose."[51]

Although Abul Fazl may not have been actively at work on the *Akbarnama* until 1590, there is evidence that he had begun researching the manuscript as early as 1587-88. In that year Jawhar Aftabchi wrote his memoirs of Humayun's reign in response to an imperial decree that, "those who from old service remembered, with certainty or with adminicle of doubt, the events of the past, should copy out their notes and memoranda and transmit them to court."[52] This order[53] was issued in the thirty-third year of the Divine Era (1587-88).[54] Despite Akbar's orders several courtiers did not respond and in 1589[55] "a second command shone forth from the holy Presence-chamber; to wit—that the materials which had been collected, should be faired out and recited in the royal hearing, and that whatever might be written down afterwards, should be introduced into the noble volume as a supplement."[56] At least two other members of the emperor's court responded to the emperor's call for information concerning the events of the first years of the dynasty: Akbar's aunt, Gulbadan Begam (*Humayunnama*), and Bayazid Biyat, the superintendent of the imperial kitchen (*Tazkira-i Humayun va Akbar*). It is also possible that Abd ar-Rahim's translation of the *Baburnama* was in response to this decree.

In preparing the *Akbarnama*, Abul Fazl also had access to the detailed information contained in documents of the imperial Records Office which had been established at Fatehpur-Sikri in 1574-75.[57] Akbar appointed fourteen clerks—two for each day of the week—to this office. They were charged with writing down,

the orders and the doings of His Majesty and whatever the heads of the departments report; what His Majesty eats and drinks; when he sleeps, and when he rises; the etiquette in the State hall; the time His Majesty spends in the Harem; when he goes to general and private assemblies...when he marches and when he halts; the acts of His Majesty as the spiritual guide of the nation; vows made to him; his remarks; what books he has read out to him.[58]

The importance of the records office for Abul Fazl's work can be gleaned from a passage in the *Akbarnama*:

I obtained the chronicle of events beginning at the nineteenth year of the Divine Era...and from its rich pages I gathered the accounts of many events. Great pains too, were taken to procure originals or copies of most of the orders which had been issued to the provinces from the Accession up to the present date which is the dawn of fortune's morning. Their sacred contents yielded much material for the sublime volume.[59]

After gathering his data, Abul Fazl made five drafts of the *Akbarnama* before he was satisfied with it. Fayzi was supposed to further revise these drafts in order to render them into harmonious and elegant prose. The latter died in 1595, however, having worked on only the first ten years of the initial volume. While we do not know the exact chronology of the manuscript, progress must have been fairly rapid as Badauni refers to it as early as 1590[60] and Nizam ad-Din Ahmad in 1592-93.[61] Two profusely illustrated copies of the *Akbarnama* have survived: one generally attributed to the 1590s (now in the Victoria and Albert Museum) and containing one hundred and seventeen illustrations of events between 1560 and 1578 (NOS. 4, 14,

15, 16, 17, 32) and the other now shared between the Chester Beatty Library and the British Library except for several dispersed pages. The latter (datable to around 1604 or slightly later on the basis of a marginal inscription) was copied by Muhammad Husayn Zarin Qalam (NO. 18) and has one hundred paintings covering Akbar's reign through March, 1589. The numerous miniatures of these manuscripts depict in bold detail the events that shaped the emperor's life from the birth of his sons (NO. 14, fig. 2) to the battles he won (NO. 4) and the activities of his court (NO. 17). Although the miniatures in the later *Akbarnama* tend to follow those of the earlier one, the number of illustrations and the subject matter of certain paintings vary between the two.

32. *Akbar at the Chishti Shrine in Ajmer* (Akbarnama, ca. 1590).

During the late 1580s and 1590s two other historical manuscripts were illustrated for Akbar: the *Baburnama* and the *Chingiznama*. The former was translated by Abd ar-Rahim from Babur's original Turki, and presented to Akbar on November 24, 1589.[62] At least four copies of the manuscript are known—all illustrated by artists from the imperial ateliers—suggesting that it was greatly admired by the emperor and his family. The first of these copies (now dispersed), which may have been the manuscript actually presented to Akbar, can be attributed to around 1589 and originally contained one hundred and ninety-one illustrations (NOS. 33, 34). Subsequent copies were made ca. 1591 (British Library), ca. 1593 (State Mu-

35. *Chingiz Khan Dividing His Empire between His Sons* (Chingiznama, *ca. 1596*).

seum of Oriental Cultures, Moscow and the Walters Art Gallery, Baltimore), and in 1597-98 (National Museum of India).[63] Although all of the illustrated manuscripts of the *Baburnama* are based on Abd ar-Rahim's translation, several earlier translations had been made such as Zayn ad-Din Khwafi's, done during Babur's lifetime, and Mirza Payandah Hasan Ghaznavi's of 1584.[64] The illustrations of the manuscript—which follow the text closely in the earliest copy and deviate from it in the latter ones—can be divided into two groups: narrative events such as "Babur Restoring

33. *Babur Restoring Ulugh Beg's Garden at Istalif* (Baburnama, *ca. 1589*).

34. *Feast at Sultan Jalal ad-Din's House at Karrah* (Baburnama, *ca. 1589*).

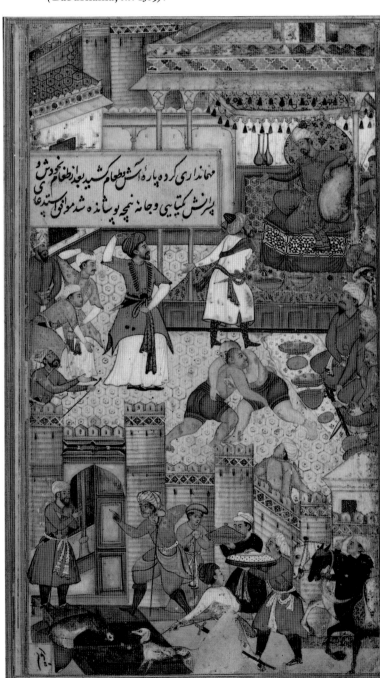

74

36. *Abaqa Khan Enthroned* (Chingiznama, *ca. 1596*).

Ulugh Beg's Garden at Istalif" (NO. 33) designed by Miskin and painted by Gwaliori, and depictions of the flora and fauna of India. The latter images reflect Babur's intense interest in his environment and establish an attitude towards nature shared by almost all of his descendants.

The *Chingiznama* (NOS. 2, 35, 36, 37), like the *Tarikh-i Khandan-i Timuriyya*, describes the life of one of Akbar's most revered ancestors. It actually forms part of the *Jami at-Tavarikh*, the extraordinary world history written by Rashid ad-Din (1247-1313) around 1307. The Mughal copy of the *Chingiznama*,[65] dated May 25, 1596, though incorrectly referred to as the *Jami at-Tavarikh* after its parent manuscript, focuses uniquely on the life of Chingiz Khan and his immediate decendants as can be seen in "Chingiz Khan Dividing His Empire Between His Sons" (NO. 35) designed by Basawan and executed by Bhim Gujarati.

Taken as a group, the historical manuscripts made for Akbar follow a logical progression. The earliest one, the *Tarikh-i Alfi*, examines the great kings of Islam. The next one, the *Tarikh-i Khandan-i Timuriyya*, traces the history of one dynasty in particular. Finally, the later manuscripts (with the exception of the *Chingiznama*) glorify the lives of Akbar and the Mughals, the last of the Timurids. Within the context of these manuscripts, the *Akbarnama* is without doubt the most revealing as it both defines Akbar's world as he wished it to be seen and established his relationship to the past. Although the manuscript was begun after the emperor had moved from Fatehpur-Sikri to Lahore, it is clear that his years at Fatehpur-Sikri played a major role in the formation of his character and attitude towards history. It was there, for instance, that he established most of the institutions described in the *Ain-i Akbari* and consciously set about documenting, in minute detail, the events of his reign. The city also left a strong imprint on the visual memory of the emperor's artists, who were able to paint its buildings and accurately describe events that took place there long after they had presumably moved to the Panjab. Basawan, for instance, was able to recall the punishment of Masud Husayn in 1573 (see p. 48 and NO. 17) in even greater detail than Abul Fazl, while Kesu the Elder (NO. 14) and Tulsi the Elder (NOS. 15, 16) were able to depict with precision the gateways, palaces and surroundings of Fatehpur-Sikri even though such detail is not found in the text.

Indeed, the presence of several illustrations in the Victoria and Albert Museum's copy of the *Akbarnama*

37. *A Fortress under Siege* (Chingiznama, *ca. 1596*).

38. *A Cow and Calf (ca. 1570).*

40. *Dervish (ca. 1570-75).*

39. *Two Mullas (ca. 1565-70).*

that do not follow the text closely raises the possibility that some of the miniatures in the manuscript were either originally intended for an earlier biography of Akbar[66] or painted prior to the actual writing of the book. Since Abul Fazl began researching the manuscript at least two years before he started to write, it is conceivable that a number of miniatures – of either general interest, such as the "Construction of Fatehpur-Sikri" or of particularly memorable events like the "Punishment of Masud Husayn" – were worked on during this period and then inserted into the book at appropriate places. The lack of text on these images as well as their formal qualities, which relate more to paintings of the late 1580s, if not earlier, than they do to miniatures of the 1590s, further supports this possibility.[67]

In addition to the manuscripts they illustrated, the artists of the imperial atelier painted numerous individual images. The earliest of these miniatures (NO. 38) can be attributed to the first years of Akbar's stay at Fatehpur-Sikri. These were either portraits (NOS. 39, 40, 41, 42), studies of local flora and fauna (NO. 43), or landscape studies (NO. 44) which grew out of the Mughals' awareness of their environment. Sometimes, as in "A Flowering Pomegranate Tree" (NO. 43), an intense observation of nature mixed with mythical figures leads to an amusing contrast between reality and fantasy. But for the most part these studies tend to be precise depictions of the animals and plants that caught the attention of the emperor or his artists. The birds (NO. 45) and the family of cheetahs (NO. 46), both curiously painted on cotton, are superb examples of this tradition.

In the *Ain-i Akbari,* Abul Fazl records that "At His Majesty's command portraits have been painted of all of His Majesty's servants and a huge album has been

41. *A Learned Man (ca. 1575-80).*

42. *A Schoolmaster and Pupil (ca. 1585).*

79

44. *Landscape Fragment (ca. 1585-90)*.

43. *A Flowering Pomegranate Tree (ca. 1570-75)*.

45. *Two Birds in a Landscape* (Berlin Jahangir album) *ca. 1580-85*.

made."[68] While these portraits "gave the dead a new life and the living an eternity" they also provided the emperor with a visual record that enabled him to "see" the various members of his court without having to read about them. In doing so they reflect the same attitude towards administrative detail and interest in the activities of the empire that prompted the establishment of the Records Office and they may well have been begun around 1574 as a visual equivalent to the documents of that office. Differences in size and setting suggest that at least two major portrait albums were formed: one with relatively large figures painted against light green backgrounds (NO.47), and one with smaller, usually finer, figures placed within landscapes (NO. 48). There are, as well, many other portraits that do not seem to belong to either of these groups. While it is possible that all of these images once formed part of a single album, it is more likely that they did not and there is no reason why several albums could not have been assembled, one for the emperor and others for his leading courtiers and perhaps even for the women of the harem.

Although the genre of portraiture was not a Mughal innovation, the Mughals' emphasis on verisimilitude distinguishes their images from the more generalized types found in fifteenth- and sixteenth-century Persian painting. Taken as a whole, the portraits made for Akbar give us a unique glimpse of the many people who were part of the emperor's court. From artists (NO. 49), to dancing girls (NO. 50), and Chaghatay women (NO. 51), as well as noblemen (NO. 52) and soldiers (NO. 53), these portraits provide us with a

46. A Family of Cheetahs (ca. 1575-80).

47. Raja Rai Singh of Bikaner (ca. 1590).

48. *Wandering Ascetic (ca. 1585).*

49. *Self Portrait by Kesu Das (ca. 1570).*

50. *Courtesan (ca. 1585).*

51. *A Chaghatay Noblewoman (ca. 1595).*

82

52. *A Muslim Courtier (ca. 1585).*

53. *A Rajput Soldier (ca. 1575).*

54. *Portrait of Raisal Darbari (ca. 1580-85).*

55. *Portrait of Tansen (ca. 1580).*

vivid picture of life in Akbar's India. The custodian of the imperial harem, Raisal Darbari (NO. 54) appears in a miniature of the mid-1580s as a man of great power and stern disposition, dressed in red and blue robes that barely conceal his muscular arms and strong limbs. According to Abul Fazl, he was the son of Raja Soja, a Shaykhawat Rajput.[69] Shah Nawaz Khan adds that:

Raja Raisal through his good fortune became a favourite of Emperor Akbar, and excelled his peers in intimacy and trust. As his good nature and understanding were apparent, he gradually rose in position of trust, and was put in charge of the royal seraglio... He was long lived, and had 21 sons, each one of whom had many children.[70]

In 1602, Raisal was raised to the rank of commander of 2,500 men and 1,250 horses indicating his importance at court.[71] Under Jahangir he served in the Deccan and was not only promoted to a commander of 3,000 but also granted an imperial flag.[72] In another portrait, Tansen, Akbar's greatest musician (NO. 55), can be seen leaning on a staff, bells dangling from his waist. He is shown in this painting as a man of about forty years with a long aquiline nose and sharp well-defined eyes. In 1562, Akbar sent Jalal ad-Din Qurchi to lure Tansen away from his patron Ram Chand of Panna. The latter:

received the royal message and recognized the sending of an envoy as an honour, and sent back with him suitable presents of elephants of fame and valuable jewels, and he also gave Tan Sen suitable instruments and made him the cheek-mole of his gifts... As he had an upright nature and an acceptable disposition he was cherished by a long service and association with H. M., and great developments were made by him in music and in composition.[73]

Tansen spent most of his time under Akbar at Fatehpur-Sikri, where he perfected his talents. When he died on April 26, 1589, Akbar ordered all his musicians and singers to accompany Tansen's body to his grave and to make melodies as if it were a marriage.[74]

The women of Mughal India are also revealed in detail in these portraits. The courtesan (NO. 50) with her mirror and many tassels was painted sometime in the late 1570s or early 1580s. Could she have been an employee in the suburb known as Shaytanpura (Devil's Town) that Akbar constructed outside of Fatehpur-Sikri for the city's growing population of prostitutes? In order to maintain control over the inhabitants of this area and pleasure-seekers from the Court the emperor,

appointed a keeper, and a deputy, and a secretary for this quarter, so that any one who wished to associate with these people, or take them to his house, provided he first had his name and condition written down, might with the connivance of the imperial officers have connection with any of them he pleased. But he did not permit any man to take dancing-girls to his house at night, without conforming to these conditions.[75]

Despite these measures the emperor's courtiers continued to see the prostitutes and dancing-girls of the city without official permission. Eventually Akbar was forced to call several well-known prostitutes from Shaytanpura to his palace in Fatehpur-Sikri in order to inquire about their seducers.[76] Among the noblemen uncovered in this way was Raja Birbar, one of Akbar's closest companions and friends, and a man of allegedly outstanding virtue.[77]

Although the emperor's library was the most important center for production and collection of books in India, it was not the only one. A number of Akbar's courtiers maintained libraries, some containing as many as four or five thousand books, while others even had the capacity to produce illustrated manuscripts. Their miniatures, however, are invariably painted in a rougher, less sophisticated manner than those of imperial manuscripts. Among the noblemen with the largest libraries were Fayzi (see Chapter IV), Abd ar-Rahim Khan Khanan and Mirza Aziz Koka. As many as five calligraphers, including Abd ar-Rahim al-Haravi and Mawlana Baqir, both of whom eventually went to work for Akbar, and eight painters were employed in the Khan Khanan's library which was also a gathering place for large group of scholars, poets, and writers.[78] A copy of the *Ramayana* begun in 1587-88 and completed in 1598-99, based directly on the translation of the manuscript prepared for Akbar, containing one hundred and thirty well executed paintings, suggests both the size and importance of the Khan Khanan's library.[79]

The earliest dated sub-imperial manuscript extant, however, is the *Kitab-i Saat* (NO. 56), an astrological treatise copied for Mirza Aziz Koka at Hajipur by Muhammad Yusuf. The manuscript, which contains twelve miniatures, was completed on November 7, 1583 and reflects the growing power and wealth of the leading members of Akbar's court due to the stability and prosperity of the emperor's years at Fatehpur-Sikri. As one of Akbar's foster brothers and good friends, Mirza Aziz was in a unique position to benefit from the enhanced conditions of the empire. He was renowned for amusing comments: "A man said something, and I thought it was true. He was vehement about it, and I began to doubt. When he swore to it, I knew it was a lie."[80] Mirza Aziz was also an accomplished calligrapher and a pupil of Mawlana Baqir, the son of the great Persian master of *nastaliq,* Mir Ali.[81]

Although there has yet to be a detailed study of imagery in Akbari manuscripts, it is clear that the emperor often followed older patterns. It has recently been shown that within the Islamic tradition of book illustration different types of texts tended to evolve different illustrative traditions, with text and paintings generally transmitted as a complete unit.[82] The major distinction lies between historical manuscripts characterized by their greater number of illustrations, larger format, and bolder manner of painting, and poetic texts whose illustrations are far fewer in number but extraordinary in terms of quality. Under Akbar's patronage the same pattern is visible. The two miniatures illustrated here from the pocket-sized *Divan* of Anvari (NOS. 26, 27) are among only fifteen spread throughout the manuscript's three hundred and fifty-four folios, but one hundred and thirty-two large paintings are distributed through the three hundred

and eighty-eight surviving folios of the almost contemporary *Tarikh-i Khandan-i Timuriyya* (fig. 8). Just as Akbar appreciated the inherent qualities of different Arabic scripts in the field of calligraphy, he did not look for identical qualities in illustrations from different types of texts. None of the paintings on the history-laden pages of the *Tarikh-i Alfi* (NO. 31) would ever have been intended to match the intimate precision of a miniature such as the "Boat and Landscape" (NO. 23) from an unidentified poetic manuscript. Nevertheless, in addition to the traditional scenes of enthronements, battles, and sieges, official celebrations, and hunting excursions, a new imagery evolved based on drawing from life and techniques found in European works of art. It is the interaction between these poles of aesthetic experience that guided the development of the visual arts under Akbar's patronage.

56. *Mercury in Gemini* (Kitab-i Saat, *1583*).

CHAPTER IV

THE KITABKHANA AS A CENTER OF COLLECTION

APART FROM being a center of manuscript production, Akbar's *kitabkhana* was also the principal repository for the imperial collection of manuscripts, and albums of paintings and calligraphies. The emperor acquired his collection in four different ways: inheritance, conquest, purchase, and gifts. Akbar was highly acquisitive, so much so that Monserrate, who never quite approved of the flamboyant, worldly side of the emperor's character, was led to bemoan in a letter to his superior in Goa that "Akbar does not see a thing without trying to get a similar one."[1] Although most of the works that Akbar acquired or inherited were of non-Indian origin, once they became a part of the imperial collection, they were enthusiastically studied and enjoyed by the emperor as well as his artists and courtiers.

Akbar's collection can be divided into two broad categories: Persian manuscripts, paintings and calligraphic folios, and non-Persian (mainly European) books, prints, and paintings. The emperor's collection of Persian material can be broken down into three further categories. The most precious group consists of Timurid manuscripts from Herat, and was collected with an eye towards the work of great masters of painting and calligraphy illuminating the chief themes of imperial power. The second, and later, category to be collected consists of manuscripts from Bukhara. Here the main interest focused on versions of the standard masterpieces of Persian literature by one particularly admired calligrapher. The last category is comprised of unfinished manuscripts that were subsequently illustrated in Akbar's *kitabkhana*.

Works, not always genuine, by the great early calligraphers Ibn Muqla (886-940), Ibn al-Bawwab (d. 1022) and Yaqut al-Mustasimi (d. 1298), and the latter masters of *nastaliq* such as Mir Ali at-Tabrizi (ca. 1360-1420) and Sultan Ali al-Mashhadi (1442-1519) were highly sought after throughout the eastern Islamic world. Another passion of aesthetically-minded princes was the desire to own works by great individual painters such as Ustad Kamal ad-Din Bihzad (ca. 1455-1535), whose fame was beginning to rival that of the greatest calligraphers. Increased international trade contacts and diplomatic missions throughout the area stretching from Europe to China also stimulated a taste for foreign curiosities and exotica alongside that for past wonders of the Islamic artistic tradition.

The downfall of the Timurids in Herat, which caused the dispersal of many truly extraordinary works of art, provided wonderful opportunities for princely connoisseurs. The death of Sultan Husayn Mirza (the patron of both Sultan Ali and Bihzad) in 1506 was immediately followed by frenzied activity on the part of those seeking to assume the mantle of Timurid political power to obtain Timurid works of art and, if possible, actual artists, the ultimate cultural status symbols of the early sixteenth century. Among the participants in this highly charged art market were the Uzbeks (who captured Herat and its artisans in 1507), the Safavids (who defeated the Uzbeks in 1510 and moved a good deal of the contents of the former Timurid library to Tabriz), and the Ottoman Turks (who sacked Tabriz four times in the first half of the

Cupola-like Structures (chatri) *on the Roof of the Single-Pillared Pavilion in the Palace Complex (Plan: 63)*

sixteenth century and carried masses of booty back to Istanbul, where much of it still survives in the Topkapu Saray Library). Luckily for Akbar, Babur also entered the fray and taking full advantage of the situation made some brilliant acquisitions. In fact, both Babur and Humayun were inveterate collectors and connoisseurs of books, especially illustrated manuscripts, and they are the ones who set Akbar on a similar path. Furthermore, what they acquired and passed on formed the basis of Akbar's collection at Fatehpur-Sikri.

It is not known exactly when and where Babur managed to obtain the famous copy of the *Shahnama* prepared and illustrated for Prince Muhammad Juki around 1440 (fig. 10). Muhammad Juki was a grandson of Timur and a brother of the more prolific patron Prince Baysunghur, who wrote the preface for this recension of the Persian "Book of Kings." Babur's seal (at the upper left corner of the fly-leaf) is dated "96," which probably stands for the year A. H. 906 (1500-01). A more likely time for him to have acquired this manuscript, though, would have been during his forty-day visit to Herat in late 1506, just a few months after Sultan Husayn's death, when it might have been given to him as a gift by his Timurid relations. It is also possible that it was acquired by force at some time after the Uzbek conquest of Herat. Babur notes, for example, that when he re-captured Samarqand in 1511 after a nine-year absence he was accompanied by his "muddle-headed" librarian Darvish-i Ali Beg, the younger brother of Sultan Husyan's famous poet, confidant, and statesman Mir Ali Shir Navai (1440-1501). It would have been the librarian's responsibility to find masterpieces such as this *Shahnama* in any recently captured library and add them to his master's collection.

Even before the viewer's eyes fall on the manuscript's thirty-one miniatures and two brilliantly colored and illuminated chapter headings, the Juki *Shahnama* stands out as an extremely impressive object. Approximately thirty-two centimeters (thirteen inches) high and twenty-two centimeters (nine inches) wide, it contains five hundred and thirty-six folios of lustrous pale brown paper set within more recent lighter margins, the fifty thousand or so couplets of the text written in a fine and uncrowded *nastaliq* hand. The thirty-one paintings, which in most cases occupy at least three-quarters of the page, are truly exciting with their rare combination of narrative power and otherworldy luminosity. Small elegant figures act bravely against expansive backdrops of fantastic architecture and stylized rocky landscapes, rendered in coral, turquoise or lavender, of an intensely

hallucinogenic nature. In the folio illustrated here, the final dramatic duel between Prince Isfandiyar and the evil Turanian king Arjasp is almost lost in the huge courtyard of the brilliantly decorated palace, which floats on an ethereal cloud of blue-tinged lavender cliffs – a fantastic realm contrasting dramatically with the often stark reality of Babur's native Central Asian environment.

The awe with which Babur and his descendants must have held this manuscript is amply demonstrated by their seals and inscriptions on the burnished gold fly-leaf (fig. 9) which stands out as a memorial to the Mughal passion for collecting art. At the upper left corner is Babur's seal, executed in a bold script (*thuluth*) and referring to himself as a *qurkani* (son-in-law), alluding to the relationship through which Timur was connected with Chingiz Khan. Across the center of the seal runs a Mongol heraldic device, incorporating the three small circles arranged as a triangle that Timur used as his state or dynastic symbol.[2] At the middle left of the page is a fragment of an early Humayuni seal, in the same style as that of his father and presumably affixed before his exile from India, followed at the top center of the page by a second seal in an elegant *nastaliq* script that reflects the influence of his stay at the Safavid court in Iran.[3] Below this is Jahangir's seal and then to the right is that of Shah Jahan, in which he again picks up the Timurid connection by describing himself as the second Lord of the Auspicious Conjunction of Planets (*sahib-i qiran*), a title originally adopted by Timur.

In the center of the page, Shah Jahan has left an autograph note recording how the manuscript entered his library on the day of his accession to the throne in 1628. Directly beneath is the seal of Aurangzeb who inherited this *Shahnama* almost a century and a half after it was first acquired by Babur. Although Akbar's own seal is missing from this page, there is no doubt that he too was once its proud owner, for during the 1580s or 1590s one of his artists was commissioned to repaint the background landscape of the miniature illustrating "Yazdigird Hiding in the Mill."[4] In 1582 Akbar commissioned a new copy of the *Shahnama* to be transcribed and illustrated in his *kitabkhana* at Fatehpur-Sikri,[5] but it is doubtful whether this now-lost version ever fully matched the emotional value of the Juki "Book of Kings" first acquired by his grandfather.

Babur's interest in collecting books continued once he entered India. On his way to Delhi at the beginning of 1526 he managed to capture the fort of Milvat from Ghazi Khan, the son of Dawlat Khan Lodi (whose wavering loyalty later caused an exasperated Babur to describe his as a "rustic blockhead"[6]). Ghazi Khan was an acclaimed poet and man of learning, so it was with great expectation that Babur entered the fort and sought out his library. In the words of his close companion Zayn Khan, "Having cast his glance personally on some of the books, he [Babur] left the work of examination and investigation of the rest to the judges and scholars who had been attending on his victorious stirrups."[7] The general conclusion was that not many books were of special interest or value, certainly far fewer than they had expected. Nevertheless some of the better ones were presented to Humayun, who had taken part in the initial examination and was referred to in this regard by Zayn Khan as "the true judge of books,"[8] while others were sent to his brother Prince Kamran in Qandahar. Humayun's original anticipation must have soured even further when he discovered that his story-teller had been struck by an arrow and killed on the battlefield during the capture of Ghazi Khan's fort.

Expectations of bibliographic loot were again heightened upon the final defeat of Sultan Ibrahim Lodi at Panipat three months later. While Babur relaxed in Delhi and visited its many monuments and famous tombs, an advance party including Humayun, the treasurer Amir Wali Qizil, and Babur's long-serving librarian Amir Abdullah Beg was sent to subdue Ibrahim's fortress in Agra and to take charge of its treasures. It is unfortunate that no mention is made in the histories as to what they found in the way of books that belonged to the former sultans of Delhi. If any illustrated manuscript did fall into their hands, however, it is fair to assume that they would have found the paintings crude in comparison with the fine Timurid miniatures in the works they already possessed.

Humayun inherited the incipient Mughal collection in 1530. According to Abul Fazl, he regarded the especially rare books as his "real companions" and always kept them with him—in boxes strapped on the back of camels during his many campaigns.[9] How-

57. *Timur Granting an Audience* (*Zafarnama, ca. 1467*).

FIG. 9. Flyleaf from the *Shahnama* of Firdausi, ca. 1440: Royal Asiatic Society, London (Ms. 239).

ever, because of his increasingly tenuous political status this turned out to be a questionable policy. In late 1534 he set off from Agra in order to conquer Gujarat and first caught up with its ruler, Sultan Bahadur Shah, in eastern Rajasthan. He then pursued him, books in tow, on a triumphant chase through Mandu, Champanir, Cambay, and Diu before he succeeded in driving him out of Gujarat in 1535. It was while encamped at Cambay, savoring this stunning victory, that Humayun's luck ran out. Just before dawn one day a band of five thousand tribal rebels fell upon the Mughal camp and in the ensuing fracas managed to plunder many of the emperor's rarest and most beloved books. Among the works taken, according to the slightly confused account of Abul Fazl, was a copy of "the *Timurnama*, transcribed by Mulla Sultan Ali and illustrated by Ustad Bihzad, and which is now in the Shahinshah's library [i.e. Akbar's]."[10]

Despite Abul Fazl's description, there can be no doubt that the manuscript in question is actually a copy of Sharaf ad-Din Yazdi's *Zafarnama* copied by Shir Ali in 1467-68 for Sultan Husayn Mirza and containing miniatures attributed to Bihzad (NO. 57).[11] Completed in 1424-25, the *Zafarnama* is an account of the life and times of Timur, a subject of obvious interest to the Mughals. Surprisingly, in this manuscript the program of illustration consists only of six double-page miniatures, a format that was previously reserved almost exclusively for the frontispiece of a manuscript, but was later widely used by Akbar's artists. This device allows these magnificent miniatures of royal audiences and military engagements an expansiveness, coupled with a wonderful sense of exciting detail, that would otherwise have proved impossible in a manuscript measuring only about twenty-one centimeters (eight and one quarter inches) high and about twelve centimeters (four and three-quarters inches) wide. The pages illustrated here show Timur granting an audience in a garden at Balkh on the occasion of his succession to the line of the Chaghatay Khans (see above, p. 14), a moment of great political importance for the Mughals. Could the Mughals ever have found an image more to their liking than this spectacular representation of Timur seated on a wooden throne in front of a splendid imperial domed tent or yurt? The idyllic nature of the garden setting is only rivalled by the vibrancy of the assembled textiles, the animal-head design seen on the roof of the yurt being similar to one that was later used on carpets woven in Akbar's own workshops (see Chapter V).

The subsequent history of this manuscript is a testimony to the remarkable adventures that awaited valuable Timurid manuscripts in the volatile sixteenth century—and the seemingly magnetic drawing power of the Mughal library by the time of Akbar. After being looted from Humayun's camp in Gujarat in 1535, its travels remain a mystery until the 1570s, after which a series of seals and autograph inscriptions of the Mughal emperors on the manuscript's flyleaf take over the story.[12] Under the crudely written word "Farvardin" (the first month of the Persian solar year), Jahangir recorded in his own shaky hand that, "This word is in the blessed handwriting of his late departed Majesty [Akbar], now in heaven, and Mir Jamal ud-Din Husayn Inju [who had entered the emperor's service at some time before the battle of Pattan in early 1573]

FIG. 10. "Isfandiyar Slays Arjasp in the Iron Fortress," *Shahnama* of Firdausi, ca. 1440: Royal Asiatic Society, London (Ms. 239, f. 278).

presented this copy to his Majesty in the capital of the caliphate, Agra."[13] How delighted, and surprised, Akbar must have been to recover such a prized possession of his late father. From a series of notes on the last page of the manuscript, we also know that it was originally appraised, presumably by Akbar's librarian, at 1,550 rupees, but after Akbar had looked through it he decided that its exceptional quality warranted its value being nearly doubled to 3,000 rupees.[14]

As was the case with the Juki *Shahnama,* family appreciation for this copy of the history of their illustrious ancestor continued, and Jahangir's second note, at the bottom right corner of the flyleaf, records that it was transferred into his library during the first year of his reign (1605), and also confirms Abul Fazl's belief that the miniatures were painted by Bihzad. Later on, Shah Jahan added a more elegantly written note in the top right corner of the page to the effect that the manuscript entered his library on the day of his accession to the throne, the same day on which he inscribed the Juki *Shahnama.* After the death of Shah Jahan it passed into the possession of Aurangzeb whose seal, dated 1659-60, also figures on the flyleaf.

What was left of the core of the Mughal library survived Humayun's exile in Iran, largely due to the loyal efforts of the librarian Mulla Balal, who accompanied the emperor throughout his unhappy peregrinations.[15] Nevertheless Humayun had not learned a lesson from his disastrous loss at Cambay and in mid-1550 he again sallied onto the battlefield with his camel-back library–this time against his brother Kamran. His forces lost the rather confused encounter and in the ensuing chaos the camels disappeared with the books. As the lost goods presumably included the Juki *Shahnama,* it is not hard to imagine the grief Humayun felt at this latest in a series of unfortunate setbacks.

Soon, however, Humayun's situation took a definite turn for the better and a few months later he was able to recapture Kabul, where he had an emotional reunion with the eight-year-old Prince Akbar who had been held hostage there by Kamran. No sooner had they finished embracing when, in the words of Abul Fazl,

Two camels loaded with boxes and without drivers were seen on the field of battle. His Majesty said "every one is having his plunder, let mine be these two camels!" He went himself and taking their nose-strings, ordered that they should be made to kneel and that the boxes should be opened, so that he might see what was inside. By a beautiful coincidence it was found that special, royal books which were lost at the battle of Qibcaq were in these boxes and in perfect condition. This was the occasion for a thousand rejoicings.[16]

The emotions that Humayun exhibited upon the return of these precious manuscripts must have left a lasting impression on Akbar, who was then old enough to recognize that, for his father at least, books had a value far beyond that of the text alone.

Apart from family heirlooms such as the Juki *Shahnama* and the 1467-68 *Zafarnama,* Akbar's *kitabkhana* contained a range of Persian material whose time and place of accession into the Mughal collection is more difficult to ascertain. Some of these works might have been procured by Babur or Humayun but others found their way to India as a result of Akbar's almost insatiable appetite for books. The zeal with which rare manuscripts were chased down in this period is well illustrated by a case involving Abd ar-Rahim Khan Khanan. In an autograph note on a manuscript of the *Khamsa* of Amir Khusrau Dihlavi he managed to piece together in 1617, Abd ar-Rahim notes how he had first sent one of his librarians (Mir Baqi Samarqandi) all the way to Gujarat in 1603-04 with a large sum of money and firm orders to buy up any stray folios he could lay his hands on.[17]

Loose paintings as well as manuscripts were a prime target for collection, and one of Akbar's most prized possessions must have been a painting by Bihzad of two camels fighting completed when the artist was seventy years old ca. 1525.[18] Now in the collection of the Gulistan Museum in Tehran, it is mounted with a later copy made in India for Jahangir, who added an autograph note to the new version saying that Bihzad's painting "was seen and copied by Nanha the painter according to my orders" in 1608-09.[19] Thanks to a recently discovered copy, painted by Abd as-Samad around 1585 (NO. 58), it is now evident that Bihzad's original also once belonged to Akbar. Intriguingly, Abd as-Samad's version (which is reversed and extended at the top) is a stylistically freer adaptation than that of Nanha, who strained to make an extraordinarily exact copy for Jahangir.[20] The heavier shading on the tree in the right background, the weightier human figures, and the less stylized representation of the field on which the camels are engaged in battle all stamp Abd as-Samad's work as unmistakably Mughal. It also shows the great sense of experimentation that characterized Akbar's *kitabkhana* at Fatehpur-Sikri, where even works by Bihzad were subject to close scrutiny and subtle re-interpretation as part of the quest to formulate a new mode of painting. An exact copy would have been of no interest to Akbar.

From the middle of the sixteenth century onwards, Bukhara replaced Herat as the main source of Persian manuscripts for Akbar's collection. In 1500, the Uzbek

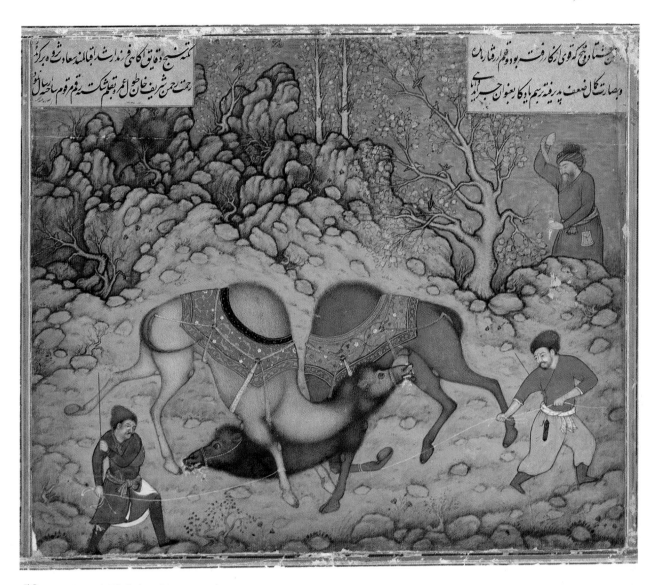

58. *Two Camels Fighting (ca. 1580-90).*

Shaybani Khan captured most of Transoxiana from the Timurids and followed this up in 1507 with the conquest of Herat. There, the highly literate but immodest Uzbek ruler inherited the Timurid *kitabkhana* and, according to a shocked Babur, even had the nerve to take pen in hand and correct the calligraphy of Sultan Ali and the drawing of Bihzad.[21] In 1510 Shaybani lost Herat to the Safavids, but the Uzbeks in Bukhara never gave up their claim to the city and its cultural legacy and attacked it frequently before Shaybani's nephew Ubaydullah Khan finally recaptured it in 1528-29. On this occasion a number of Herati artisans were taken back to Bukhara, where they received renewed, if enforced, patronage.

Painting, clearly imbued with the influence of Bihzad, flourished under Ubaydullah in Bukhara, and upon his death in 1539 it reached new heights under the guidance of his son Abd al-Aziz Khan, who ruled until 1549. In an anthology composed in 1566, Hasan Nisari left a glowing description of the Uzbek *kitabkhana*: "the gilders and illuminators of the studio, having brought decoration and painting to perfection, with a single hair point depicted faces so that in portrait drawing [even] a hair tip of a person depicted had no flaw – and in art everyone of them was another Mani and better than Bihzad's pupils."[22] Among those brought to Bukhara from Herat in 1528-29 was the calligrapher Mir Ali al-Husayni, a former student of Sultan Ali, and a great admirer of Babur, in whose honor he wrote a number of poems (see above, p. 17). Mir Ali excited great interest among the later Mughal emperors, suggesting that when collecting non-Mughal manuscripts it was often the work of the calligrapher rather than the painters who illustrated it

93

that was most keenly sought.[23] Mir Ali's acceptance of Babur as the savior of the Timurid dynasty also increased his popularity with the Mughal emperors. But such widespread popularity could be inherently dangerous for a sixteenth-century calligrapher, as one of Mir Ali's own poems poignantly attests:

A long life of exercise bent my body like a harp,
Until the handwriting of this unfortunate one had become
    of such a canon
That all the kings of the world sought me out, whereas
In Bukhara, for means of existence, my liver is steeped in
    blood
My entrails have been burnt up by sorrow. What am I to do?
    How shall I manage?
For I have no way out of this town,
This misfortune has fallen on my head for the beauty of my
    writing.
Alas! Mastery in calligraphy has become a chain on the feet
    of this demented one.[24]

Many Bukharan works of this period ended up in India, some of them surprisingly soon after they were finished. Two illustrated and beautifully illuminated manuscripts calligraphed by Mir Ali are typical with respect to the path they followed into Akbar's India. The earlier of the two is a *Bustan* (Flower Garden) of Sadi copied in Bukhara in 1531-32 with three miniatures retouched by artists working for Jahangir in the early part of the seventeenth century.[25] The second is a copy of Jami's *Tuhfat al-Ahrar* (Gift of the Free) apparently copied in Bukhara in the 1540s, also with three miniatures.[26] Both manuscripts carry virtually identical autograph notes by Jahangir giving a partial history of how they came into his collection, but unfortunately he does not explain how or when they left Bukhara. According to Jahangir, they at first belonged to his younger brother Murad and then upon this prince's death in 1599 they passed into Akbar's *kitabkhana*. Jahangir inherited them from his father with the throne in 1605.

How the manuscripts came into the possession of Murad is a mystery. Although there is a purported mark of Akbar's librarian in the *Tuhfat al-Ahrar* dated to the first year of Akbar's reign (1556),[27] this seems to be an almost impossibly early date for it to have left Bukhara. Furthermore, this would require it to have been collected by Humayun, whose seal is nowhere to be found in either this manuscript or the *Bustan*. None of the histories mention Murad as a bibliophile, but his background and education would not preclude such interests. In fact, he was probably the best educated of Akbar's sons, his formal education having been entrusted both to the poet Fayzi (when he was eight years old) and shortly afterwards, to the Jesuit

fathers who taught him Portuguese over a number of years.

One answer to the puzzle might be that the two manuscripts were presented to Murad in Kabul (the closest he ever came to Bukhara) in 1581 when, as an eleven-year-old, he led the imperial army to victory against Mirza Hakim Muhammad. Another possibility is that he came across them after 1583 when he was appointed to manage the administration of the royal household. Significantly, he was aided in this position, which included jurisdiction over the imperial workshops, by Abd as-Samad.[28] Whatever the case may be, by around 1580 there were enough high-quality manuscripts on the market to ensure that serious book-collecting was no longer the prerogative of emperors alone.

Another Bukharan manuscript to enter Akbar's collection is a copy of the *Gulistan* of Sadi now in the British Library (NO. 59). Its colophon, which is dated A. H. 975 (1567-68), gives the name of its calligrapher as Mir Ali al-Husayni.[29] The manuscript contains thirteen miniatures executed at two different times: six painted in a Bukharan manner contemporary with the date in the colophon, and the remaining seven added by Mughal artists during the first decade of the seventeenth century. Illustrated here is one of the four paintings in the first group, signed by the artist Shahm Muzahhib (Shahm the Illuminator). Painted in a manner that clearly belies the artist's Bukharan origins, it illustrates a prince and his courtiers watching a wrestling contest between an old master and his arrogant young pupil. The face of the prince is rendered as a portrait of the young emperor Akbar and the canopied throne in which he sits is inscribed, "It was ordered in the days of the prosperity of the great king Jalal al-Din Muhammad Akbar, may Allah perpetuate his kingship and sovereignty."[30]

This Mughal intrusion, along with the fact that all the paintings are larger than the text panels, allows one to conclude that the seven "Bukharan" miniatures were actually added after the manuscript arrived in India.[31] The existence of another painting in Shahm's hand in Akbar's 1570 *Anvar-i Suhayli* further suggests that the manuscript was illustrated in India around 1570.[32] One wonders, in fact, whether the manuscript might have been brought to India by Shahm himself: an example of an international trade in manuscripts ready for illustration carried out by unemployed artists seeking work at the courts of newly active patrons

59. *The Old Wrestler Who Overthrew an Arrogant Pupil* (Gulistan *of Sadi, 1567-68*).

94

such as Akbar. Shahm never again received any commissions from Akbar, however, and consequently Bukharan painting had virtually no effect on the development of Mughal art.

Two Persian manuscripts of uncertain lineage are examples of early material that was considerably altered and embellished by Akbar's artists once it came into his possession. The first is an exquisite copy of the *Khamsa* of Nizami measuring about 16 by 10 cm. and now part of the Keir collection.[33] According to three colophons found in different sections of the manuscript, it was calligraphed in the Iranian city of Yazd by Ali ibn Mubarak al-Fahraji between 1502 and 1506. By the 1580s it was in the hands of Akbar who ordered that the thirty-five spaces for illustrations, left blank in Yazd, be filled in by his own painters. These new Akbari miniatures can be dated to the second half of the 1580s on the basis of the presence of work by the artist Farrukh Beg, who only arrived at Akbar's court from Iran in 1585. If indeed the text and the artist

FIG. 11. Page from a *Divan* of Hafiz, margin figures added in late sixteenth century (ex-Bute collection).

arrived in India simultaneously, Farrukh Beg's presence at court with a conveniently unillustrated manuscript would strike an interesting parallel with the case of Shahm and the unfinished Bukharan *Gulistan* described above.

Another non-Mughal manuscript embellished in Akbar's *kitabkhana* is a *Divan* of Hafiz (fig. 11), the text of which is said by Shah Jahan, in an autograph note on the book's flyleaf, to have been written by the celebrated Timurid calligrapher Sultan Ali al-Mashhadi.[34] The style of the illuminated frontispiece confirms a date in the first half of the sixteenth century, but the manuscript's sumptuously decorated new margins were only added towards the end of the century after it had come into Akbar's possession.[35] The decoration, which closely prefigures the elaborate margins favored by Jahangir, consists of human and animal figures portrayed either against highly stylized landscapes or within small rosettes and cusped medallions. It is almost entirely executed in gold, although some of the human figures, shown in a variety of poses, are enlivened with touches of color. Like the earlier illustrated Timurid manusripts, this *Divan* of Hafiz was dutifully passed down from father to son by the later Mughal emperors until at least the reign of Aurangzeb, whose seal surmounts the ornate illumination on the first page of the text.

Always on the lookout for new sources of luxury goods and items of curiosity, Akbar took full advantage of the growing European trade with India. While the most significant outcome of this interest was the arrival of a Jesuit mission in Fatehpur-Sikri in 1580, this was by no means Akbar's first contact with Europeans and their art. The initial contact had in fact taken place during the siege of Surat in early 1573 when the inhabitants of the fort sought help from the Portuguese, who had occupied Goa in 1510. But when the Portuguese reinforcements arrived at Surat they soon took stock of Akbar's strength and decided instead to pass themselves off as ambassadors to his court. According to Abul Fazl's description of this meeting, "They produced many of the rarities of their country, and the appreciative Khedive [Akbar] received each one of them with a special favour and made inquiries about the wonders of Portugal and the manners and customs of Europe. It seemed as if he did this from a desire of knowledge, for his sacred heart is a depot of spiritual and physical sciences."[36] European art, however, had already made its presence felt in Mughal painting before this historic meeting.

Even in the very earliest productions of Akbar's patronage one can discern a Mughal awareness of European art. In the "Storm at Sea" from the ca.

1560-65 *Tutinama* (NO. 10), a blond passenger wears a European-style costume, and a figure at the very bottom left-hand corner of a miniature in the 1568 *Ashiqa* is also portrayed in distinctly European garb.[37] More importantly, a painting by Basawan from the same early *Tutinama* proves that an anonymous European engraving, dated 1544, after one by Georg Pencz (Nuremberg, ca. 1500-50) had reached Akbar's *kitabkhana* by at least the mid-1560s.[38] It was the figure leaning on a crutch at the right of this print of "Joseph Telling His Dream to His Father" (NO. 62) that provided Basawan with the model for a figure of a hunter in the *Tutinama* miniature.

The European print presumably reached Mughal India from Goa, which was well connected with Antwerp by ship, but the convincing portrayal of two Europeans in a miniature from a *Zafarnama* illustrated for Shah Tahmasp in 1529[39] leaves open the possibility that this type of material could have been brought to India from Iran, perhaps as part of an artist's scrapbook. The influence of this print went beyond its role as a new source of stock figures for the Mughal *kitabkhana*, for Basawan, along with certain other Mughal artists, also responded to its technique. This copy after Pencz, and especially the detail of the old man with the crutch, proved to be an extraordinarily popular source of subject matter for artists working in Akbar's *kitabkhana* throughout the rest of the century. Prior to the time of Fatehpur-Sikri, European prints occupied a rather modest position in the Mughal collection. They were used more as source material for his artists than admired by Akbar as precious objects in their own right.

According to Abul Fazl, one of the outcomes of Akbar's contact with the Portuguese in 1572-73 was a growing awareness on his part of the "curiosities and rarities of the skilled craftsmen of that country."[40] In fact, the emperor's interest in European articles soon reached such a level that in late 1575 he dispatched an artistic mission to Goa from Fatehpur-Sikri under the command of Haji Habibullah. In the words of Abul Fazl, he "was appointed to take with him a large sum of money, and the choice articles of [Mughal] India to Goa, and to bring for H. M.'s delectation the wonderful things of that country. There were sent along with him many clever craftsmen, who to ability and skill added industry, in order that just as the wonderful productions of that country (Goa and Europe) were being brought away, so also might rare crafts be imported (into Akbar's dominions)."[41]

The mission stayed in Goa for almost two years, in a remarkable display of early cultural exchange. In December, 1577 they arrived back and Haji Habibullah,

60. *The Head of Saint John the Baptist (ca. 1580).*

"attended by a large number of persons dressed up as Christians and playing European drums and clarions," paid homage to Akbar, who was encamped at the time between Delhi and Fatehpur-Sikri. Abul Fazl's account continues that after the Haji had placed some of the choice articles of Goa before Akbar, "Craftsmen who had gone to acquire skill displayed the arts which they had learnt and received praises in the critical place of testing."[42] An object that might have been made by one of these Mughal artists in Goa is a small, yellowish sandstone plaque showing the head of St. John the Baptist being presented to Salome (NO. 60). Miniature bas-relief carving in stone was virtually unknown in Mughal India, but one of the main aims of the mission was just this type of experimentation with new media. In Goa the artist who produced this object had plenty of opportunity to copy his composition from a European representation of the same scene. Nevertheless the way in which he transformed a foreign composition in a strange medium leaves little doubt of his Mughal background, especially in his handling of the drapery and architectural setting.

A number of European musical instruments were also brought back from Goa but none of them caused as much excitement as an elaborate organ that was exhibited to the public in Fatehpur-Sikri at the beginning of 1581. According to the description of the event left by a bemused Badauni, "It was like a great box the size of a man. A European sits inside it and plays the strings thereof, and two others keep putting their fingers on five peacock-wings, and all sorts of sounds come forth. And because the emperor was so pleased, the Europeans kept coming at every moment in red and yellow colours, and went from one extravagance to another. The people at the meeting were astounded at this wonder, and indeed it is impossible for language to do justice to the description of it."[43]

In March, 1578, just a few months after the first mission had returned from Goa, Father Pereira, the Jesuit Vicar-General of Bengal, arrived in Fatehpur-Sikri at Akbar's invitation. In many discussions concerning the nature of Christianity, Pereira encouraged Akbar to make contact with the Jesuit missionaries at the College of St. Paul in Goa, to whom an embassy was dispatched soon afterwards. Akbar's embassy, which arrived in Goa in September, 1579, carried a letter from the emperor addressed to the Jesuit fathers and asking them to send to Fatehpur-Sikri, "two learned priests who should bring with them the chief books of the Law and the Gospel. . . . The moment my ambassadors return let them not hesitate to come with them and let them bring the books of the Law."[44] Eagerly responding to Akbar's invitation, the Jesuit mission, comprised of Fathers Acquaviva, Henriques and Monserrate, set out from Goa in November, 1579 and reached Fatehpur-Sikri on the last day of February, 1580.

Within a week of their arrival in Fatehpur-Sikri the priests, with the exception of Father Monserrate, who was ill from the journey, left their noisy quarters in the caravanserai and proceeded up to the palace where they presented Akbar with seven of the eight volumes of the Antwerp *Polyglot Bible* (NO. 61). According to a joint letter written by the priests shortly after the event, "On the day we made the presentation he [Akbar] performed such an elaborate ceremonial that we were altogether surprised. He caught hold of each individual tome and, after kissing it, placed it on the head with great reverence in front of all his grandees and captains and the rest of the people gathered in the vast courtyard of the palace, and everyone was amazed."[45] The account is continued in another joint letter written to the Father Provincial in Goa: "Thereafter, while he commanded us to go inside, he leafed through those books with great reverence and delight and wished that it should be left to him. He now keeps it in his residence (where he is most of the time), in a new desk [or box], which he ordered specially for this purpose."[46]

As both a great bibliophile and seeker after knowledge, Akbar not surprisingly was excited about the addition of the *Polyglot Bible* to his collection. Prepared under the sponsorship of Philip II of Spain and the editorial supervision of his personal chaplain, it was printed in four languages (Hebrew, Chaldean, Latin and Greek) by Christophe Plantin in Antwerp between 1568-72.[47] The bold juxtaposition of the four different scripts in the text would have immediately fascinated Akbar, but what must have really captured his imagination were the title pages engraved by a variety of Flemish artists such as Pieter van der Heyden, Pieter Huys, and the Wiericx brothers. Even if their complex symbolism needed some explanation in the beginning, they served as useful didactic tools for the Jesuits. Monserrate relates how during the campaign to put down Mirza Hakim Muhammad in 1581, Akbar "ordered the sacred volumes to be brought and the Priest to be called . . . Then [after a long monologue] the Priest, at the King's command, unrolled the books; and seizing his opportunity, explained the pictures."[48] There is no doubt that they were also closely scrutinized within the *kitabkhana*.[49]

The Jesuit missionaries brought to Fatehpur-Sikri at least two European altarpieces that were highly admired by Akbar and his courtiers. Approximately a month after the Jesuits arrived in the city, and just one day after they had moved to new quarters within the palace precincts, Akbar came alone to pay them a visit. This was almost immediately recorded in a letter by Henriques: "The first thing he [Akbar] did was to go into the church, which was well appointed with its perfumes and fragrance. On entering he was suprised and astonished and made a deep obeisance to the picture of Our Lady that was there, from the painting of St. Luke, done by Brother Manuel Godinho, as well as to another beautifully executed representation of Our Lady brought by Fr. Martin da Silva from Rome, which pleased him no end.[50] After stepping outside briefly to discuss these pictures with his attendants, he came back in with his "chief painter" and other painters, "and they were all wonderstruck and said that there could be no better paintings nor better artists than those who had painted the said pictures."[51] In a letter written a couple of months after the visit, Acquaviva further recalls that Akbar "prayed before the picture of Christ and the Virgin, venerating thrice, once in our manner, the other in that of the Muslims and the third in the Hindu fashion, that is to say prostrate, saying that God should be adored with every form of adoration."[52]

The first painting mentioned by Henriques was copied by Brother Manuel Godinho in Goa[53] from another copy made in Rome of the Madonna and Child in the Borghese Chapel of the Church of Santa

Maria Maggiore. The earlier copy of this famous painting popularly attributed to St. Luke had been made by order of St. Francis Borgia with the express permission of Pope Pius V and sent to Goa in 1578.[54] A number of copies were evidently made at the same time in Rome, for in 1578 Spanish Franciscans arrived in Macao with one, and then in 1581 another larger copy arrived in the same Portuguese post on the coast of China, destined for the Jesuit mission there.[55] The identity of the second altarpiece is less clear, but comments made by one of Akbar's courtiers, on a subsequent visit, to the effect that "it was truly that of the heavenly queen seated on her throne"[56] at least give a basic idea of the painting's iconography.

The second visit to see the altarpieces took place just one week after the first one, but this time Akbar was accompanied by his three sons, Abul Fazl, and three other senior government officials. He instructed them to leave their shoes outside and then specifically warned his sons to behave respectfully inside the dimly lit chapel. Once in front of the St. Luke Madonna, however, the young princes, according to an effusive letter from Henriques, "could no longer contain their joy at seeing the Infant Jesus in his Mother's arms, and it seemed as if they would have liked to play with him and talk to him if they could only approach him."[57] Seeing how enamoured he was with their altarpieces, the Jesuits offered Akbar the one that Father da Silva had brought from Rome. Akbar "was full of joy over it, and wrapping it with much reverence, he took it home."[58] Soon afterwards the latest acquisition to the imperial collection was put on public display outside one of the palaces.[59]

Almost immediately, Akbar started to order that copies of the Jesuit material be made by his artists. Replicas of crucifixes, for example, were made in gold and ivory, and he also had a gold reliquary made for himself.[60] This round of activity might also be considered as an alternative origin for the small sandstone plaque showing the head of St. John the Baptist (NO. 60; see above p. 97). Akbar also ordered copies of the altarpieces to be made by his painters. Unfortunately, no contemporary copies of the St. Luke Madonna and Child have survived, but there is a later version in a Jahangiri album in the Gulistan Palace Library in Tehran.[61] A Mughal enthroned Madonna and Child from around this period does, however, suggest itself as possibly being one of the original copies made of the so far unidentified painting brought from Rome by Father da Silva.[62] More significantly, this flurry of activity around the material brought to Fatehpur-Sikri by the Jesuits caused a new wave of interest in European prints.[63]

61. *Polyglot Bible (1568-72).*

One of the prints brought out again for copying by the Mughal artists was the anonymous European engraving after Georg Pencz's "Joseph Telling His Dream to His Father" (NO. 62). This time, Kesu Das, who along with Basawan was one of the artists most responsible for integrating Europrean subjects and techniques into the Mughal idiom, made a full copy of the Pencz composition which can be dated on stylistic grounds to 1580-85.[64] Kesu Das added a new background to this otherwise faithful version, which shows that another painting of the same scene he did only about five years later (NO. 63) was recopied from his earlier painting rather than from the print.[65] The second version, which has been extended at the top by the addition of two oversized birds in order to better fit the dimensions of the Jahangiri album in which it was later included, shows a more sophisticated inte-

gration of European techniques. It appears that after the initial excitement over the Jesuit material had died down following the departure of the first mission from Fatehpur-Sikri in 1583, the mere presence in a Mughal painting of easily indentifiable European forms was not enough to satisfy Akbar's continually developing taste. In the case of Pencz's "Joseph Telling His Dream to His Father," it can easily be seen how the influence of just one European print could reverberate throughout Mughal painting for a period of decades, even though the original probably was in the emperor's private possession most of the time.

The older practice of using single figures, or groups of figures, from European sources as part of larger compositions continued with greater frequency after 1580 as the number of prints available to Akbar's artists in the *kitabkhana* increased. In most cases their foreign

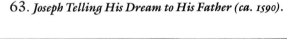

62. *Joseph Telling His Dream to His Father (1544).*   63. *Joseph Telling His Dream to His Father (ca. 1590).*

origin would have been obvious to the Mughal viewer even though they were set in a purely Mughal landscape. Such an example is a painting of ca. 1590 from the Chester Beatty Library of two winged angels attending another one seated in a European chair (NO. 64). Here the exoticism of the angels is brought to the forefront of the image, whose appeal would also have been heightened by the amusingly foreign notion of angels engaging in an exchange of fish. Even more exotic to the Indian eye must have been a pastiche, from ca. 1585-90, of at least two separate pairs of figures brought together to form a splendidly incongruous court scene (NO. 65). As an amateur shoe designer and fashion innovator (see above, p. 50), Akbar must have keenly relished the golden boots of the seated nobleman! Perhaps the finest painting of this genre, however, is an image of the Madonna and Child reclining on a dazzling gold carpet in front of an open pavilion (NO. 66). This miniature, attributed to Basawan, is a glowing testament to the sensitive integration of European subject matter and technique within Mughal painting.

Prints, paintings and other European objects with religious themes were far outnumbered in Akbar's collection by Mughal and Persian material, even though the former had the edge in terms of novelty. In fact, Monserrate records in one of his letters how in September, 1580 a mulla from Mecca presented a Koran "excellently bound and written" to Akbar in Fatehpur-Sikri.[66] The pilgrimage to Mecca was always a prolific source of books and other objects, purchased either during the journey itself, or from other pilgrims in the holy city. One can imagine Akbar eagerly awaiting the return from Mecca each year of the official

64. *Three Angels in a Landscape (ca. 1585).*

65. *Four Europeans (ca. 1590).*

66. *Madonna and Child*
    (ca. 1599-1600).

67. *A Scholar with His Pupil (ca. 1570-80).*

pilgrimage leader with gifts ranging from minor trinkets to texts reflecting the latest trends in religious scholarship.

Books from India also entered Akbar's collection in a steady flow, whether as gifts or as the spoils of military campaigns. Although manuscripts were illustrated in the pre-Mughal Islamic courts of India, they must have left Akbar singularly unimpressed, for there is not one record of his depositing any into his *kitabkhana,* and indeed none has yet to be found with Mughal seals or inscriptions. As an illustration of the low esteem in which Akbar held Indian books, Badauni mentions that a number of books captured from Itimad Khan, the former governor of Ahmadabad in Gujarat, when he surrendered to the Mughal forces in 1572, were taken out of the library in Fatehpur-Sikri by the emperor one night in 1585 and distributed among the learned and pious men in the House of Worship.[67]

68. *A Prince and a Hermit (ca. 1580-85).*

Gifts of books also flowed in the other direction for, as a sign of respect to the emperor, courtiers with a scholarly or literary bent would never fail to present Akbar with a copy of their latest works. In terms of quantity, however, the biggest windfall for Akbar's collection came in 1595 when he inherited four thousand six hundred "valuable bound books" from the library of his recently deceased poet-laureate Fayzi, who had carefully catalogued them in three sections: verse, medicine, astrology, and music; philosophy, religious mysticism, astronomy, and geometry; and, finally, commentaries on the Koran, the traditions of the prophet Muhammad, and books on theology, and all other subjects connected with the sacred law.[68] Although none of these books is said to have been illustrated, the fact that most of them were autograph copies or at least were written in their authors' time was thought to significantly increase their value.

When Akbar died in 1605 after a long and active life of patronage and collecting, no fewer than twenty-four thousand volumes were housed in his *kitabkhana,* according to an early-seventeenth-century Flemish writer.[69] In view of the four-thousand-six-hundred-volume windfall from Fayzi's library alone, there is little reason to doubt this figure. But Akbar's library was more than an ostentatious display of accumulated wealth. The stunning array of Persian and European material that Akbar was able to add to the library throughout his reign provides another important clue to understanding his taste and motivation as a connoisseur of painting and calligraphy. The material Akbar collected formed a spectacular complement to the books and albums that were actually calligraphed, illustrated, and illuminated in his *kitabkhana.*

One outcome of this passion for collecting was a growing tendency on the part of the Mughal emperors to treat inherited objects as vital components of their imperial and dynastic paraphernalia. Numerous Mughal manuscripts contain handwritten inscriptions by Jahangir and Shah Jahan attesting to the fact that one of their very first acts upon ascending the throne was to formally add their father's most precious manuscripts to their own libraries. Objects also acquired an auspicious aura beyond their sentimental value. One example is the case of a huge ruby that had been given to Akbar by his mother, Maryam Makani, on the occasion of Jahangir's birth at Fatehpur-Sikri in 1569, when it had been valued at 125,000 rupees. First Akbar and then Jahangir wore it for many years as a flamboyant ornament on their turbans. But in his memoirs for the year 1617, Jahangir records that "apart from its value and delicacy, as it had come down as of auspicious augury to the everlasting State, it was bestowed on my son [Shah Jahan]."[70] Manuscripts such as the Juki *Shahnama,* however, were never passed on by a living Mughal emperor.

The presence of non-Indian manuscripts and paintings, either inherited or collected by Akbar, also had a crucial impact on the goals Akbar set for the productions of his *kitabkhana.* Timurid masterpieces, including sumptuous versions of the *Shahnama* and the *Zafarnama* exuding overt imperial imagery, collected by Babur and Humayun reflect a very traditional princely taste. Owning these works, which included paintings by the great master Bihzad, represented the peak of their artistic experience. When Akbar inherited this type of manuscript from his father, along with a proclivity for the Timurid aesthetic, he was faced with a choice. He could either continue established patterns of collecting, although finding works by the likes of Bihzad and Sultan Ali was presumably becoming much more difficult by the second half of the sixteenth century, or he could try to outdo these Timurid masterpieces with the productions of his own *kitabkhana.* With the help of artists such as Mir Sayyid (NO. 67), Abd as-Samad (NOS. 68, 69), Daswanth (NO. 8, fig. 8) and Basawan (NOS. 9, 17, 41), and calligraphers such as Muhammad Husayn "Zarin Qalam" (NO. 20), Akbar boldly set off along the second, more challenging path.

It was with these aims and ideals in mind that Akbar became deeply interested in European art. At the first contact with it, his curiosity and taste for exotica had been aroused, but after the mission to Goa between 1575 and 1577 his interest became more profound. The new techniques learned by his artists in Goa, followed by a second influx of European material with the arrival in Fatehpur-Sikri of the first Jesuit mission in 1580, presented Akbar and his artists with an extra dimension of inspiration. Apart from their value as dazzling luxury objects, the non-Indian works collected in Akbar's *kitabkhana* acted as a major catalyst for new developments in Mughal painting.

69. *A Prince Hunting with Falcons (ca. 1585).*

CHAPTER V

THE KARKHANAS: THE IMPERIAL WORKSHOPS

Akbar's patronage of the arts was not limited to the *kitabhana*. He also supported a vast network of imperial *karkhanas* (workshops) that produced everything from perfume to clothes, guns, and tents. The emperor took a keen interest, bordering on the obsessive, in the various items produced in his workshops. Monserrate, who, impressed by Akbar's devotion to the arts, noted with awe that, "the king is considered by some to be mad, because he is very dextrous in all jobs, because I have seen him making ribbons like a lace-maker, and filing, sawing, and working very hard."[1] Akbar did not hesitate to watch and even practice, "for the sake of amusement, the craft of an ordinary artisan."[2] The emperor's desire to learn the trades of his craftsmen grew out of his conviction that ideas must be tempered by experience. As he put it, "Although knowledge in itself is regarded as the summit of perfection, yet unless displayed in action it bears not the impress of worth; indeed, it may be considered worse than ignorance."[3] True greatness, according to Akbar and Abul Fazl, "does not shrink from the minutiae of business, but regards their performance as an act of Divine worship."[4] This attitude, which led Akbar to quarry stone alongside his workmen at Fatehpur-Sikri, and to devise a way to prefabricate many of the city's buildings in order to cut down on the noise of the stone-masons,[5] also led to his patronage of talented courtiers such as Mir Fathullah Shirazi. The latter entered the emperor's service at Fatehpur-Sikri in 1582-83 and exemplified the kind of person Akbar was trying to attract to his court. He was not only skilled in all sciences from astrology to Koranic studies but he was constantly inventing devices, such as a self-driven flour mill, a kaleidoscope, and a wheel that cleaned twelve gun-barrels at once.[6]

Although the exact location of individual workshops at Fatehpur-Sikri has yet to be identified, some of them were in cells adjacent to the emperor's palace.[7] The House of Perfume, for instance, which was transformed into a residence for the Jesuits in 1580, was actually built against a wall of the palace.[8] Other workshops were also constructed near the palace including "studios and work-rooms for the finer and more reputable arts, such as painting, goldsmith work, tapestry-making, carpet and curtain-making, and the manufacture of arms."[9]

The imperial workshops and storerooms were administered as part of the emperor's extensive household. In 1595 alone 7,729,669 rupees were spent on the expenses of this administrative unit, which included "one hundred offices and workshops each resembling a city, or rather a little kingdom."[10] The administration of the imperial stores and *karkhanas* was the responsibility of the *mirsaman* and the *nazir-i buyutat*.[11] These officers reported to the emperor's minister in charge of financial matters.[12] In 1583, after Akbar's extensive administrative reorganization of the empire, management of the royal household was entrusted to Prince Murad. He was aided in this position by Raisal Darbari, Muhammad Ali Khazanchi, Karmullah, and Abd as-Samad, the latter presumably chosen for his intimate knowledge of the arts.[13] Different officers were put in charge of each of the household's departments and workshops. Itimad Khan Gujarati, Baqi Khan, Jagmal, and Hakim Ain al-Mulk among others supervised the buying and selling of jewels, while Nawrang Khan, Qasim Khan, Makhsus Khan, and Latif Khwaja were responsible for overseeing Akbar's many building projects.[14] In addition to the many clerks, servants and artisans who worked there, each

107

Carved Sandstone Wall of the Pavilion by the Anup Talau Tank

70. *A Courtier with a Winecup (ca. 1570).*

had its own treasurer charged with keeping daily, monthly, quarterly, and yearly accounts.[15]

The artisans of the *karkhanas* produced the luxurious furnishings required for Akbar's princely lifestyle at Fatehpur-Sikri, ranging from sumptuous carpets that could seat an entire assembly to small gold or jade cups that were seldom touched by any hands but the emperor's. The prolific output of the Mughal workshops was supplemented by a much smaller number of imported rarities. Other items from the *karkhanas* served a more public function. When an important guest arrived at Fatehpur-Sikri, such as Mirza Sulayman in 1583 (see above p. 44), an array of textiles that bordered on the sculptural in their golden richness was brought out to decorate the road all the way out to the formal reception point sixteen kilometers (ten miles) from the city. Similar goods were used to decorate the palace on great feast days, such as the New Year which, according to Monserrate, Akbar celebrated at Fatehpur-Sikri in 1582, "with such lavish expenditure of money, with such magnificence of clothing, ornament and all manner of appurtenances and with such gorgeous games, that the like, we are told, had not been seen for thirty years."[16] Monserrate's description of this Mughal pomp adds that the walls and colonnades of the State Hall were covered with gold and silk cloths and a jewel-encrusted throne was set up for Akbar under one of the awnings.

The principal surviving goods made in Akbar's *karkhanas* include textiles, metal and wooden objects, and jade and stone carvings. Because so few Akbari decorative works of art are inscribed, their attribution (or reattribution) to Akbar's reign is, by necessity, based on formal and conceptual similarities to paintings from dated manuscripts and architectural ornament found on buildings of the period. A great deal of imagery is, in fact, shared among these related arts.

Akbar was particularly fond of textiles. Cloths from all over the world were imported by the emperor and copied by his artisans. Foreign weavers, mainly from Iran, directed studios[17] in Lahore, Agra, and Ahmadabad as well as Fatehpur-Sikri.[18] According to Abul Fazl the emperor himself:

acquired in a short time a theoretical and practical knowledge of the whole trade; and on account of the care bestowed upon them the intelligent workmen of this country soon improved. All kinds of hair-weaving and silk-spinning were brought to perfection; and the imperial workshops furnished all those stuffs which are made in other countries. A taste for fine material has since become general, and the drapery used at feasts surpasses every description.[19]

In addition to the textiles manufactured in the *karkhanas* there were velvets from Europe, Iran, and

Gujarat, satin and silk from Yazd, Mashhad, Herat, and Europe and broadcloth from Turkey, Portugal, and Nagor.[20]

Akbar was somewhat of a couturier, designing new fashions as he pleased and often dressing in garments of silk combined with long cloaks of his own design.[21] Each year one thousand costumes were made for the imperial wardrobe and one hundred and twenty of these were always kept in readiness for the emperor.[22] These clothes were arranged according to the days, months, and years of their entry into the wardrobe, and according to their color, price, and weight.[23] Abul Fazl adds that:

All articles which have been brought, or woven to order, or received as presents, are carefully preserved; and according to the order in which they were preserved, they are again taken out for inspection, or given out to be cut and to be made up, or given away as presents.[24]

Although few imperial textiles of the period have survived, a silk hanging now in the Los Angeles County Museum of Art (NO. 70) indicates the artistic heights many of these items reached. Woven into the background of the textile is a standing figure with a long cape and an elaborate turban. A boldly patterned geometric border surrounds the figure and creates the impression of an arched doorway or niche. The figure's elongated body, long narrow hands, and large oval face are almost identical to those of several of the figures in the *Hamzanama,* and suggest the hanging may have been made during the late 1560s or early 1570s. Later on in the seventeenth century, similar hangings depicting European figures, were used to decorate one of Jahangir's palaces.[25]

Akbar's interest in textiles also extended to carpets, which were used to cover the floors of palaces, tombs and tents.[26] By the end of the sixteenth century Abul Fazl was able to write that:

His Majesty has caused carpets to be made of wonderful varieties and charming texture; he has appointed experienced workmen, who have produced many masterpieces. The *gilims* [kilim] of Iran and Turan are no more thought of, although merchants still import carpets from Goshkan (a town between Kashan and Isfahan), Khuzistan, Kirman and Sabzwar. All kinds of carpet weavers have settled here, and drive a flourishing trade. These are found in every town, especially in Agra, Fathpur and Lahor.[27]

A number of carpets can be attributed to Akbar's reign even though some of them have traditionally been attributed to a later date. Among the most important of these rugs are:

An animal carpet, in fragments (NO. 71), now in several private and public collections in America and Europe.

71. *Fragment of an Animal Carpet (late 1500s).*

72. *Pictorial Carpet,* detail *(ca. 1580-90).*

A fragment of an animal-and-tree carpet in the collection of Howard Hodgkin.

A rug with birds among trees in the Österreichisches Museum für angewandte Kunst, Vienna.[28]

A fragment of a bird-and-beast carpet now in the collection of Howard Hodgkin.

A hunting carpet formerly in the Yerkes collection.[29]

A fragment of an animal carpet now in the Musée des Arts Décoratifs, Paris.[30]

A pictorial carpet in the Museum of Fine Arts, Boston (NO. 72).

An animal rug in the National Gallery of Art, Washington known as the Widener carpet (NO. 73).

An animal-and-tree carpet now in the Metropolitan Museum of Art, New York (fig. 12).

A fragment of a rug depicting two elephants fighting in the Textile Museum, Washington, D. C.[31]

An animal carpet now in a private collection in Great Britian.[32]

73. *The Widener Animal Carpet (late 1500s).* **Detail, right.**

FIG. 12. Detail of animal and tree carpet, late sixteenth century: The Metropolitan Museum of Art, New York, Gift of J. Pierpont Morgan, 1917 (17.190.858).

All of these carpets except for the fragment in the Musée des Arts Décoratifs and the rug in the private British collection (which have deep bluish-green fields) are woven against dark red backgrounds in either silk or wool. Catalogue number 71 is generally considered to be from the earliest extant Mughal rug.[33] The fragments of this carpet are composed of recurring motifs such as six-headed birds, leopards' heads with sharp fang-like teeth, and exuberant, if not awkward, forms that distinguish them from other early Mughal textiles. Only the Hodgkin animal-and-tree carpet, with its large, stiffly drawn lion and telescopic flower, comes close to sharing the odd and enigmatic feeling created by the images of these early pieces; their boldness of design reflects the same taste for drama and action that characterizes the paintings of the *Tutinama* and *Hamzanama*.

Models for the grotesque imagery of these pieces can be found in representations of fifteenth-century Iranian textiles, like the fabric covering the yurt behind the enthroned figure of Timur in the 1467-68 *Zafarnama*[34] (NO. 57) and such sixteenth-century textiles as the small imperial rug, possibly from Tabriz, now in the Museu Calouste Gulbenkian in Lisbon.[35] Persian carpets – if not craftsmen – also provided the inspiration for many of the other rugs woven for Akbar. A series of late-sixteenth-century animal carpets from eastern Iran,[36] are clearly the prototype for such Mughal rugs as the Widener carpet (NO. 73). The Iranian carpets are composed of intricately scrolled vines that entwine a variety of animals – some real and some mythical – against a rich red background of wool pile on a warp and weft of silk. Large floral medallions punctuate the vines and create a counterpoint to the animals. The same kind of pattern, using almost identical motifs, is established in the Mughal rugs.

The Indian carpets, however, differ from their Iranian models in two ways: their fields are more open and the animals that populate them are drawn with a greater sense of naturalism. Instead of being abstract elements of an elaborate pattern, the animals and flowers in Indian rugs are treated as individual studies. Note, the carefully drawn rhinoceros and full-bodied elephant in the Widener carpet which immediately bring to mind the almost contemporary "portrait" of a family of cheetahs (NO. 46).

The figures in many of these rugs are related to – if not derived from – contemporary Mughal drawings and paintings. The two camels fighting in the Widener carpet are based on a famous painting by Bihzad, or a very close copy of it, which had found its way during the third quarter of the sixteenth century to India

where it was copied by Abd as-Samad (NO. 58). Similarly, figures from the Boston pictorial carpet (NO. 72) have their origins in miniatures from the great manuscripts of the 1580s and 1590s. The two men conversing in their simple house with its second-story pavilion are closely related to the foppish dervish in the 1595 *Baharistan* of Jami,[37] while the driver and his bullock cart are extremely close to an image from the Victoria and Albert Museum's copy of the *Akbarnama*.[38]

The relationship of these carpets to imperial paintings clearly indicates that Akbar's artists worked with his weavers in developing new designs. Mir Sayyid Ali, for example, has been credited with the design of the early animal carpet (NO. 71),[39] which, if correct, means tht the rug must have been worked on prior to 1572, when he left India for Mecca. Formal conventions used in illustrating manuscripts were transferred to woven goods and the results were often spectacular. A large animal-and-tree carpet belonging to the Metropolitan Museum of Art (fig. 12) also suggests a connection between the decorative arts and the architectural decoration of cities such as Fatehpur-Sikri. It is composed of a repeating series of palm and flowering trees, birds, tigers, antelopes, and griffins against a finely woven red background. Each component of the rug's eight meters (twenty-seven feet) – from the birds to the palm trees and leaping gazelles – is rendered in minute detail. The movement from the branches of one tree to the next creates a web-like effect that holds the composition together and leads the viewer around the carpet. While it is difficult to date this rug with precision, the closeness of its design to several of the intricately carved stone panels in the pavilion by the Anup Talau at Fatehpur-Sikri (see p. 106), indicates that it may have been woven around 1580. Both have similarly drawn palm trees with scaly trunks and feathery branches and angular flowering bushes held together by the interaction of their branches.

At Fatehpur-Sikri Akbar's most valuable textiles were kept in the *farrashkhana* (private storehouse). Akbar considered this one of the most important parts of his household and looked upon the efficiency of its administration as an "insignia of Divine worship,"[40] for it was these textiles that were used to display the full range of his power during festivals and welcoming ceremonies for revered guests. The majority of textiles stored in the *farrashkhana*, however, were related to the construction and decoration of the emperor's tents, which ranged from relatively simple affairs to large multi-storied designs that took days to erect.[41] On journeys these tents, with their many awnings,

74. *One of a Pair of Lion Heads (ca. 1550-1600).*

FIG. 13. Detail of bronze lion, private collection

carpets, wooden screens and panels and other accoutrements, were transported by a vast caravan of elephants, mules, and camels.[42] Specially trained workmen in conjunction with the quartermaster were responsible for selecting sites for pitching the tents and making sure that they were properly laid out according to rigidly established camp protocol.

A devastating fire destroyed much of the *farrashkhana* at Fatehpur-Sikri in 1579. Arif Qandahari records the vast range of material that was burnt:

> Approximately one crore [10,000,000] pieces of awnings (*shamiyana*), tents (*kargah* and *khayama*) and screens (*saraparda*) made from gold cloth, European velvet, woolen cloth, Damask silk, satin and brocade, brocaded carpets and European velvet, gold cloth and embroidery of an amount beyond description were all burnt and lost. Due to the dignity of power of the one of lofty nest [Akbar] and the unbounded benefits of his generosity, the dust of anger never reached the noble and the most holy mind of His Majesty and he never asked again for any of these burnt articles.[43]

Textiles were not the only products of the imperial workshops at Fatehpur-Sikri that gave visual expression to Akbar's great wealth and taste as a connoisseur. By the time of his death in 1605, the emperor had accumulated an assortment of golden and silver furniture and plate as well as golden images of elephants, horses, and camels in addition to silver cups, discs, candelabra, and columns said to be worth 93,820,068 rupees.[44] While many of these objects have been lost or destroyed, the pages of sixteenth-century manuscripts depict similar works of art.

A pair of spectacular gilded bronze lion heads (NO. 74), now in the Museum für Ostasiatische Kunst in Cologne, are among the few objects from this period still extant. Each of the boldly cast heads weighs about fifty kilos (one hundred and ten pounds) and measures thirty-two centimeters (fifteen inches) high by forty-five centimeters (eighteen inches) deep. Both have large, almond-shaped eyes, flaring nostrils, small pointed ears, and flowing manes that are as majestic as they are dramatic. Except for minor variations in the articulation of the manes, the heads are identical and were presumably cast from the same mold.

Only one other early Mughal bronze, a lion standing on its hind legs (fig. 13), can be compared to the Cologne lion heads. With its muscular torso, sharply delineated forms, and carefully drawn face, it conveys the same sense of power that the lion heads exude. Both also share a number of formal features, such as the swirling lines and rippling knots of their manes, open mouths with thin protruding tongues, and heavily worked eyes with deeply furrowed brows. These features relate closely to contemporary Mughal paintings of lions. The rearing lion, for instance, is almost identical in shape and design to a lion depicted in a Mughal *Zafarnama*,[45] while the Cologne heads have the same broad smiling faces, slightly crossed eyes and well-modelled features as the lions in the painting of "Noah's Ark" from an unidentified manuscript illustrated ca. 1590.[46]

The backs of the lions' heads reveal their function. Each one has a deep V-shaped well. Two rectangular prongs – one at the top and one at the bottom of each head – extend backwards almost twenty-five centimeters (ten inches). Slots in the prongs provide a means of securing them. This design is well suited to attaching the heads to the prow or stern of a ship. According to Abul Fazl, "His Majesty had the sterns of the (imperial) boats made in the shape of wonderful animals, and thus combines terror with amusement."[47] Many Akbari miniatures show these boats with finely wrought elephants, antelope, and leopard-headed prows and an illustration from the Chester Beatty Library *Tutinama* (f.86a) depicts one with a gilded lion-headed prow almost identical to the remarkable examples from Cologne. In 1574 Akbar set out from Fatehpur-Sikri for Bengal by ship and Abul Fazl's account of the event indicates the efforts that went into making the emperor's boats both awe-inspiring and attractive:

Such wonderfully fashioned boats were made under his directions as to be beyond the powers of description. There were various delightful quarters and decks, and there were gardens such as clever craftsmen could not make on land on the boats. The bows (*sir*), too, of every one of those waterhouses were made in the shape of animals, so as to astonish spectators... There were wonderful instances of architecture, and various canopies and extraordinary decorations, etc., so that if this writer should proceed to describe them he would be thought to be exaggerating.[48]

A large number of the objects made in the imperial workshops were associated with needs of the emperor's kitchen, which operated around the clock in order to satisfy Akbar's dietary idiosyncrasy – eating only one meal a day at irregularly spaced intervals.[49] The emperor's food was served on dishes of gold, silver, stone and earthenware. According to Abul Fazl:

During the time of cooking, and when the victuals are taken out, an awning is apread, and lookers-on kept away... The gold and silver dishes are tied up in red cloths, and those of copper and china in whiter ones. The *mir bakawal* (superintendent of the kitchen) attaches his seal, and writes on it the names of the contents whilst the clerk of the pantry writes on a sheet of paper a list of all the vessels and dishes which he sends inside, with the seal of the *mir bakawal,* that none of the dishes may be changed.[50]

These elaborate precautions were taken to insure that the emperor's food was not poisoned. A gem-studded golden spoon,[51] a large wine bowl with an inscription to 1583 given to the shrine of Abu Abdallah al-Husayn,[52] a vase,[53] and a ewer,[54] and several fragments of Ming dynasty blue-and-white ware (fig. 14) reflect the objects either made in the *karkhanas* or kept in the storerooms that were used in the preparation and serving of Akbar's food. Some of these objects like the humble lion-headed ewer[55] and the simple brass vase were obviously utilitarian and employed on a daily basis. Others like the dazzling gold spoon with its emeralds, diamonds, and rubies and the wine bowl, which has a lengthy inscription around its rim and detailed champlevé designs on the lower part of its body, probably served ceremonial purposes.

While little is known about the Chinese porcelains collected by the Mughals, by the 1580s an abundant

FIG. 14. Ming Chinese ceramic fragments from Chia-ching reign (1522-67: Emperor Shiah-tsung), excavated at Fatehpur-Sikri.

supply of blue-and-white ware had made its way to Akbar's court. The miniatures of such manuscripts as the *Hamzanama*[56] and *Akbarnama* depict these vessels in quantity and show them serving a variety of functions from containing food to decorating the niches of palaces. The Mughals came into contact with Chinese porcelain as early as 1497, when Babur noted that one of Ulugh Beg's pavilions at Samarqand was known as the *chinikhana* (Porcelain House).[57] Later, in 1519, the emperor complained of losing a China cup and a spoon when his raft overturned on a river.[58] During the second half of the sixteenth century Chinese porcelains[59] became extremely popular in India as evidenced by the vast number of fragments of Ming bowls excavated recently at Fatehpur-Sikri (fig. 14) and other sites such as Din-panah in Delhi.[60]

In addition to the metal and ceramic objects made for Akbar, works of wood and jade and other stones were produced in the imperial ateliers. Jade vessels were among the Mughals' most prized possessions. Akbar and his many descendants supported a thriving industry that turned out exquisitely carved rings, dagger hilts, drinking cups, and related goods. The models for most of these objects – especially the

75. Small Fluted Vessel (late 1500s).

vessels – were Timurid jades brought to India during the latter half of the sixteenth century. An exquisite white tankard with inscriptions to Ulugh Beg, Jahangir, and Shah Jahan[61] and a highly polished dark-green wine cup inscribed for Jahangir at Fatehpur-Sikri in 1619,[62] are examples of this important trade.

Jade reached the Mughals through middlemen who plied the commerical routes between India and China. Khwaja Muin, who came to Akbar's court in 1562-63 had a monopoly on jade from Kashgar and was presumably a major supplier to the Mughals.[63] Although there are no jades that have inscriptions dating them to Akbar's reign, at least one vessel, a small jar or ink pot (NO. 75), can be attributed to this period.[64] The simplicity of the pot's design with its full, almost heavy, features contrasts with the thinner and more refined jades of the seventeenth century,[65] and relates it to such jars as the ones that appear in "A Muslim Teacher with His Pupils" (NO. 67) which can be ascribed to the 1570s and "Mercury in Gemini" (NO. 56) from the 1583 *Kitab-i Saat*[66]

Wood was one of the most popular materials used by Akbar's craftsmen. Abul Fazl, records that eight kinds of wood were in general use during the sixteenth century, including *susau,* mulberry and *babul.*[67] Akbar was apparently so interested in the structural properties of this material that he had seventy-two types of wood weighed in order to determine their relative density. From this knowledge the emperor was able to improve building methods as well as to invent a variety of new carts and carriages that eased the burdens of travel. One of these, a large cart drawn by an elephant, contained several bathrooms providing Akbar with a mobile pleasure pavilion.[68]

A large box and a chair, both inlaid with ivory, and a panel possibly from a throne, are among the few wooden objects of Akbar's reign still extant. The box, now in the National Museum, Stockholm (fig. 15). is divided into a series of rectangular units by the ivory inlays. In the center of each of these units is a finely executed arabesque emanating from an oval form. Flowers and buds punctuate various points along the arabesques and add both complexity and excitement to the design. A similarly decorated lid covers the box The coat of arms and initials of Clas Fleming (married 1573 and died 1597) and his wife Ebba Stenbock (who died in 1614) are engraved on the top of the box,[69] indicating that it must have been in Sweden by the end of the sixteenth century. Similar boxes abound in contemporary Mughal paintings.[70] The chair, now in Uppsala, has almost identical ivory inlays to the box.[71] A cartouche at the back of the chair has the name Cathar(ina) Stenbock Reg(ina) engraved on it.[72]

FIG. 15. Inlaid wooden box, late sixteenth century: National Museum, Stockholm (NM KHV 277/1907).

Catharina was the last consort of Gustavus I Vasa (1523-60) and died in 1624. The fact that she was also Ebba Stenbock's sister, suggests that the box and chair were imported from India at the same time.

These items reflect the beginning of a burgeoning trade between Mughal India and Europe that was established while Akbar was at Fatehpur-Sikri. Haji Habibullah's mission of 1575 (see pages 97-98) forged artistic and commerical links with the Portuguese in Goa that resulted ultimately in the exportation of a vast quantity of Mughal goods – from spices and tex-tiles to jewels and furniture – and the importation of everything from prints and engravings to textiles and musical instruments. The arrival from London of John Newberry, Ralph Fitch, and William Leedes at Fatehpur-Sikri in 1583 opened further possibilities of European trade. In fact, Leedes, a jeweler, entered Akbar's service and was given a house, five slaves, a horse, and a stipend by the emperor.[73] Leedes and his compatriots brought with them a letter from Queen Elizabeth seeking "suitable privileges" from the Mughals. Although the letter did not result in any immediate benefits, it set the stage for Sir Thomas Roe's mission of 1615 and the subsequent success of the East India Company.

The long and narrow panel, now in the Hodgkin collection (NO. 76), depicts a ruler, probably Akbar, seated on a low throne watching two pairs of combatants fighting with heavy swords and parrying with small round shields. Three attendants stand by the ruler's side, while a retainer bearing a long standard and preceded by two elephants, approaches from the right.[74] According to eyewitness accounts, Akbar was "fond of watching fencing bouts; and on certain occasions, after the manner of the ancient Romans, he made gladiators fight before him; or fencers were made to contend until one had killed the other."[75] At Fatehpur-Sikri these contests took place on the *maydan* outside of the Elephant Gate by the edge of

76. *Throne Panel (ca. 1550-1600).* **Detail, below.**

FIG. 16. Detached heads of Jaimal and Patta, 1568-69: Red
Fort Museum, Delhi.

the lake.[76] here the emperor employed several different kinds of gladiators, each capable of performing
remarkable feats:

> In fighting they show much swiftness and agility, and join
> courage to skill in stooping down and rising up again. Some
> of them use shields in fighting, others use cudgels. The latter
> are called *lakrait*. Others again use no means of defence, and
> fight with one hand only; these are called *yakhath*. The
> former class come chiefly from the eastern districts, and use a
> somewhat smaller shield; which they call *chirwa*. Those who
> come the southern districts make their shields large enough
> to conceal a horseman.[77]

The combatants in the Hodgkin panel, with their
bold gestures and lively movements, are part of a
standard iconography of kingship found throughout
the Muslim world. Their ritualized fighting was meant
to entertain their royal patrons while symbolizing the
martial arts. This imagery was ideally suited to the
adornment of such imperial equipment as thrones.
Akbari thrones were made of gold, silver, and carved
wood, often inlaid with precious stones.[78] The pages
of the emperor's historical manuscripts record many
of these thrones, which consisted of low square or octagonal platforms with raised backs ending in either
polylobed medallions or arches. Narrow panels of
wood similar in shape as well as design to the Hodgkin

panel decorated their edges, enhancing their beauty
and emphasizing the ruler's status.[79]

Abul Fazl boasts that clever workmen could chisel
the red sandstone from Fatehpur-Sikri more skillfully
than carpenters could turn wood. Their creations, in
his opinion, vied with the picture book of Mani – the
paradigm of artistic perfection.[80] The elaborately
carved walls of the pavilion by the Anup Talau at
Fatehpur-Sikri as well as the finely worked columns
and reliefs at the Red Fort in Agra, and the citadel at
Lahore testify to the accuracy of Abul Fazl's words.
Akbar's master stone-masons and designers were not
limited in their production to architectural decoration. They also made monumental stone sculptures
such as the red sandstone statues of the great Rajput
warriors Jaimal and Patta (fig. 16), and the massive
elephants that guard the main gate at Fatehpur-Sikri
(see p. 45). Jaimal and Patta, defended Chittorgarh
against Akbar in the siege of 1567-68 (NO. 4), and were
both killed during the battle – the former shot by a
bullet from the emperor's favorite gun, Sangram.

The statues of Jaimal and Patta were originally
mounted on the backs of large black elephants[81] driv-
en by mahouts, which stood in front of the Elephant
Gate at the Red Fort in Agra, completed according to
Badauni in 1568-69.[82] During the seventeenth century

they were moved to the fort at Shahjahanabad in Delhi where the French traveller, François Bernier, among others, saw them.[83] At some point, possibly during the reign of Aurangzeb, they were dismantled and buried in the grounds of the fort where they were eventually uncovered in 1863.[84] While it is impossible to know whether or not the statues of Jaimal and Patta were conceived as part of the original setting of the gate, they were definitely in place by 1580 when Monserrate visited the fort and observed that:

> In front of the gateway are statues of two petty kings, whom Zelaldinus [Akbar] himself shot with his own musket; these are seated on life-size statues of elephants on which the kings used to ride when alive. These statues serve both as trophies of the King's prowess, and as monuments of his military victories.[85]

A miniature (ca. 1593) from the *Baburnama,* showing Babur entering the fort at Agra in 1526 depicts Jaimal and Patta in detail.[86] The Rajputs and their mahouts straddle the backs of their mounts, which stand on low platforms on either side of the fort's gate. Brightly colored cloths cover the elephants' backs and act as a visual counterpoint to the darkness of their skin. Though clearly anachronistic, the inclusion of Jaimal and Patta in a scene from the *Baburnama* is not surprising since the artists of the manuscript painted the fort at Agra as they saw it in the early 1590s rather than as it would have been seventy years earlier. A second painting, dated 1610, by Ustad Salivahana leaves no doubt that the statues at Agra were of Jaimal and Patta.[87] Like the miniature from the *Baburnama,* it portrays the entrance to the Elephant Gate and shows the two elephants and their riders at either side of the gate. But here the artist has added in Devanagri script the names of the two Rajputs next to the elephants.

The heads of Jaimal and Patta, though slightly worn and no longer attached to the warriors' bodies, are as boldly conceived as they are strong.[88] Their well-modelled faces exude a sense of power and determination. Look, for example, at the sharply defined lines of their eyes and ears, and the full, rounded folds of their turbans. Similarly accomplished forms can be seen in the elephants that decorate the brackets of Akbari buildings at the fort in Lahore (which date to the 1590s) as well as the serpents and other animals that adorn the walls and brackets of the so-called Jahangiri Mahal at Agra.

Akbar's interest in the appearance of his world and his desire to leave his mark on almost every aspect of his empire extended to such areas as the mint and the Office of Administration. Gold and silver, because of the emperor's attention, noted Abul Fazl, "have been brought to the greatest degree of purity (and), in like manner the form of the (emperor's) coins has also been improved."[89] Gold coins (NO. 77) served primarily as reserve coinage, while silver (NO. 78) and copper money (NO. 79) were used as a circulation currency. Akbar's finest engravers, such as Mawlana Maqsud

77. *Gold Coins (1578-79 and 1579-80).*

78. *Silver Coins (1577-78 and 1578-79).*

79. *Copper Coins (1578-79 and 1579-80).*

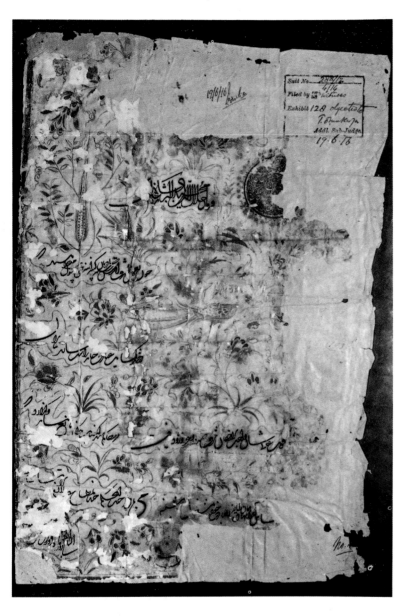

80. *Farman (ca. 1598)*.

and Mulla Ali Ahmad, were responsible for preparing the finely cut dies for casting gold coins that included inscriptions by poets such as Fayzi.[90] Mawlana Maqsud came from Herat and served under Humayun before going to work for Akbar, who greatly admired his astrolabes, globes, and copying-boards, as well as his engravings.[91] Mulla Ali, a native of Delhi, was Akbar's finest engraver. According to Abul Fazl he was "unsurpassed as a steel-engraver, so much that his engravings are used as copies."[92] He learned his trade from his father, Shaykh Husayn, and studied the work of Mawlana Maqsud before surpassing both of them.

Two superbly cast gold *mohurs,* one dated 1578-79 and another possibly from 1579-80, and two silver *rupees* dated 1577-78 and 1578-79, all minted at Fatehpur-Sikri, are evidence of the skill of Akbar's die-cutters and engravers. The *mohurs,* in particular, with their finely shaped lines and large flowing letters set deeply into the gold show how important coinage was for the Mughals. Indeed, each coin represented not only a specific weight but also a symbol of the emperor. Although this extension of the emperor's persona to his coins was by no means unique to the Mughals, Akbar sought to make it explicit through the use of inscriptions. For the *sahansah,* a heavy round coin, Fayzi composed the following lines:

It is the sun from which the seven oceans get their pearls,
The black rocks get their jewels from his lustre.
The mines get their gold from his fostering glance,
and their gold is ennobled by Akbar's stamp
This coin, which is an ornament of hope,
Carries an everlasting stamp, and an immortal name.
As a sign of its auspiciousness, it is sufficient
That, once, for all ages the sun has cast a glimpse on it.[93]

While Akbar was at Fatehpur-Sikri, in 1577-78, he ordered a complete revision of the operation of his mints. Abd as-Samad was appointed master of the mint and he became rsponsible for the overall administration of the imperial mints of Lahore, Gujarat, Jaunpur, Patna, and Bengal in addition to the mint at Fatehpur-Sikri.[94] As part of the reorganization of the mints the emperor also ordered that square coins be produced. Although it took several years for these wishes to be carried out, the result of Akbar's efforts was the standardization and centralization of his mints and a dramatic increase in the quality of the coins they produced.[95] The extraordinary refinement of the *mohurs* and the visually arresting design of the *rupees* are in direct response to the emperor's reforms and reflect his impact on the development of Mughal coinage.

The imperial mints and workshops depended upon the efficiency of the Office of Administration for their success. At Fatehpur-Sikri this office was in a large hall and, as Monserrate noted, it was:

presided over by a chieftan of great authority and ability who signs the royal *farmans* (orders). These are eight days afterwards sealed by one of the queens, in whose keeping is the royal signet-ring and also the great seal of the realm. During these eight days' interval every document is most carefully examined by the confidential counsellor and by the King himself, in order to prevent error and fraud. This is done with special care in the case of gifts and concessions conferred by royal favor.[96]

All appointments and financial transactions had to be recorded by the imperial clerks and authorized by the relevant superintendents and ministers before being given royal approval. This meant that vast amounts of paper work had to be processed daily and that each order had to have its authenticity certified. consequently, seals were affixed to all *farmans* in order to guarantee their veracity. The *Ain-i Akbari* describes in detail the various kinds of documents issued by the records office from *sanads* (vouchers) to *sayurghals* (royal grants) and *parwanchas* (stipends), and stipulates the precise order in which the different seals were to be applied to these papers. Each document was divided into several folds beginning at the bottom of the page and ending at the top with the emperor's *tughra* (monogram):

On the first fold which is less broad, at a place towards the edge where the paper is cut off, the *Vakil* puts his seal; opposite to it, but a little lower, the *Mushrif* of the *Diwan* puts his seal, in such a manner that half of it goes to the second fold. Then, in a like manner, but a little lower, comes the seal of the *Sadr*... The seals of the *Diwan* and the *Bakshi* do not go beyond the edge of the second fold, whilst the *Diwan-i juz*, the *Bakshi-yi juz* and the *Diwan-i buyutat* put their seals on the third fold. The *Mustawfi* puts his seal on the fourth, and the *Sahib-i Tawjih* on the fifth fold. The seal of His Majesty is put above the *Tughra* lines on the top of the *Firman*, where the princes also put their seals in *Taliqas*.[97]

Many of the same artists who worked on the dies for Akbar's coins made his seals. Mawlana Maqsud designed one of the emperor's earliest seals as a circular form containing the names of Akbar and his ancestors back to Timur written in *riqa*. He also created a similar seal using *nastaliq* characters, but this one only had Akbar's name on it. These seals were put on letters to foreign kings and on documents relating to royal appointments. A second kind of seal, called a *mihrabi*, used for judicial transactions, was six-sided and included the words "uprightness is the means of pleasing God; I never saw any one lost in the straight road."[98] For other orders a square seal, with the words *Allahu Akbar jalal jalalahu*, which can be construed either as "God is Great" or "Akbar is God," was employed.

Mulla Ahmad Ali recut several of the emperor's seals and in a long letter to Badauni – a close friend of his – he describes his work on the circular seal containing the names of Akbar and his forebears, a task which took four months to complete:[99]

My employment from the 1st of Zi-l-Hijjah to the end of Rabi'u-l-awwal [year unknown] has been the engraving of the seal of the just king, the perfect Khalifah on which are engraved his sublime titles and the names of his exalted ancestors as far as Amir Timur, the lord of the (fortunate) conjunction. The seal is wide and round and contains eight circles, one in the middle, and the rest clustered around it.[100]

In addition to Akbar's name, located in the central circle, and Timur's which is directly above Akbar's, the seal bears the names of Humayun, Babur, Umar Shaykh Mirza, Sultan Abu Said Mirza, Sultan Muhammad Mirza, and Jalal ad-Din Miran Shah.[101]

This seal can be seen in the upper right hand corner of a beautiful, though partially damaged *farman* (NO. 80) now in the archives of the Catholic Archdiocese of Agra. Surrounding the outer circle of the seal is a series of red and gold flecks that give the impression that it is enclosed by a halo. Immediately to the left of the seal is Akbar's *tughra* and below it in a fine hand is the text which grants permission to a group of Jesuit fathers to build a "house of worship" in Cambay and implores the ruler of that city not to stand in their way.[102] Gold flowers, trees and birds, highlighted in blue and red, decorate the page and reflect the document's royal origin. Although the date of the *farman* is no longer entirely legible it must have been issued sometime prior to 1598 when Father Xavier noted in a letter to the General of the Society of Jesus that:

After much vacillation and much obstruction from our opponents, he (Akbar) gave us leave to build a church at Cambay; the same favour could not be obtained in the case of Sindh, on account of the vehement opposition encountered.[103]

The importance of this *farman* for the history of the Jesuits in India is obvious. Its exquisite illumination – which differs from most surviving Akbari *farmans* – suggests that the emperor considered it a significant document and enhanced its appearance in order to emphasize either his support of the Jesuits or, by extension, his commitment to religious tolerance.

CHAPTER VI

AKBAR AND THE POWER OF IMAGES

He [God] knows the visible and the unseen.
He is the Mighty One, the Merciful, who excelled
in the making of all things. He first created man
from clay, then bred his offspring from a drop of
paltry fluid. He moulded him and breathed into
him of His Spirit.

(KORAN 32:6-9)

THE IDEA OF human creativity in the Islamic world has to be seen in the light of God's original act of creation. The princely patron of the arts was always aware that God was the only true creator of forms, and the only one who could instill life into those forms. It is not surprising, therefore, that in sixteenth-century India theoretical discussion of the arts centered on how forms were able to transmit meaning rather than on artistic creativity itself. Few patrons were as interested as Akbar in the functioning of signs and the communication of ideas. In 1579-80 he even went so far as to establish a "House of the Dumb" (*gang mahall*) just outside Fatehpur-Sikri in order to see what language children would acquire if they were totally isolated from all speech, with a staff of dumb wet-nurses.[1] After three or four years the children were discovered to be as functionally dumb as their nurses. Fortunately, Akbar's involvement with the visual arts was far more successful.

The best understanding of how Akbar thought images could, and should, function is found in the writings of Abul Fazl, who developed a highly poetic explanation of how ideas are communicated. In a wonderful passage from the *Akbarnama*, Abul Fazl related that when Akbar commissioned him to write the history of his reign, "Wings came to my soul, and strength to my tongue, and in an admirable manner I brought the hidden things of the heart from the soul's

ocean to the shore of paper."[2] Later, in the *Ain-i Akbari*, Abul Fazl further embellished his metaphor. The spoken word, he wrote, "steps forward on man's tongue, and enters, with the assistance of the conveying air, into the windows of the ears of others. It then drops the burden of its concrete component, and returns, as a single ray, to its old place, the realm of thought." But occasionally, he continued, an idea takes "a different direction by means of man's fingers, and having passed along the continent of the pen and crossed the ocean of the ink, alights on the pleasant expanse of the page, and returns through the eye of the reader to its wonted habitation."[3]

Under Akbar's enthusiastic and free-ranging patronage the same metaphor was valid for artistic creation in all the media, as the "ocean of ink" was transformed into a more profound reservoir of techniques, colors, and forms. The political and cultural goals that motivated Akbar in his patronage of the arts have been discussed in earlier chapters. What remains to be defined is the nature of the conventions that guided Akbar's artistic aspirations from the "realm of thought" to the reality of the finished product, and the philosophical issues that helped shape his interests.

Safely ensconced in his new City of Victory, Akbar personally participated in a wide range of artistic activity, trying his hand at everything from quarrying stone and playing the kettledrum to determining which

Room with Stone Screens on the North Façade of "Jodh Bai's Palace"

scenes should be illustrated in the various manuscripts under production in his *kitabkhana*. Such all-round virtuosity inevitably led Abul Fazl to compare Akbar, in his remarkably long list of epithets at the beginning of the *Ain-i Akbari*, to the legendary Iranian king Jamshid, who is traditionally credited with introducing the crafts to mankind.[4] Although such comparisons are a common literary device, Akbar's activities at Fatehpur-Sikri certainly confirm the aptness of the link with Jamshid. It might even be suggested that a magnificent figure of a gold-clad Jamshid in a miniature painted by Abd as-Samad in 1588 was intended as an ideal representation of Akbar, a visual parallel to Abul Fazl's written praise.[5] Ironically, the only area of the arts in which no expertise was claimed for Akbar was calligraphy, the Islamic princely art par excellence. It may thus be no coincidence that calligraphy was the art form that changed the least at Akbar's court.

Akbar's appreciation of art was encouraged by the writings of Nasir ad-Din Tusi, whose *Akhlaq-i Nasiri* was singled out for copying and illustration in the early 1590s. Of all the proclamations found in this text, the one perhaps quoted most often by Akbar in the company of his artists would have been the following admonition for the pursuit of excellence in craft, which was interpreted as encompassing everything from the act of kingship itself to the daily chores of the lowly street-sweeper: "All who are characterized by a trade should make advance and seek perfection therein, not showing contentment with an inferior degree or acquiescing in meanness of aspiration. It should be recognized that men have no finer ornament than an ample subsistence, and the best means of acquiring a subsistence lies in a craft."[6] This advice is well reflected in the quality of almost every object produced for Akbar, from luxurious illustrated manuscripts to the seals affixed on official documents.

Another passage in the *Akhlaq-i Nasiri* talks about "Masters of Tongues"(*dhawu al-alsina*), defined as those whose craft comprises the "sciences" of Scholastics, Jurisprudence, Elocution, Rhetoric, Poetry, and Calligraphy.[7] It is at this very point in the above-mentioned manuscript of this text that Akbar boldly ordered the most detailed painting we have of his *kitabkhana* (NO. 19). As Akbar clearly intended this as a statement that not only his calligraphers but also his artists were "Masters of Tongues," it must be asked by what means or signs did he think they were able to communicate and what it was that he wanted them to communicate. Such questions lead us into especially fascinating territory when they are applied to the new developments in painting that occurred during the Fatehpur-Sikri years.

Akbar's entire reign was characterized by the way in which the arts were rendered open to dramatic changes in matters of content and mode of representation. Even Abul Fazl regarded the dense and long-winded literary style he adopted in the *Akbarnama* as something entirely new (and praiseworthy!) and sought to contrast positively his "new gait" with the "fantastic embellishments" of other writers both past and present.[8] It was at Fatehpur-Sikri, the new capital of his enlarged Indian empire, that Akbar began in earnest to mediate a permanent reconciliation between his Central Asian ancestry and the political, social, and geographical realities of India. The main reward for his daring initiatives was an overall stability in the empire that allowed for considerable refinements to be made in almost all areas of Mughal political and cultural life. Even though Akbar's stay at Fatehpur-Sikri is traditionally regarded as sadly truncated, by the standards of the Mughals themselves fourteen years must have seemed almost an eternity. Neither Babur nor Humayun ever had the luxury of that long a stay in any one place. Planned anew literally from the ground up, Fatehpur-Sikri afforded Akbar a perfect stage on which to act out his self-chosen role as the semi-divine emperor, the "Shadow of God on Earth." For Akbar this included both theoretical and practical leadership in the arts, and it was at Fatehpur-Sikri that Akbar's ideas in this area crystallized into a coherent and consistent vision.

The field of painting, the best preserved and documented of all the media utilized by Akbar's artisans, serves as the best model for a study of the exciting changes that took place in the visual arts under Akbar's patronage. The seeds for this new mode of painting had been sown in the early 1550s just before Akbar ascended the throne. At this stage paintings such as the St. Louis "Youth and Musician" (NO. 5) the Fitzwilliam "Prince Hunting" (NO. 7), and such portraits as that of Shah Abu al-Maali by Dust Muhammad (NO. 81) took the first tentative steps away frm purely Safavid conventions that nevertheless remained an important element in Mughal painting (unlike Safavid culture in general which was never appreciated at Akbar's court). Even in the *Tutinama* begun ca. 1560, when Akbar was in his late teens (NOS. 8, 9, 10), one immediately becomes aware of the deft combination of seemingly unrelated forms that characterize Akbari painting as being receptive to "foreign" elements (both Indian and European) without ever losing track of its own originality.

Illustrations from the *Hamzanama* – painted between 1562 and 1577 (NOS. 11, 12) – fulfill the possibilities of a uniquely dynamic manner of painting that had been hinted at in certain epsiodes from the *Tutinama* such as the "Storm at Sea" (NO. 10). Bold modelling, extremely expressive gestures, and a rarely matched liveliness of action set the *Hamzanama* apart as the high point of early Akbari painting. From here on there could never be any turning back towards the refined purity of its Safavid stylistic roots. Even an old Safavid master like Abd as-Samad was unable to conceal the effects of this exciting new approach when he copied Bihzad's painting of fighting camels that had come into Akbar's possession (NO. 58). Later in Akbar's reign, during the years surrounding Akbar's departure from Fatehpur-Sikri, there was an evolution towards a somewhat more refined manner, especially in illustrations painted for a series of deluxe poetic manuscripts such as the Keir *Khamsa* of Nizami, the

1588 *Divan* of Anvari and the 1597-98 "Dyson Perrins" *Khamsa* of Nizami. In a different category, by 1602, three years before Akbar's death, the forty-one miniatures in the *Jog Bashisht* (NO. 30) show a quality of emotional depth and painterly finish that is both astonishing and profoundly moving.

Writing in the second half of the 1590s, Abul Fazl boasted that "His Majesty has looked deep into the matter of raw materials and set a high value on the quality of production," and that consequently "colouring has gained a new beauty...and finish a new clarity."[9] But refinement in techique does not alone explain the development of the mature Akbari aesthetic. While it has been astutely observed that "the rhythmic and coloristic violence of the *Hamza-nama* is a formal expression of the struggle of Akbar's intellect against

81. *Shah Abu al-Maali (ca. 1556-60).*

the manifold problems of an empire in the making," and "conversely, the calmer, more delicate forms of the later pictures mirror Akbar's peace of mind which came with the increased security in the empire,"[10] this interpretation still leaves certain interesting avenues unexplored. Could there be a more deep-seated philosophical basis for the development of the characteristic tendencies of Mughal painting during Akbar's reign, and how do they tie in with the Mughals' concepts of creativity, communication, and meaning?

By the sixteenth century, Muslim thought in India was thoroughly permeated by the theory of *wahdat al-wujud* (literally, "the oneness of being"), a pantheistic belief in the unity of being formulated by the Spanish mystic Ibn al-Arabi (1164-1240) and later popularized by such famous poets as Jami (1414-92). According to Ibn al-Arabi this indivisible Reality can, however, be viewed from two different angles: "the Real," standing for God and the essence of all phenomena, and "the Many," standing for the phenomenal world of appearances. On the broadest level a distinction is thus set up between "inner meaning" or "esoteric content" (*manavi*[11]) and "outer form" (*surat*[12]); in other words, between what might be termed the spiritual and material worlds. Ibn al-Arabi's favorite metaphor to stress that he was not proposing a theory of duality was that outer form represents a mirror-image or shadow of "the Real" beyond.[13]

This theory of *wahdat al-wujud,* supported by liberal thinkers such as Abul Fazl and his brother Fayzi but bitterly opposed by more orthodox courtiers such as Badauni, had a number of important political and cultural ramifications for Akbar's India. On the one hand, the closeness of this world view to Hindu monism had already played a key role in opening up a dialogue between Muslim and Hindu mystics in pre-Mughal India, a process Akbar chose to continue and expand in such forums as the House of Worship at Fatehpur-Sikri. On the other hand, Abul Fazl was extremely fond of using this metaphysical vocabulary, which was frequently employed rhetorically in the Persian literary tradition,[14] when attempting to describe Akbar's universal power and authority. Standard allusions, reminiscent of Ibn al-Arabi's original metaphor, to emperors as the "Shadow of God on Earth" were in fact so frequent that Fayzi felt it appropriate to re-amplify Akbar's supposedly divine origins in the following undated verse: "Although kings are the shadow of God on earth, he [Akbar] is the emanation of God's light. How then can we call him a shadow?"[15]

In his discussion of calligraphy and painting in the *Ain-i Akbari,* Abul Fazl interprets the dichotomy between the spiritual or inner world (*manavi*) and the material or external world (*surat*) in a much more specific manner, and uses it as the very backbone of his argument. Initially he takes care to identify Akbar as an emperor particularly interested in this metaphysical distinction as it applies to the perception of visual objects, describing him at one point as the "Depicter of the External and Revealer of the Internal,"[16] and later on as the "Perceiver of the Links between the Visible and Invisible Worlds."[17] Although the parallel with the opening line of the Koranic verses quoted at the beginning of this chapter is striking, Abul Fazl has gone beyond the bounds of mere eulogy and has, in fact, pinpointed the reasons for Akbar's great interest in painting. Art provided Akbar with a unique opportunity to combine the pursuit of aesthetic pleasure with an investigation into the nature of the universe. As Abul Fazl clearly states, "His Majesty, from his earliest youth, has shown a great predilection for this art, and gives it every encouragement, as he looks upon it as a means, both of study and amusement."[18]

Observation of nature and the production of images were thought to go hand in hand towards providing a fuller understanding of the world at large, and Abul Fazl implies that this realization was one of the key factors behind the heightened interest in the arts that is so apparent at Akbar's court. This addition of a metaphysical component to the art of painting led Abul Fazl to write that, "It is indeed amazing that from a cultivation of the habit of observing [*surat bini*] and making of images [*tamthal arai*]—which is by itself a source of indolence—came the elixir of wisdom and a cure for the incurable sickness of ignorance, and those many haters of painting who blindly followed their predecessors had their eyes opened to Reality."[19] Under Akbar's patronage outer form and inner meaning become the two poles for criticism of painting, and we are assured by Abul Fazl that the emperor was an excellent judge of both.[20] Outer form had to be depicted in such as way as to lead the viewer to the inner, esoteric meaning. The desirability of this relationship is further expressed on the walls of the palace at Fatehpur-Sikri popularly known as the *Sunahra Makan* or "Maryam's House":

The garden of its pictures is in the color of [just like] the garden of paradise...
In elegance it is like the gilded vault of the firmament. In grace it is like the turquoise-colored place of the firmament...
Its beautifully drawn paintings are a meaning-displayed

form. Its meaning-displaying form is the ravisher of the heart of men of certainty.[21]

Such sentiments would have been firmly instilled in the artists of Akbar's *kitabkhana*. According to Badauni, for example, an otherwise unknown painter by the name of Payravi ("the Follower") attained a degree of brilliance "by means of studying the outward form to hidden truths," and wrote a now lost poetic treatise on their relationship which began as follows:

O Lord, I am unable to grasp hidden truth [*mana*]!
Forgive me, for I am too much a worshipper of the outward form [*surat*]
Of thy grace, O most Pure God
    Thou hast so fashioned the outward form of our earthly tabernacles
That every (fair) form which I see
Points out to me the way to the hidden truths of Thine Essence.[22]

What Akbar desired to create and codify was a new pictorial language in which ideas would be given a formal representation, or set of signs, as effective as the letter in the fields of writing, where Abul Fazl noted, "the written shape guides to letter and word and from there the content [*mana*] is found out."[23] However, in order for painting to acquire the potent ability to communicate the subtleties of the world already vested in writing, new forms or signs had to be devised to better express the desired inner meanings. It is clear that painters who "blindly followed their predecessors" were of little interest to Akbar, just as Abul Fazl avowed that the emperor was not concerned with poets because "he attaches no weight to a handful of imagination."[24] New directions in painting had to be be investigated and on this daring journey two exciting paths were open to Akbar: the first emphasized the observaton of nature and drawing from life, while the second was based on the study of European techniques that had come to Akbar's attention.

Part of the motivation behind taking up the challenge of the first path was succinctly stated by the Safavid artist Sadiqi Beg[25] in *The Canons of Painting:* "when there has already been a Mani and a Bihzad, how else [except through the direct observation of Nature] could one break free of the crushing weight of past perfection?" But increased exposure to a wide range of new art forms seems to have shaken Akbar's belief in the "perfection" of Bihzad and other past masters of the Persian tradition, and opened up the possibility of setting his own standards of brilliance. The second path was made all the more enticing by the way in which European paintings and prints, of which

Akbar was aware by the 1570s at the latest, seemed to be able to represent the subtelties of nature so successfully. Abul Fazl recorded the reaction these works engendered upon their arrival at the Mughal court: "Although in general a picture represents a material form...the painters of *firanq* [Europe] quite often express, by using rare forms, our mental states and [thus] they lead the ones who consider only the outside of things to the place of inner meaning."[26] It is safe to assume here that Abul Fazl had in mind the highly emotional reception Akbar accorded the two altarpieces brought to Fatehpr-Sikri by the Jesuit mission in 1580. But just as the detailed study of nature had great ramifications throughout Mughal painting and not only on the actual production of human portraits or animal studies, Akbar's interest in European works went far beyond the production of exact copies. Instead, foreign techniques were made subservient to the Mughal ideals being expressed and explored.[27]

Akbar directed a corps of well over one hundred artists along a path that eventually led to the achievements found in such later manuscripts as the *Jog Bashisht* (NO. 30). The concept of what a painting should be was given a new theoretical foundation and an explicit set of goals. To meet this challenge, new formal and technical conventions were brought into currency. Realism combined with a highly charged emotional content brushed aside the dazzling surface brilliance of Safavid and Timurid paintings with their emphasis on the perfection of form. Even the old Safavid masters who had been brought to India by Humayun were encouraged to alter their manner of painting, and Abul Fazl wrote that although Abd as-Samad "knew this art before he joined the royal service, the transmuting glance (*iksri-i binish*) of the king [Akbar] has raised him to a more sublime level and his images have gained a depth of spirit" (literally, his outer forms turned their face to inner meaning).[28] Soon Abul Fazl was able to answer Sadiqi Beg's challenge with the claim that "such excellent artists have assembled here [in Mughal India] that a fine match has been created to the world-renowned unique art of Bihzad and the magic making of the Europeans."[29] Few would challenge his assertion that Akbar's bold experiments with new directions in painting were a great success.

In fact, claims were soon made to the effect that through the fine qualities of painting under Akbar "inanimate objects appear to come alive" and that by the commissioning of state portraits "the dead have gained a new life, and the living an eternity."[30] Remembering the Koranic proclamations, however, about God being the only true creator, and fearing that the emperor's motives might be misunderstood, Abul Fazl hurried to quote a disclaimer concerning the role of the artist as creator made by Akbar during a private assembly one day: "I cannot tolerate those who make the slightest criticism of this art. It seems to me that a painter is better than most in gaining a knowledge of God. Each time he draws a living being he must draw each and every limb of it, but seeing that he cannot bring it to life must perforce give thought to the miracle wrought by the Creator and thus obtain a knowledge of Him."[31] Through this statement the emperor was able to deftly move aside any orthodox religious opposition to his infatuation with the visual arts.

Akbar demanded that equal attention be paid to both a subject's inner essence and its outer form. His determination that any given form should lead the viewer to a deeper, esoteric meaning is one of the main factors that makes Mughal painting from Akbar's reign so visually and emotionally satisfying. Some of these new powers of artistic expression had a decidedly practical use, allowing Akbar to gauge, for example, the true character of a courtier through his portrait and also strengthened the didactic possibilities of painting. On a metaphysical level, the search for the inner essence behind a given outer form was ultimately seen to bring both patron and artist to a fuller awareness of the Divine, and the power of God the creator.

25b. *Detail of Manuscript of the* Gulistan *of Sadi (1582-83).*

NOTES

CHAPTER 1 (pp. 13-33)

1. *Letters from the Mughal Court: The First Jesuit Mission to Akbar (1580-1583)*, ed. John Correia-Afonso. (Bombay: Heras Institute of Indian Culture, 1980).

2. Abul Fazl, *Akbarnama,* Vol. I, tr. H. Beveridge (Delhi: Ess Ess Publications, 1973), pp. 519-20.

3. *Ibid.,* p. 520.

4. This painting is in the Gulistan Museum, Tehran and is illustrated in Laurence Binyon, J.V.S. Wilkinson, and Basil Gray, *Persian Miniature Painting,* (New York: Dover Publications, 1971), pl. CIVb (No. 230).

5. *Akbarnama,* Vol. I, p. 179.

6. *Ibid.,* p. 180.

7. As tr. by Oleg Grabar in his review of A. A. Semenov, "Inscriptions on the Tombs of Timur and his Descendants in the Gur-e Amir," *Epigrafika Vostoka,* 2, 49-62, published in *Ars Orientalis,* Vol. II, 1957.

8. *Ibid.,* pp. 553-54.

9. *Akbarnama,* Vol. I, pp. 197-98.

10. Zahir ad-Din Muhammad Babur, *Baburnama,* tr. A. S. Beveridge (New Delhi: Oriental Books Reprint Corporation, 1970), p. 340.

11. Qazi Ahmad, *Calligraphers and Painters,* tr. V. Minorsky (Washington: The Smithsonian Institution, 1959), pp. 128-129.

12. *Baburnama,* p. 518.

13. Zayn Khan, *Tabaqat-i Baburi,* tr. Sayed Hasan Askari (Delhi: Idarah-i Adabiyat-i Delli, 1982), p. 163.

14. Abul Fazl, *Ain-i Akbari,* Vol. III, H. Blochmann, 2nd ed. rev. D. C. Phillot (New Delhi: Munshiram Manoharlal, 1977), pp. 8-10.

15. For details concerning Akbar's conquests during the 1560s and 70s see S. Roy, "Akbar" in *The History and Culture of the Indian People,* Vol. VII (Bombay: Bharatiya Vidya Bhavan, 1980), pp. 115-133.

16. *Akbarnama,* Vol. II, p. 475.

17. *Ain-i Akbari,* Vol. III, p. 451.

18. *Ibid.,* p. 429.

19. The Persian term is *ibadatkhana.*

20. *Ain-i Akbari,* Vol. III, p. 433.

21. Abd al-Qadir Badauni, *Muntakhab at-Tavarikh,* Vol. II. tr. W. H. Lowe (Delhi: Idarah-i Adabiyat-i Delli, 1973), p. 280.

22. Marshall Hodgson, *The Venture of Islam* (Chicago: University of Chicago Press, 1974), Vol. III, pp. 61-65, provides a more thorough discussion of these aspects of Akbar's government.

23. *Ibid.,* p. 65.

24. *Ain-i Akbari,* Vol. III, pp. 449-50.

25. *Ibid.,* p. 449.

26. Tr. in our *Fatehpur-Sikri: A Sourcebook* (Cambridge, Massachusetts: Aga Khan Program for Islamic Architecture, 1985), pp. 290-91.

27. Hodgson, *The Venture of Islam,* Vol. III, p. 76.

28. *Akbarnama,* Vol. III, p. 298.

29. *Ain-i Akbari,* Vol. I, p. 3.

30. *Ibid.,* Vol. III, p. 450.

31. *Ibid.,* Vol. II, p. 174.

32. *Ibid.,* Vol. I, p. 632.

33. *Muntakhab at-Tavarikh,* Vol. II, p. 276.

34. *Akbarnama,* Vol. II, p. 502.

35. Illustrated in Binyon, Wilkinson and Gray, *Persian Miniature Painting,* pl. CV No. 232.

36. *Akbarnama,* Vol. II, p. 67.

37. For a detailed discussion of these artists see Pramod Chandra, *The Tuti-Nama of the Cleveland Museum of Art* (Graz: Akademische Druck-u. Verlagsantalt, 1976), pp. 16-26.

38. Jawhar Aftabchi, *Tazkirat al-Vaqiat,* tr. Charles Stewart (Delhi: Idarah-i Adabiyat-i Delli, 1972), p. 43.

39. Now on deposit at the Walters Art Gallery (TL 6.1950). See No. 57.

40. Reproduced in Binyon, Wilkinson and Gray, *Persian Miniature Painting,* pl. CV-B.

41. *Ibid.,* pl. CIV-B.

42. Now part of the *Muraqqa-i Gulshan* in Berlin. Reproduced in Ernst Kühnel and Herman Goetz, *Indische Buchmalereien aus dem Jahangir-Album des Staatsbibliothek zu Berlin* (Berlin: Scarabaeus Verlag, 1924), pls. 4, 32.

43. Fitzwilliam Museum, P. D. 138-1948.

44. British Museum, 1913, 2-8 I.

45. Reproduced in part and discussed at length in Chandra, *The Tuti-Nama,* pp. 44-46, pls. 97-105.

46. Reproduced in Stuart Cary Welch, *Wonders of the Age: Masterpieces of Safavid Painting,* (Cambridge, Massachusetts: The Fogg Art Museum, Harvard University, 1979), pl. 75.

47. Reproduced in A. U. Pope, ed., *Survey of Persian Art,* 6 Vols. (London: Oxford University Press, 1938-52), pl. 913-B.

48. Quoted in Chandra, *The Tuti-Nama,* pp. 172-3.

49. Illustrated in S. C. Welch, *Wonders of the Age,* p. 178.

50. Despite the assertion in Humayun's letter (quoted by Bayazid Biyat) that Mir Sayyid Ali and Abd as-Samad arrived at Kabul in 1552, both artists appear to have entered the emperor's service in 1549. See, for instance, the *Akbarnama,* Vol. I, p. 552.

51. Chandra, *The Tuti-Nama,* pp. 44-5.

52. *Akbarnama,* Vol. I, p. 634.

53. *Ain-i Akbari,* Vol. I, p. 113; as tr. by C. M. Naim in Chandra, *The Tuti-Nama,* p. 182.

54. Annemarie Schimmel, *Calligraphy and Islamic Culture* (New York: New York University Press, 1984), p. 184.

55. *Muntakhab at-Tavarikh,* Vol. II, p. 329.

56. Chandra, *The Tuti-Nama,* p. 69.

57. *Akbarnama,* Vol. II, pp. 343-44.

58. Chandra, *The Tuti-Nama,* p. 180.

59. See for instance, S. C. Welch, *Imperial Mughal Painting* (New York: George Braziller, 1978), p. 21.

60. *Baburnama,* p. 280.

CHAPTER II (pp. 35-55)

1. *Akbarnama,* Vol. II, p. 503.

2. *Ibid.,* Vol. II, p. 530.

3. *Khanqah.*

4. Quoted by Nizam ad-Din Ahmad Haravi, *Tabaqat-i Akbari,* tr. B. De. (Calcutta: Asiatic Society of Bengal, 1927-39), Vol. II, p. 358.

5. *Ibid.*

6. Rabi II, A. H. 979. Muhammad Arif Qandahari, *Tarikh-i Akbari,* ed. Muin ud-Din Nadwi, Azhar Ali Dihlavi and Imtiyaz Ali Arshi (Rampur: Raza Library, 1962), pp. 149-50.

7. In his memoirs, however, Jahangir states that the city only

received the additional name of "City of Victory" after Akbar's conquest of Gujarat in 1573: Nur ad-Din Muhammad Jahangir, *Tuzuk-i Jahangiri*, ed H. Beveridge and tr. A. Rogers (New Delhi: Munshiram Manoharlal, 1968), Vol. I, p. 2.

8. *Hatyapul*.

9. Father Monserrate, *The Commentary of Father Monserrate*, S. J., J. S. Hoyland (London: Oxford University Press, 1922), pp. 200-01.

10. *Tarikh-i Akbari*, p. 150.

11. *Ibid*.

12. Monserrate, *The Commentary*, p. 36.

13. *Tarikh-i Akbari*, p. 150.

14. It seems likely, however, that Muhammad Qasim Khan, who carried the joint titles of "Master of the Land and Sea Routes" *(mir-i barr u bahr)* and "Master of Pyrotechnics" *(mir-i atish)* and who was responsible for the construction of the Agra fort, would have played a leading role.

15. *Tarikh-i Akbari*, pp. 144-45.

16. Monserrate, *The Commentary*, p. 201.

17. *Akbarnama*, Vol. II, p. 530.

18. *Baburnama*, p. 588. For a miniature from the ca. 1593 illustrated *Baburnama* (State Museum of Eastern Cultures, Moscow) depicting this platform, see S. Tyulyayev, *Miniatures of Baburnama* (Moscow: State Fine Arts Publishing House, 1960), pl. 65. The platform is also illustrated in the ca. 1591 version (British Library: Or, 3714, f. 459r) and the 1597-98 version (National Museum of India: f. 327v).

19. Ralph Fitch, in *Early Travels in India 1583-1619*, ed. William Foster (London: Humphrey Milford and Oxford Univeristy Press, 1921), p. 18.

20. *Tarikh-i Akbari*, p. 46.

21. *Muntakhab at-Tavarikh*, Vol. II, p. 176.

22. *Ibid.*, p. 219.

23. *Ibid.*, p. 220.

24. Alluding to Koran 9:109. *Tarikh-i Akbari*, p. 151.

25. For a more detailed description of the buildings at Fatehpur-Sikri, see S. A. A. Rizvi and V. J. Flynn, *Fathpur-Sikri* (Bombay: Taraporevala, 1975). For a collection of passages discussing Fatehpur-Sikri and its buildings taken from a variety of sources, ranging from contemporary Persian accounts to those left by later European travellers, see our *Fatehpur-Sikri: A Sourcebook*.

26. *Muntakhab at-Tavarikh*, Vol. II, pp. 277-78.

27. *Ain-i Akbari*, Vol. I, p. 309.

28. *Muntakhab at-Tavarikh*, Vol. I, p. 311.

29. *Ain-i Akbari*, Vol. I, p. 311.

30. Attilio Petruccioli, "The Process Evolved by the Control Systems of Urban Design in the Moghul Epoch in India: the Case of Fathpur Sikri," *Environmental Design* 1 (1984), 22-23.

31. *Naqqarakhana*.

32. *Daftarkhana*.

33. For a fuller discussion of the make-up of Akbar's nobility, see Iqtidar Alam Khan, "The Nobility under Akbar and the Development of His Religious Policy, 1560-80," *Journal of the Royal Asiatic Society*, (1968), 29-36, and M. Athar Ali, *The Mughal Nobility under Aurangzeb* (Bombay: Asia Publishing House, 1968), pp. 14-20.

34. *Muntakhab at-Tavarikh*, Vol. II, p. 352.

35. For a discussion of this process, see the introduction in our *Fatehpur-Sikri: a Sourcebook*, pp. 12-13.

36. Monserrate, *The Commentary*, p. 199.

37. *Ibid.*, appendix, p. XXVIII.

38. *Ain-i Akbari*, Vol. I, p. 165. The three branches of government are the Imperial Household, the Army, and the Administration.

39. *Ibid*. In the English translation of this passage, Blochmann writes that Akbar "is visible from outside the awning," but the Persian word in question *(shadurvan)* clearly refers to the "curtain wall" of the palace in another contemporary text *(Tarikh-i Akbari*, p. 147).

40. *Muntakhab at-Tavarikh*, Vol. II, p. 336. Badauni uses the Persianized spelling *"jharuka."*

41. Monserrate, *The Commentary*, p. 184.

42. *Akbarnama*, Vol. III, p. 557. *Dawlatkhana* and *divankhana*, whether standing alone or modified by the adjectives *amm* (public) or *khass o amm* (private and public), both appear to refer to the State Hall, but describe a different structure or space when modified by the adjective *khass* (private).

43. *Muntakhab at-Tavarikh*, Vol. III, p. 142.

44. *Akbarnama*, Vol. III, p. 56. Basawan's more vivid recollection is supported by Badauni's account of the event *(Muntakhab at-Tavarikh*, Vol. II, p. 163).

45. Popularly known as the *"Divan-i Khass."*

46. Awnings *(shamiyanas)* and screens *(sarapardas)* were among the textiles destroyed by a huge storehouse fire in Fatehpur-Sikri in 1579 (see p. 114).

47. *Tabaqat-i Akbari*, Vol. II, p. 555.

48. *Ain-i Akbari*, Vol. I, p. 287.

49. Monserrate, *The Commentary*, p. 198. Monserrate also claims (p. 28) that in private Akbar was fond of wearing a scarlet Portuguese cloak with gold fastenings. For Akbar's taste in clothing, see also *Ain-i Akbari*, Vol. I, pp. 93-102.

50. *Muntakhab at-Tavarikh*, Vol. II, p. 268. For Humayun's practices in this respect, see Khwandamir, *Qanun-i Humayuni*, tr. B. Prashad (Calcutta: Royal Asiatic Society of Bengal, 1940), pp. 51-54.

51. *Muntakhab at-Tavarikh*, Vol. II, pp. 265-67.

52. As tr. by S. A. A. Rizvi, *Religious and Intellectual History of the Muslims in Akbar's Reign* (New Delhi: Munshiram Manoharlal, 1975), p. 145. For contemporary accounts of this event, see *Akbarnama*, Vol. III, pp. 396; *Muntakhab at-Tavarikh*, Vol. II, pp. 276-77; *Tabaqat-i Akbari*, Vol. II, pp. 520-21.

53. The best discussion of this controversial issue can be found in Rizvi, *Religious and Intellectual History*, pp. 374-417.

54. *Akbarnama*, Vol. III, p. 158.

55. *Ibid.*, pp. 368-69.

56. *Muntakhab at-Tavarikh*, Vol. II, p. 213. The important reference to the *jizya* tax is not mentioned in Lowe's translation of this passage. For a further discussion of this matter see, Iqtidar Alam Khan, "The Nobility under Akbar," p. 32.

57. *Akbarnama*, Vol. III, pp. 346-47.

58. *Ibid.*, p. 549.

59. Iqtidar Alam Khan, "The Nobility under Akbar," p. 33.

60. *Akbarnama*, Vol. II, p. 599.

61. *Maktabkhana*.

62. *Dar az-Zarb*.

63. There is no evidence to support the popular theory that the city was abandoned due to a shortage of water.

64. *Akbarnama*, Vol. III, p. 748.

65. *Tuzuk-i Jahangiri*, Vol. I, p. 3.

66. Muhammad Salih Kambu, *Amal-i Salih*, ed. Ghulam Yazdani (Calcutta: Royal Asiatic Society of Bengal, 1912-39) Vol. I, p. 127; Abd al-Hamid Lahawri, *Padshahnama*, ed, K. Ahmad and M. A. Rahim (Calcutta: Asiatic Society of Bengal, 1867-68), Vol. I, part 1, p. 243.

CHAPTER III (pp. 57-85)

1. M. S. Simpson, "The Production and Patronage of the Haft Aurang by Jami in the Freer Gallery of Art," *Ars Orientalis*, Vol. XIII, pp. 93-100.

2. Monserrate, *The Commentary*, p. 60.

3. *Ain-i Akbari*, Vol. I, pp. 109-110.

4. *Muntakhab at-Tavarikh*, Vol. II, p. 328.

5. "Kitabkhana," *Encyclopedia of Islam*, 1st ed., 4 Vols. (London: E. J. Brill, 1913-18), p. 1046.

6. *Ibid.*

7. *Ibid.*

8. *Ibid.*

9. *Ibid.*

10. *Ibid.*, p. 1047.

11. Qazi Ahmad, *Calligraphers and Painters*, p. 158.

12. A similar page from the same album is now in the Staatsbibliothek Preussischer Kulturbesitz, W. Berlin and is reproduced in Kühnel and Goetz, *Indische Buchmalereien*, pl. 20 (fol. 18a).

13. *Akbarnama*, Vol. III, p. 125.

14. *Ain-i Akbari*, Vol. I, p. 517.

15. *Ibid.*, p. 110.

16. *Ain-i Akbari*, Vol. I, p. 103.

17. *Ibid.*

18. *Ibid.*

19. *Ibid.*, p. 109.

20. *Ibid.*, p. 114; as tr. by Naim in Chandra, *The Tuti-Nama*, p. 183.

21. *Ibid.*

22. *Ibid.*, p. 114; as tr. by Naim in Chandra, *The Tuti-Nama*, pp. 183-84.

23. Milo C. Beach, *The Imperial Image; Paintings for the Mughal Court* (Washington: Freer Gallery of Art, 1981), p. 24.

24. *Ain-i Akbari*, as tr. by Naim in Chandra, *The Tuti-Nama*, p. 184.

25. *Muntakhab at-Tavarikh*, Vol. III, p. 283.

26. The Persian term used, *tasvirkhana*, means literally "painting-house" and is only used by Abul Fazl in the *Ain-i Akbari*. It is not clear whether this was an invention on his part or a standard means of referring to a library's studios.

27. Quoted in Sir Thomas W. Arnold, *Painting in Islam*, (Oxford: Clarendon Press, 1928), p. 151.

28. J. V. S. Wilkinson, *The Lights of Canopus* (London: The Studios Limited, 1929).

29. British Library, Or 4615.

30. Chester Beatty Library, Ms. 15.

31. Royal Asiatic Society, Ms. 258.

32. B. W. Robinson et al, *Islamic Painting and The Arts of the Book* (London: Faber and Faber, 1976), pp. 238-248.

33. Chester Beatty Library, Ms. 21.

34. Jeremiah P. Losty, *The Art of the Book in India* (London: British Library, 1982), p. 87.

35. *Ain-i Akbari*, Vol. I, p. 112.

36. Abdul Aziz, *The Imperial Library of the Mughals* (Delhi: Idarah-i Adabiyat-i Delli, 1974), p. 46.

37. *Muntakhab at-Tavarikh*, Vol. II, p. 186.

38. *Ibid.*, p. 330.

39. *Ibid.*, pp. 329-30.

40. *Ibid.*, p. 328.

41. *Ibid.*

42. *Ain-i Akbari*, Vol. I, p. 113.

43. *Muntakhab at-Tavarikh*, Vol. II, p. 329.

44. Beach, *The Imperial Image: Paintings for the Mughal Court*. p. 94.

45. F. 278b.

46. Although there is no specific information in the *Akbarnama* concerning when the manuscript was begun, Abul Fazl does mention that the manuscript took seven years to write (*Ain-i Akbari*, Vol. III, p. 456) and that it was completed in 1597-98 (*Ain-i Akbari*, Vol. III, p. 476).

47. *Ain-i Akbari*, Vol. III, p. 476.

48. *Akbarnama*, Vol. II, p. 544.

49. Chester Beatty Library, Ms. 3, f. 176b.

50. *Ain-i Akbari*, Vol. III, p. 476-76.

51. *Ibid.*, p. 456,

52. *Akbarnama*, Vol. I, p. 30.

53. *Akbarnama*, (Ms. 117 in the Royal Asiatic Society), as quoted in the introduction, *Akbarnama*, Vol. I, p. 33.

54. *Akbarnama*, Vol. I, p. 33 provides a discussion of the dates given in this manuscript.

55. *Ibid.*, p. 33.

56. *Ibid.*, p. 30.

57. *Ibid.*, p. 29.

58. *Ain-i Akbari*, Vol. I, p. 268.

59. *Akbarnama*, Vol. I, p. 31.

60. *Muntakhab at-Tavarikh*, Vol. II, p. 388.

61. *Tabaqat-i Akbari*, Vol. I, p. 1.

62. *Akbarnama*, Vol. III, p. 862.

63. Ellen Smart, "Six Folios from a Dispersed Manuscript of the Baburnama," in *Indian Painting* (London: Colnaghi, 1978), pp. 111-114.

64. C. A. Storey, *Persian Literature: A Bio-Bibliographical Survey*, Vol. I, part 1, pp. 532-33. (London: Luzacs and Co., 1927-29).

65. Mentioned as one of the manuscripts illustrated for Akbar by Abul Fazl in the *Ain-i Akbari*, Vol. I, p. 115.

66. Beach, *The Imperial Image*, p. 85.

67. *Ibid.*

68. *Ain-i Akbari*, Vol. I, p. 115; as tr. by Naim in Chandra, *The Tuti-Nama*, p. 184.

69. *Ain-i Akbari*, Vol. I, p. 462.

70. Shah Nawaz Khan, *Maathir al-Umara*, tr. H. Beveridge, 3 vols. (Patna: Janaki Prakashan, 1979), Vol. II, pp. 564-65.

71. *Akbarnama*, Vol. III, p. 1215.

72. *Tuzuk-i Jahangiri*, Vol. I, p. 17.

73. *Akbarnama*, Vol. II, p. 280.

74. *Ibid.*, Vol. III, p. 816.

75. *Muntakhab at-Tavarikh*, Vol. II, pp. 311-12.

76. *Ibid.*

77. *Ibid.*

78. Beach, *The Imperial Image*, p. 134 and M. Mahfuzul Haq, "The Khan Khanan and His Painters, Illuminators and Calligraphists," *Islamic Culture*, Vol. 5, no. 4, 1931, pp. 621-630.

79. See Beach, *The Imperial Image*, (pp. 128-156), for a detailed discussion and analysis of this manuscript.

80. *Maathir al-Umara*, Vol. I, p. 331.

81. *Ibid.*

82. Marie Lukens Swietochowski, "The Development of Traditions of Book Illustration in Pre-Safavid Iran," *Iranian Studies*, 7, Nos. 1-2 (1974), p. 49; Priscilla Soucek, "Comments on Persian Painting," *Iranian Studies*, 7, Nos. 1-2 (1974), p. 73.

CHAPTER IV (pp. 87-105)

1. Letter dated September 9, 1580 from Monserrate to Father Vicente: *Letters from the Mughal Court*, p. 82.

2. For a description of Timur's use of this device based on the older Buddhist *cintamani* symbol, see Clavijo, *Embassy to Tamerlane 1403-1406*, tr. Guy Le Strange (London: George Routledge and Sons, 1928), pp. 208-209. Clavijo also states that "The lord (Timur) has these three O's on his seals, and he has ordered those who are tributary to him have it stamped on the coins of their countries" (p. 209 and n.5).

3. This interpretation was suggested to us by Wheeler Thackston.

4. J. V. S. Wilkinson and Laurence Binyon, *The Shah-Namah of Firdausi: The Book of the Persian Kings* (London: Oxford University Press, 1931), pl. 24.

5. *Muntakhab at-Tavarikh*, Vol. II, p. 329. It has been suggested that a detached miniature now in the Keir collection originally belonged to Akbar's copy of the *Shahnama*: Robert Skelton, "Indian Painting of the Mughal Period," in *Islamic Painting and the Arts of the Book*, ed. B. W. Robinson (London: Faber and Faber, 1976), pp. 237-38 and color plate 31.

6. *Baburnama*, p. 459.

7. *Tabaqat-i Baburi*, p. 58.

8. *Sadr al-kitab: Tabaqat-i Baburi*, p. 58.

9. *Akbarnama*, Vol. I, p. 309.

10. *Ibid.*, pp. 309-10.

11. Like the *Timurnama* composed in verse by Abdullah "Hatifi" Jami around 1500, the prose *Zafarnama* completed by Sharaf ad-Din Yazdi in 1424-25 is a history of Timur. It seems highly unlikely that copies of both works could have been stolen from Humayun before eventually finding their way back into the Mughal library in the time of Akbar. The anonymous *Tarikh-i Khandan-i Timuriyya* (fig. 8) written and illustrated for Akbar ca. 1584 is an entirely different book.

12. Sir Thomas W. Arnold, *Bihzad and his Paintings in the Zafarnamah MS.* (London: Bernard Quaritch, 1930), facing p. 1.

13. *Ibid.*, p. 2.

14. *Ibid.*, pp. 3-4.

15. *Akbarnama*, Vol. I, p. 452. Mulla Surkh, another one of Humayun's librarians, had deserted the emperor in ca. 1541 and entered the service of his Rajput rival Raja Maldeo of Jodhpur according to Gulbadan Begam, *Humayunnama*, tr. A. H. Beveridge Delhi: Idarah-i Adabiyat-i Delli, 1972, p. 154.

16. *Akbarnama*, Vol. I, p. 571.

17. The note is written around the *shamsa* (illuminated medallion) at the very beginning of the manuscript, which is now in the collection of the Museum für Islamische Kunst in East Berlin (Ms. Orient, Fol. 1278).

18. Binyon, Wilkinson and Gray, *Persian Miniature Painting*, pp. 130-31 and pl. LXXXVII A.

19. *Ibid.*, p. 131 and pl. LXXXVII B.

20. There is no doubt that Nanha, as stated by Jahangir, made his copy from Bihzad's original and not from Abd as-Samad's version.

21. *Baburnama*, p. 329.

22. Khwaja Hasan Nisari Bukhari, *Muzzakir al-Ahbab*, cited and tr. by Mudaddema Mukhtarovna Ashrafi-Aini, "The School of Bukhara to c. 1550," in *The Arts of the Book in Central Asia: 14th-16th Centuries*, ed. Basil Gray (Boulder, Colorado: Shambala/UNESCO, 1979), p. 264.

23. Mir Ali's son Mirza Baqir later migrated to India and found work in the *kitabkhana* of Abd ar-Rahim Khan Khanan (M. Mahfuzul Haq, "The Khan Khanan and His Painters, Illuminators and Calligraphers," *Islamic Culture*, Vol. 5, no. 4 (1931), p. 626, before entering the service of Akbar. Jahangir avidly collected calligraphic folios by Mir Ali, many of which were included in his albums.

24. Quoted by Qazi Ahmad, *Calligraphers and Painters*, pp. 130-131.

25. Fogg Art Museum, Harvard University, 1979, 20; Welch, *The Art of Mughal India* (New York: Asia Society, 1963), NO. 23.

26. Chester Beatty Library, Ms. 215. The colophon is dated "A. H. 915" (1509) but this must be an error for Mir Ali was not in Bukhara at that time. Since one of the miniatures is dated A. H. 955 (1548-49) it has been suggested that this, or A. H. 951 (1544-45), was the intended date in the colophon: Binyon, Wilkinson and Gray, *Persian Miniature Painting*, p. 124 pl. LXXXI B.

27. Binyon, Wilkinson and Gray, *Persian Miniature Painting*, p. 124.

28. *Akbarnama*, Vol. III, p. 598.

29. A further discussion of this problematic colophon can be found in the catalogue entry.

30. Norah M. Titley, *Miniatures from Persian Manuscripts* (London: British Library, 1977), p. 147.

31. Chandra, *The Tuti-Nama*, p. 73; Losty, *The Art of the Book*, p. 86.

32. Chandra, *The Tuti-Nama*, p. 73 and pl. 42.

33. Skelton, "Indian Painting of the Mughal Period," pp. 238-48, plates V.7-41, and color plates 32-33; Losty, *The Art of the Book in India*, cat. no. 61 and color plate XXIII.

34. Apart from a few dispersed pages, the bulk of the manuscript, which formerly belonged to the Marquess of Bute, is now in the collection of the British Library (Or. 14139).

35. Skelton, "Indian Painting of the Mughal Period," p. 251.

36. *Akbarnama*, Vol. III, p. 37.

37. Losty, *The Art of the Book*, pl. XX.

38. Beach, "A European Source for Early Mughal Painting," *Oriental Art*, n.s. 22 (1976), pp. 181-84.

39. Gulistan Palace Library, Teheran, folio 520: Basil Gray, *Persian Painting* (New York: Skira/Rizzoli, 1977), p. 132.

40. *Akbarnama*, Vol. III, p. 207.

41. *Ibid.*, p. 207.

42. *Ibid.*, p. 322.

43. *Muntakhab at-Tavarikh*, Vol. II, p. 299.

44. Quoted in Sir Edward Maclagan, *The Jesuits and the Great Mogul* (London: Burns, Oates and Washbourne, 1932), p. 24.

45. Joint letter from March-April, 1580 to the Captain of Daman: *Letters from the Mughal Court*, pp. 29-30.

46. Joint letter dated July 13, 1580 to Father Vicente: *Letters from the Mughal Court*, p. 42.

47. A detailed description of the Polyglot Bible is given by Ebba Koch in "The Influence of the Jesuit Mission on Symbolic Representations of the Mughal Emperors," *Islam in India, Studies and Commentaries*, ed. C. W. Troll, Vol. 1 (1982), pp. 15-16.

48. Monserrate, *The Commentary*, pp. 136-38.

49. For a detailed discussion of the effect these images and their intended use had on Mughal painting, see Koch, "The Influence of the Jesuit Mission."

50. Letter from Henriques to Father Peres, from a compilation of letters written in March-April, 1580: *Letters from the Mughal Court*, pp. 30-31.

51. *Ibid.*, p. 31.

52. Letter dated July 18, 1580 from Acquaviva to Father Mercurian: *Letters from the Mughal Court*, p. 58.

53. *Ibid.*, p. 60.

54. Maclagan, *The Jesuits*, p. 227.

55. John E. McCall, "Early Jesuit Art in the Far East, IV," *Artibus Asiae*, II (1948), p. 47. The second larger copy is reproduced as fig. 22, and a Chinese copy as fig. 25.

56. Joint letter to the Captain of Daman from a compilation of letters written in March-April, 1580: *Letters from the Mughal Court*, p. 33. In another letter (quoted on p. 48) this same comment is said to refer to the copy made by Godinho, but this cannot be possible, as the St. Luke Virgin is not depicted seated on a throne.

57. *Ibid.*

58. Joint letter dated July 13, 1580 to Father Vicente: *Letters from the Mughal Court*, pp. 48-49.

59. Joint letter to the Captain of Daman from a compilation of letters written in March-April, 1580: *Letters from the Mughal Court*, p. 34.

60. *Ibid.*, p. 33. More information on the reliquary in another letter is given on p. 59.

61. Ashok Kumar Das, *Mughal Painting during Jahangir's Time* (Calcutta: The Asiatic Society, 1978), p. 237 and pl. 69.

62. Private collection. Illustrated in S. C. Welch, *Room for Wonder: Indian Painting during the British Period 1760-1880* (New York: The American Federation of the Arts, 1978), fig. 1.

63. For additional information about which prints found their way into the Mughal collection see, Beach, "The Gulshan Album and its European Sources," *Bulletin of the Museum of Fine Arts, Boston*, 332 (1965), pp. 63-91.

64. Beach, "The Mughal Painter Kesu Das," *Archives of Asian Art*, 30 (1976-77), pp. 39-42 and fig. 9. The painting is now in the collection of the Chester Beatty Library (Ms. 41, no. 2).

65. *Ibid.*, pp. 39-42 and fig. 57.

66. Letter dated September 9, 1580 from Monserrate to Father Vicente: *Letters from the Mughal Court*, p. 76.

67. *Muntakhab at-Tavarikh*, Vol. II, p. 205.

68. *Ibid.*, Vol. III, p. 421.

69. Joannes de Laet, *The Empire of the Great Mogol*, tr. J. S. Hoyland (Delhi: Idarah-i Adabiyat-i Delli, 1975), p. 108. De Laet did not actually visit India himself but compiled his book from the first-hand accounts of others.

70. *Tuzuk-i Jahangiri*, Vol. I, p. 409.

CHAPTER V (pp. 107-121)

1. *Letters from the Mughal Court*, p. 81.

2. Monserrate, *The Commentary*, p. 201.

3. *Ain-i Akbari*, Vol. III, p. 430.

4. *Ibid.*, Vol. I, p. 11.

5. See Chapter I, p. 20.

6. *Maathir al-Umara*, Vol. I, pp. 545-46.

7. Brand and Lowry, *Fatehpur-Sikri: A Sourcebook*, p. 36.

8. Monserrate, *The Commentary*, p. 58.

9. *Ibid.*, p. 201.

10. *Ain-i Akbari*, Vol. I, p. 12.

11. *Ibid.*, p. 6.

12. *Ibid.*

13. *Ibid.*, p. 598.

14. *Ibid.*, p. 599.

15. *Ibid.*, p. 14.

16. Monserrate, *The Commentary*, p. 175.

17. *Pishgah-i huzur* is the term used by Abul Fazl.

18. *Ain-i Akbari*, Vol. I, p. 93.

19. *Ibid.*, p. 94.

20. *Ibid.*, pp. 98-102.

21. Monserrate, *The Commentary*, p. 198.

22. *Ain-i Akbari*, Vol. I, p. 96.

23. *Ibid.*, p. 97.

24. *Ibid.*, p. 94.

25. As can be seen in a page from the *Jahangirnama* now in the Raza Library, reproduced in *An Age of Splendour—Islamic Art in India*, ed. by K. Khandalavala (Bombay: Marg Publications, 1983), p. 41.

26. Daniel Walker, "Classical Indian Carpets," *Hali*, Vol. IV, No. 3 (1982), p. 253.

27. *Ain-i Akbari*, Vol. I, p. 57.

28. Or 292. Published in color in Erwin Gans-Reudin, *The Indian Carpet* (London: Thames and Hudson, 1984), p. 76.

29. Recently published in *The Textile Gallery*, (London: The Textile Gallery, 1984). 1984, pl. 2.

30. Inv. 5212. Published in color in *Hali*, Vol. IV, No. 3 (1982), p. 225.

31. R. 63.00.13. Published in color in Gans-Ruedin, *The Indian Carpet*, p. 67.

32. *The Eastern Carpet in the Western World: From the 15th to the 17th Century*, (London: Arts Council of Great Britain, 1983), p. 98, No. 76.

33. Robert Skelton, *The Indian Heritage: Court Life and Art under Mughal Rule* (London: Victoria and Albert Museum, 1982), p. 74.

34. Now on deposit at the Walters Art Gallery (TL 6.1950).

35. Inv. No. T. 113. *Museu Calouste Gulbenkian, Catalogo*, Lisbon, 1982, fig. 292.

36. See *The Eastern Carpet in the Western World*, p. 97 for a brief discussion of these rugs.

37. Now in the Bodleian Library. Reproduced in color in S. C.

Welch, *Imperial Mughal Painting*, pl. 8.

38. Victoria and Albert Museum, I.S. 2-1896 24/117.

39. Martin Dickson and Stuart Cary Welch, *The Houghton Shahnameh*, 2 Vols. (Cambridge, Massachusetts: Harvard University Press, 1981), p. 109.

40. *Ain-i Akbari*, Vol. I, p. 55.

41. *Ibid.*, p. 56.

42. *Tarikh-i Akbari*, tr. in our *Fatehpur-Sikri: A Sourcebook*, p. 281.

43. *Fatehpur-Sikri: A Sourcebook*, pp. 102-103.

44. De Laet, *The Empire of the Great Mogol*, p. 108.

45. British Library, Or. 1052, f. 307a.

46. Reproduced in Beach, *The Imperial Image*, p. 123.

47. *Ain-i Akbari*, Vol. I, p. 290.

48. *Akbarnama*, Vol. III, p. 120.

49. *Ain-i Akbari*, Vol. I, p. 61.

50. *Ibid.*

51. Skelton, *The Indian Heritage*, p. 151.

52. *Ibid.*, p. 144.

53. *Ibid.*, p. 145.

54. Now in a private European collection.

55. For an almost identical ewer depicted in a page from a sixteenth-century copy of the *Baburnama* see Mario Bussagli, *Indian Miniatures*, tr. R. Rudorff (New Delhi: The Macmillan Company of India, 1976), pl. 40.

56. See, for instance, no. 8770/48 from the Osterreichisches Museum für angewandte Kunst, reproduced in G. Egger, *Der Hamza Roman*, (Vienna: Osterreichisches Museum für angewandte Kunst, 1969), pl. 11.

57. *Baburnama*, p. 80.

58. *Ibid.*, p. 407.

59. For one of the most detailed records of the type of Chinese porcelains at the Mughal court see the painting of "Prince Khurram Weighed against Metals" (British Museum, 1948, 10-9-69), reproduced in S. C. Welch, *Imperial Mughal Painting*, pl. 18.

60. In addition to ceramics, other goods including paintings on silk (*Ain-i Akbari*, Vol. III, p. 458) were imported by Akbar from China.

61. *The Arts of Islam*, (London: the Arts Council of Great Britain, 1976), p. 129, no. 114.

62. Skelton, "The Shah Jahan Cup," *Victoria and Albert Museum Bulletin*, Vol. II, No. 3, 1966), p. 7.

63. *Akbarnama*, Vol. II, pp. 301-02.

64. We are grateful to Amy Poster for making available to us her unpublished paper on *The Guennol Jade Jarlet*.

65. Skelton, "The Shah Jahan Cup," p. 7. For a metal vessel with the identical design see folio 97 of the Victoria and Albert Museum *Akbarnama*.

66. Since shapes, once they entered the Mughal repertoire, tended to remain constant over long periods of time, it is also possible that the Guennol jar was made during the seventeenth century (*The Guennol Jade Jarlet*, p. 2) in which case it would still reflect a type of vessel common at Akbar's court.

67. *Ain-i Akbari*, Vol. I, p. 233.

68. *Ibid.*, p. 285.

69. Vilhelm Slohmann, "The Indian Period of European Furniture I," *Burlington Magazine*, 1934, p. 120.

70. See f. 97 of the Victoria and Albert Museum *Akbarnama*.

71. Slohmann, "The Indian Period of European Furniture I." p. 120.

72. *Ibid.*

73. Fitch, in *Early Travels in India*, p. 18.

74. For a brief discussion of this subject see Skelton, *The Indian Heritage*, p. 161, no. 543.

75. Father du Jarric, *Akbar and the Jesuits* (London: George Routledge and Sons, 1926), pp. 9-10.

76. Monserrate, *The Commentary*, p. 61.

77. *Ain-i Akbari*, Vol. I, p. 262.

78. *Ibid.*, p. 52.

79. See f. 201 of the Chester Beatty *Akbarnama*.

80. *Ain-i Akbari*, Vol. I, p. 233.

81. H. G. Keene, *A Handbook for Visitors to Delhi and its Neighbourhood* (Calcutta: Thacker Spink & Co., 1882), p. 68.

82. Vincent A. Smith, *A History of Fine Art in India and Ceylon* (Oxford: Clarendon Press, 1930), pp. 189-191.

83. François Bernier, *Travels in the Mogul Empire*, A. D. 1656-1668, ed. by A. Constable, pp. 256-7.

84. Smith, *A History of Fine Art in India and Ceylon*, pp. 189-191.

85. Monserrate, *The Commentary, p. 35.*

86. Published in *Marg*, Vol. XI, No. 3, p. 49, fig. 7.

87. Chandra, "Ustad Salivahana and the Development of Popular Mughal Art," *Lalit Kala*, Vol. I, 1960, fig. 2.

88. The torsos of the figures are also in the possession of the Archaeological Survey of India at the Red Fort in Delhi.

89. *Ain-i Akbari*, Vol. I, p. 28.

90. *Ibid.*, p. 20.

91. *Ibid.*, pp. 54-55.

92. *Ibid.*, p. 55.

93. *Ibid.*, p. 28.

94. *Akbarnama*, Vol. III, p. 320. See also J. Deyell, "Development of Akbar's Currency System and Monetary Integration of the Conquered Kingdoms," unpublished paper read at the Conference on the Monetary System of India, National Humanities Center, 1981.

95. Deyell, "Development of Akbar's Currency System," p. 18.

96. Monserrate, *The Commentary*, pp. 208-209.

97. *Ain-i Akbari*, Vol. I, pp. 273-74.

98. *Ibid.*, p. 54.

99. This must have been accomplished prior to 1594-95 when Abul Fazl mentions that Mawlana Ahmad's new seal was made over to the Khan Azam. (*Akbarnama*, Vol. III, p. 1033).

100. *Muntakhab at-Tavarikh*, Vol. III, p. 491.

101. *Ibid.*, Vol. III, p. 491. See also NO. 53.

102. We are grateful to Dr. Ziauddin A. Shakeb for translating this document for us. A complete summary of the text is given in the entry for NO. 80.

103. Cited in Maclagan, *The Jesuit*, p. 77.

CHAPTER VI (pp. 123-128)

1. *Akbarnama*, Vol. III, p. 581; *Muntakhab at-Tavarikh*, Vol. II, p. 296.

2. *Ibid.*, Vol. II, p. 553.

3. *Ain-i Akbari*, Vol. I, pp. 103-04.

4. *Ibid.*, p. 20.

5. Freer Gallery of Art, Washington, D.C., 63.4. Illustrated in color in Beach, *The Imperial Image*, p. 73.

6. Nasir ad-Din Tusi, *The Nasirean Ethics*, tr. G. M. Wickens (London: George Allen and Unwin, 1964), pp. 158-59.

7. *Ibid.*, pp. 215-216.

8. *Akbarnama*, Vol. II, p. 554.

9. *Ain-i Akbari*, Vol. I, p. 113; as tr. by Naim in Chandra, *The Tuti-Nama*, pp. 182-83.

10. S. C. Welch, *The Art of Mughal India* (New York: The Asia Society, 1963), p. 25.

11. Alternative forms of this word are *mana* and *mani*.

12. *Surat* is derived from the same Arabic root as *tasvir* (painting) and *musavvir* (painter).

13. A. E. Affifi, *The Mystical Philosophy of Muhyid Din-Ibnul Arabi* (Cambridge: Cambridge University Press, 1939), p. 16.

14. Dickson and Welch, *The Houghton Shahnameh*, p. 260, n. 2.

15. Extract from a *rubai* of Fayzi, quoted by Abul Fazl, *Ain-i Akbari*, Vol. I, p. 631.

16. *Akbarnama*, Vol. II, p. 502.

17. *Ain-i Akbari*, Vol. I, p. 18.

18 *Ibid.*, p. 113.

19. *Ibid.*, Vol. I, p. 117; as tr. by Naim in Chandra, *Tuti-Nama*, p. 184.

20. *Ain-i Akbari*, Vol. I, p. 103.

21. *Fatehpur-Sikri: A Sourcebook*, pp. 257-58.

22. *Muntakhab at-Tavarikh*, Vol. III, p. 271.

23. *Ain-i Akbari*, Vol. I, p. 102; as tr. in Ebba Koch, "Jahangir and the Angels: Recently Discovered Wall Paintings under European Influence in the Fort of Lahore," in *India and the West*, ed. Joachim Deppert (New Delhi: Manohar Publications, 1983), p. 193, n. 73.

24. *Ain-i Akbari*, Vol. I, p. 618. Nevertheless, Abul Fazl gives accounts of at least fifty-nine poets who worked for Akbar.

25. Sadiqi Beg, *The Canons of Painting*; as tr. in Dickson and Welch, *The Houghton Shahnameh*, p. 264.

26. *Ain-i Akbari*, Vol. I, pp. 102-103; as tr. in Koch, "Jahangir and the Angels," p. 193, n. 73.

27. For a fuller discussion of this phenomenon in relation to the *Polyglot Bible* see, Koch, "The Influence of the Jesuit Mission."

28. *Ain-i Akbari*, Vol. I, p. 114; as tr. by Naim in Chandra, *The Tuti-Nama*, p. 183.

29. Abul Fazl, *Ain-i Akbari*, Vol. I, p. 113; as tr. by Naim in Chandra, *The Tuti-Nama*, p. 183.

30. Abul Fazl, *Ain-i Akbari*, Vol. I, p. 113; as tr. by Naim in Chandra, *Tuti-Nama*, pp. 183-4.

31. *Ain-i Akbari*, Vol. I, p. 115; as tr. by Naim in Chandra, *Tuti-Nama*, p. 184.

CATALOGUE

CHAPTER I
Akbar and the Formation of Mughal Art

1. *The Infant Akbar Wrestling* (p.15)
with Ibrahim Mirza

From an imperial copy of the *Akbarnama*
ca. 1604
Opaque watercolor on paper
Painting: H. 21.9 cm., W. 12 cm. Page: H. 34.5 cm.,
W. 22.1 cm.
A. Soudavar Collection

The ca. 1604 illustrated version of Abul Fazl's *Akbar-nama* (see p. 73) is divided between the British Library in London (Vol. I; Or. 12988) and the Chester Beatty Library in Dublin (Vol. II and part of Vol. III; Ms. 2). According to a note on folio 1 of the manuscript by Jahangir, its calligrapher was Muhammad Husayn al-Kashmiri Zarin Qalam (see p. 60). Folio 134b is inscribed with the date Shaban 21, A. H. 1012 (January 25, 1604). For a list of other dispersed miniatures from this manuscript, see Milo C. Beach, *The Imperial Image*, Washington, 1981, pp. 116-23. This wrestling scene belongs to a series of dispersed miniatures from the manuscript that were remounted this century within borders taken from the *Farhang-i Jahangiri*, an early-seventeenth-century Mughal dictionary. It has been identified by Toby Falk (Colnaghi, *Persian and Mughal Art*, London, 1976, p. 171) as showing a wrestling contest that took place in the Shahr-ara Garden outside Kabul between the three-year-old Akbar and his slightly older cousin Ibrahim Mirza in 1545 (*Akbarnama*, Vol. I, pp. 455-56). Mirza Kamran (Humayun's brother and the father of Ibrahim Mirza) is shown seated in the center of the tent adjudicating the fight, which arose over a symbolically prestigious kettle-drum, while the woman standing on his right is presumably Babur's sister Khanzada Begam, in whose garden pavilion the young Akbar was staying at the time.

2. *Alanquva and Her Three Sons* (p. 16)

From an imperial copy of the *Chingiznama* (see NO. 35)
ca. 1596
Opaque watercolor on paper
Painting: H. 34.29 cm., W. 21.23 cm.
Los Angeles County Museum of Art (M. 78.9.9)

The text that accompanies this miniature describes it as a picture of Alanquva and her three sons. Divinely impregnated by a ray of light after the death of her first husband, Alanquva was the mythical ancestor of the Mughals. Abul Fazl, in his description of her life (*Akbarnama*, Vol. I, pp. 178-83), emphasizes the purity of her character and the sacredness of the light that caused her pregnancy. On several occasions he compares her to Mary, thus elevating her offspring to the same status as Jesus. Alanquva gave birth to triplets, Buqun Qanqi, Yusuqi Salji and Buzanjar Qaan. The descendants of these three boys, according to Abul Fazl, were known as *nairun* or light-produced. Although Buzanjar Qaan was the youngest of the triplets, it was through him that this hidden light was passed from Chingiz Khan, to Timur, and ultimately to Akbar. Presumably he is the largest of the triplets shown next to Alanquva in this miniature. For a detailed discussion of this chain of light and its implications for Mughal ideology see pp. 14-15.

3. *Battle Scene* (p. 18)

From an unidentified historical manuscript
ca. 1590
Opaque watercolor and gold on paper
Painting: H. 35.2 cm., W. 21 cm. Page: H. 42 cm.,
W. 26.4 cm.
A. Soudavar Collection

This is one of the most dramatic Akbari portrayals of armed combat. Each of the painting's figures is charged with a sense of dynamism that is accentuated by the image's bold colors and exciting juxtapositions. The enormous elephant in the lower right, for instance, provides the perfect counterpoint to the warrior above on his white steed, while the tranquil landscape in the upper portion of the picture stands in stark contrast to the battlefield strewn with decapitated heads. The miniature is mounted on an early-seventeenth-century album page that once formed part of the Gulshan Album (*Muraqqa-i Gulshan*) that used to be in the Gulistan Palace in Tehran. While it is tempting to attribute this page to a historical manuscript, such as the *Akbarnama*, its presence in an early-seventeenth-century album suggests that it may have been intended for a manuscript that was never completed, or one that was dismembered in order to be reused as part of another book (see Beach, *The Imperial Image*, p. 85, for an elaboration of this idea). On the reverse of the page is a calligraphy signed by Mir Ali.

4. *Akbar Attacking the Fortress at Chittorgarh* (p. 21)

Design by Miskin, painting by Bhura
From an imperial copy of the *Akbarnama* (see NO. 14)
ca. 1590
Opaque watercolor on paper
Painting: H. 37.5 cm., W. 25 cm.
Victoria and Albert Museum, London (I.S.2-1896, 67/117)

Akbar's decisive victory against the Rajput state of Mewar at Chittorgarh in February, 1568 is given great prominence in the ca. 1590 *Akbarnama*. Four miniatures illustrate what was arguably Akbar's single greatest military accomplishment, a victory that paved the way for the great social and political experiments of the 1570s. This miniature forms the left side of a double-page illustration depicting an accidental explosion that caused the loss of hundreds of lives on both sides as Akbar's generals were attempting to breach the fortress with mines in December, 1567 (*Akbarnama*, Vol. II, p. 468). The full painting was designed by Miskin, with Bhura painting this half and Sarwan the right half (both sides are illustrated together in R. H. Pinder-Wilson, *Painting from the Muslim Courts of India*, London, 1976, pp. 48-49). Akbar, whose resolve to capture Chittorgarh was only strengthened by this tragedy, is shown at the bottom left corner directing operations from his tented camp as the explosion turns the sky orange and red with flames.

5. *A Youth and a Musician* (p. 24)

ca. 1550-60
Opaque watercolor on paper
Painting: H. 39.7 cm., W. 28.2 cm.
The St. Louis Art Museum (42.1952)

The attribution of this painting to Mughal patronage was originally suggested to us by Stuart Cary Welch. The subject of this fascinating miniature reflects the leisurely life of the court and has its iconographic roots in tenth- and eleventh-century poetry as well as the imagery of Islamic metalware of the thirteenth and fourteenth centuries.

6. *A Young Scribe* (p. 25)

By Mir Sayyid Ali
ca. 1550
Opaque watercolor on paper
Painting: H. 31.75 cm., W. 19.8 cm.
Lent by Edwin Binney, 3rd (I 486; 57)

Mir Sayyid Ali was one of the artists who left Iran to join Humayun, first in Kabul and then in India, and was responsible for helping to develop the conventions of Mughal painting. This miniature, painted prior to Humayun's return to India, reflects the emperor's concern for naturalism and detail. The folio of writing to the right of the scribe bears two inscriptions. The upper one reads "On the frontispiece of his mind he has written, 'Better a forceful master than a father overkind?'" The lower inscription states that "Mir Sayyid Ali, who is the rarity of the realm (*nadir al-mulk*) of Humayun Shah, painted this."

7. *A Prince Hunting* (p. 26)

ca. 1550-55
Opaque watercolor on paper
Painting: H. 22.6 cm., W. 13.8 cm.
The Syndics of the Fitzwilliam Museum, Cambridge (PD 72.1948)

Hunting imagery is one of the most common features of royal Islamic art. Often, a manuscript's patron is depicted in the guise of the hunter. This important early Mughal painting seems to be a representation of the young Prince Akbar and perhaps refers to a specific event in 1555 (when he was thirteen years old) which was later recorded by Abul Fazl in the *Akbarnama* (Vol. I, p. 634). This hunt took place on the very day Humayun re-entered Delhi after his final victory over the last Suri sultan, and only one year before Akbar ascended the throne of India after his father's premature death.

8. *The Parrot Mother Cautions Her Young* (p. 27)

Attributed to Daswanth
From an imperial copy of the *Tutinama*
ca. 1560-65
Opaque watercolor on paper
Painting: H. 10.31 cm., W. 10.8 cm. Page: H. 20.32 cm., W. 13.97 cm.
The Cleveland Museum of Art, Gift of Mrs. A. Dean Perry (62.279, f. 207r)

The *Tutinama* (Tales of a Parrot) is a Persian reworking, completed by Ziya ad-Din Nakhshabi in 1329-30, of an earlier translation of the Sanskrit prose classic *Shukasaptati* (Seventy Tales of a Parrot) where stories from the *Panchatantra*, the *Sindbadnama*, and the

Kalila wa Dimna had also been inserted. The two hundred and eighteen miniatures from this, the earliest surviving Mughal illustrated manuscript, shows Akbari painting in the very process of emerging from a mixture of Persian and local Indian idioms, an evolution succinctly described by Pramod Chandra in *The Tuti-Nama of The Cleveland Museum of Art* (Graz, 1976; published in conjunction with a facsimile edition of the manuscript wherein all the miniatures are reproduced in color). For fifty-two consecutive nights, a wise parrot relates stories until dawn to a young woman named Khujasta in order to prevent her from visiting her lover during the absence of her husband. This miniature illustrates a story told during the fifth night, in which a mother parrot warns her young against playing with a seemingly friendly family of foxes who live at the foot of their tree (see Mehmed A. Simsar's complete translation of the text: Graz, 1978, pp. 36-37). The text at the bottom of the page, however, contains the beginning of her account of a chess-playing monkey who made the mistake of associating with humans. The miniature has been attributed by Chandra to the artist Daswanth (*The Tuti-Nama*, p. 88) on the basis of similarities to the miniature on the reverse side of the folio, which is ascribed to the same artist.

9. *A Donkey in a Tiger's Skin* (p. 28)

Attributed to Basawan
From an imperial copy of the *Tutinama*
ca. 1560-65
Opaque watercolor on paper
Painting: H. 13.97 cm., W. 7.77 cm. Page: H. 20.32 cm., W. 13.97 cm.
The Cleveland Museum of Art, Cleveland, Gift of Mrs. A. Dean Perry (62.279, f. 207r)

On the thirty-first night, to illustrate the point that a person of base origin will inevitably betray himself, the parrot tells a story about a poor merchant who sent his starving donkey out into another man's pasture wearing a tiger's skin (a lion's skin in the text) in order to scare the watchmen. But the donkey eventually revealed his identity by braying aloud, leading Nakhshabi to conclude in the couplets at the top of the page (Simsar, p. 199):

> O Nakhshabi, a fine robe does not make a man noble,
> Tell me when was a more pretentious man discovered?
> A donkey who presumes to appear in a lion's coat
> Would not be a lion, but an ass who was uncovered.

Chandra (*The Tuti-Nama*, pp. 131-32) has attributed this painting to Basawan, who is also represented in this manuscript by a number of ascribed paintings.

10. *A Storm at Sea* (p. 29)

From an imperial copy of the *Tutinama*
ca. 1560-65
Opaque watercolor on paper
Painting: H. 16.9 cm., W. 10.6 cm.
Lent by Edwin Binney, 3rd

On the thirty-second night, the parrot tells the story of a young woman named Khurshid who encountered numerous misfortunes on account of her great beauty. This full-page miniature illustrates an episode in which a sudden storm arose when Khurshid was sold into slavery during a voyage to Mecca (Simsar, p. 204). Elements of European costume apparent on the blond passenger near the stern of the boat, and perhaps also on the boatman, reflect the eclectic sources that inspired the development of early Mughal painting.

11. *Amr and a Fallen Stranger outside the Castle of Fulad* (p. 31)

From an imperial copy of the *Hamzanama*
ca. 1562-1577
Opaque watercolor on cotton
Painting: H. 73.02 cm., W. 56.51 cm.
The Metropolitan Museum of Art, New York; Rogers Fund, 1923 (23.264.1)

The *Hamzanama*, one of the greatest manuscripts to be made for Akbar, originally consisted of fourteen hundred illustrations, in fourteen volumes, though only one hundred and fifty are now known. The manuscript describes the adventures of Hamza, the Prophet Muhammad's uncle, and his friend Amr. Among the many calligraphers who worked on the manuscript was Mir Dawri, who was also responsible for copying the *Ashiqa* of Amir Khusrau (see pp. 27, 28, 29), another early Mughal illustrated manuscript. Although no complete study has ever been done on the manuscript it has been published extensively. Most notable among these publications are H. Gluck's seminal study *Die indischen Miniaturen des Hamza-Romanes im Österreichischen Museum für Kunst und*

Industrie in Wien und in anderen Sammlungen of 1925 and Gerhart Egger's *Hamza-nama,* Graz, 1974.

12. *Muzmahil Treating the Sorcerers* (p. 33)

From an imperial copy of the *Hamzanama*
(see NO. 11)
ca. 1562-1577
Opaque watercolor on cotton
Painting: H. 93.7 cm., W. 75.2 cm.
The Brooklyn Museum (24.29)

This painting depicts Muzmahil, the leader of a mule caravan, treating a group of sorcerers. The bright colors, lively gestures, and dramatic setting of the miniature are typical of the most exciting pages from the *Hamzanama.* The vignettes of the mendicant approaching the castle's gate, the reclining woman, and the odd figures behind Muzmahil charge the scene with a sense of immediacy. Beach has attributed this page (which is illustration No. 84 from Book XI), to Mahesh (*The Imperial Image,* p. 65).

CHAPTER II

Fatehpur-Sikri: Akbar's City of Victory

13. *Akbar Praying at a Tomb* (p. 36)

From an unidentified historical manuscript, possibly
an *Akbarnama*
ca. 1600
Opaque watercolor on paper
Painting: H. 38 cm., W. 27 cm.
The Chester Beatty Library, Dublin (Ms. 61, no. 9)

The miniature has been mounted in borders from the seventeenth-century *Farhang-i Jahangiri,* making it difficult to identify the manuscript it was originally made for. Similar pages, also mounted in borders from the *Farhang-i Jahangiri,* belong to the ca. 1604 *Akbarnama* (see NO. 1). The proportions of this page, however, are not consistent with the more vertical format of the latter. It is tempting to think that the incident depicted here represents Akbar visiting one of the white marble Chishti tombs such as that of Muin ad-Din in Ajmer or that of Nizam ad-Din in Delhi.

14. *The Birth of Prince Salim* (p. 37)

Design by Kesu the Elder, painting by Dharm Das
From an imperial copy of the *Akbarnama*
ca. 1590
Opaque watercolor on paper
Painting: H. 37.5 cm., W. 25 cm.
Victoria and Albert Museum, London
(I.S. 2-1896 78/117)

The ca. 1590 *Akbarnama* (see pp. 72-73) provides the earliest visual documentation of Fatehpur-Sikri. Both the city itself and important events that took place there were singled out for attention by Akbar's artists. Prince Salim was born at Salim ad-Din Chishti's monastery in Sikri on August 30, 1569 (*Akbarnama,* Vol. II, pp. 502-03) and although the palace setting shown in this miniature is anachronistic (Prince Salim was born in Shaykh Salim's monastery before the new city had even been planned), the artists have accurately depicted the view looking north over the lake from Akbar's palace compound as the rising sun illuminates the eastern sky. Kesu the Elder (Kesu Kalan, also known as Kesu Das) also designed the next miniature in the manuscript, showing Akbar receiving the news of Salim's birth in Agra (folio 79/117), as well as a double-page miniature depicting Akbar's return to Fatehpur-Sikri from the conquest of Gujarat (fig. 3).

15. *The Construction of Fatehpur-Sikri* (p. 39)

Design by Tulsi the Elder, painting by Bhavani
From an imperial copy of the *Akbarnama*
ca. 1590
Opaque watercolor on paper
Painting: H. 37.5 cm., W. 25 cm.
Victoria and Albert Museum, London
(I.S. 2-1896 86/117)

The construction of Fatehpur-Sikri, according to Qandahari, was ordered by Akbar sometime in 1571. According to Father Monserrate the first structure built by the emperor was a small country house of royal magnificence (*Commentary* p. 36). Although construction was well under way by the mid-1570s, large parts of the city were still being built as late as 1578-79. Tulsi the Elder's design shows considerably more detail than is given in Abul Fazl's brief mention of the construction of the city in the *Akbarnama* (Vol. II, pp. 530-31). For details on the foundation and development of Fatehpur-Sikri see Michael Brand and Glenn D. Lowry, *Fatehpur-Sikri: A Sourcebook,* Cambridge, Massachusetts, pp. 27-45.

16. *Akbar Inspecting the Construction* (p. 41)
of Fatehpur-Sikri

Design by Tulsi the Elder, painting by Bandi,
 portraits by Madhu the Younger
From an imperial copy of the *Akbarnama*
ca. 1590
Opaque watercolor on paper
Painting: H. 37.5 cm., W. 25 cm.
Victoria and Albert Museum, London
 (I.S. 2-1896 91/117)

Highlighting Akbar's interest in the construction of
Fatehpur-Sikri rather than following a specific description in the text of the *Akbarnama* (Vol. II, pp.
530-31), this miniature shows the emperor inspecting
the work of his stone-masons. If the building on the
right is, in fact, a highly schematic representation of
the Jami Masjid with the white marble tomb of Salim
ad-Din Chishti, this painting must be read as looking
south, with the palace complex on the left. Tulsi the
Elder (Tulsi Kalan) also designed the miniature showing the construction of Fatehpur-Sikri in this manuscript (NO. 15).

17. *Masud Husayn and Co-conspirators* (p. 49)
Presented to Akbar
by Husayn Quli Khan

Design by Basawan, painting by Mansur
From an imperial copy of the *Akbarnama*
ca. 1590
Opaque watercolor on paper
Painting: H. 37.5 cm., W. 25 cm.
Victoria and Albert Museum, London
 (I.S. 2-1896 112/117)

This scene is recorded in Volume III of the *Akbarnama*
(p. 56) where Abul Fazl writes: "He [Husayn Quli
Khan] brought Masud Husain M. and all the prisoners, who had fallen into his hands in the battle,
wrapped up in cowhides from which the horns had
not been removed; and thereby excited great joy at
court." Badauni also records this event. His description in Volume II of the *Muntakhab at-Tavarikh* (p.
163) is slightly more detailed than Abul Fazl's and is
consistent with Basawan's depiction of the scene. Badauni noted that the rebels, "numbered nearly 300
persons, and he brought them prisoners before the
emperor with the skins of asses, hogs, and dogs drawn
over their faces. Some of them were put to death by
various ingenious tortures, and the remainder were let
go free."

18. *Akbar Presiding over Discussions* (p. 53)
in the Ibadatkhana

By Nar Singh
From an imperial copy of the *Akbarnama* (see NO. 1)
ca. 1604
Opaque watercolor on paper
Page: H. 28 cm., W. 20 cm.
The Chester Beatty Library, Dublin (Ms. 3, f. 263v)

The episode illustrated here, from the second *Akbarnama,* occurred in the *Ibadatkhana* (House of Worship) in 1578. Father Acquaviva, one of the Jesuit
missionaries at Fatehpur-Sikri, was debating with several of Akbar's mullas when the latter began attacking
the Gospels. Acquaviva ultimately challenged the mullas by saying, "If this faction have such an opinion of
our book, and regard the Furqan (the Koran) as the
pure word of God, it is proper that a heaped fire be
lighted. We shall take the Gospels in our hands, and
the Ulama of that faith shall take their book, and then
let us enter that testing place of truth. The escape of
any one will be a sign of his truthfulness." (*Akbarnama,* Vol. III, p. 369). To Abul Fazl's delight and no
doubt also Akbar's, the mullas declined Acquaviva's
challenge.

CHAPTER III
The *Kitabkhana:*
The Imperial Library

19. *Manuscript Atelier* (p. 59)

From an imperial copy of the *Akhlaq-i Nasiri*
ca. 1590-95
Opaque watercolor on paper
Painting: H. 23.7 cm., W. 14.3 cm.
Lent by Prince Sadruddin Aga Khan (Ms. 39, f. 196a)

The *Akhlaq-i Nasiri* was one of the books Akbar would
have read out to him time and time again (*Ain-i Akbari,* Vol. I, p. 110). Written by Nasir ad-Din Tusi in
1235, the text, which has been fully translated and
annotated by G. M. Wickens (*The Nasirean Ethics,*
London, 1964), is divided into three broad discourses
dealing with ethics, economics, and politics. Lacking
earlier illustrated models with an established iconography, the selection of passages illustrated in this

Mughal manuscript takes on additional importance. It has been established by A. Welch and S. C. Welch (*The Arts of the Islamic Book,* Ithaca, 1982, p. 175) that this representation of a working *kitabkhana* or manuscript atelier illustrates a section of the *Nasirean Ethics* dealing with communication specialists" (English translation, p. 216). Here, the painters have been emphasized as masters of communications, an idea not found in the original text (see p. 58).

20. *Illuminated Calligraphic Folio* (p. 60)

By Muhammad Husayn al-Kashmiri
  Zarin Qalam
ca. 1575-1605
Ink, opaque watercolor, and gold on paper
Page: H. 40 cm., W. 29 cm.
The Chester Beatty Library, Dublin (Ms. 31)

Although Muhammad Husayn Zarin Qalam (The Golden Pen) was Akbar's favorite calligrapher and copied such major manuscripts as the 1582-83 *Gulistan* (NO. 25) and the ca. 1604 *Akbarnama,* separate calligraphic folios signed by him are extremely rare. Surrounded by the very finest of Mughal illumination, these unidentified couplets read:

Pass by Old Wife Time like a real man of God,
Look not at the ruby of her sunset or the pearl of her dawn.
For they are not rubies or pearls—for the sake of deception
It is just the evening and morning making redness and white.

The calligrapher's signature, which takes up almost one third of the page, reads: "written by the sinner, the destitute Muhammad Husayn Zarin Qalam Akbarshahi (may God forgive his sins) in the capital of the empire *(dar as-saltanat)* Agra."

21. *Koran* (p. 61)

Copied by Hibatullah al-Husayni
Dated A. H. 981 (1573-74)
246 folios
H. 33 cm., W. 22 cm.
The British Library, London (Add. 18497)
Folios 118b-119a: Double-page illumination at the beginning of Sura 19 (Mary)
Ink, opaque watercolor, and gold on paper

To date, this is the only Koran that can be securely attributed to Akbar's reign. A note on folio 246b states that it was copied by Hibatullah al-Husayni (an otherwise unknown Mughal calligrapher) for the "Sultan of Lahore" in A. H. 981 (1573-74), a time when that city was firmly under Akbar's control. This copy of the Koran has been described in some detail by Jeremiah P. Losty, who first published it in 1982 (*The Art of the Book in India,* London, 1982, p. 85). Few texts from Akbar's reign can match the bold design of this double sura-heading with its mixture of gold, blue, and red illumination, and interplay of *muhaqqaq, naskhi,* and *riqa* scripts executed in a variety of black, blue and gold ink.

22. *Murder Scene* (p. 62)

ca. 1575-80
From the Berlin Jahangir album (assembled
  ca. 1608-18)
Opaque watercolor on paper
Painting: H. 41 cm., W. 25.5 cm.
Staatsbibliothek Preussischer Kulturbesitz,
  West Berlin (Libr. Pict. A.117 f. 16b)

It has not been possible yet to identify the subject and origin of this grisly murder scene that stands among the boldest and most direct of all the paintings created for Akbar: only the *Hamzanama* (NOS. 11, 12) can match its intensity. With three actions compressed into the single picture "frame," the story unfolds by means of true continuous narrative, a rare feature in Mughal painting. The attacker, wearing a brown *jama* and a shield slung over his back, has forced his way into a conventionally represented Hindu temple by breaking through its wall with a pick. Once inside, he accosts his bearded victim and brutally twists his head off. Finally, the same attacker is seen, in smaller scale, at the top of an adjacent tower moments after he has flung the severed head into the midst of the milling crowd below. The page has been removed from its original context and in the early seventeenth century it was mounted in an album compiled for the emperor Jahangir.

23. *Boat and Landscape* (p. 63)

From an unidentified poetic manuscript
ca. 1580-85
Opaque watercolor on paper
Painting: H. 7.7 cm., W. 5.2 cm. Page: H. 14 cm.,
  W. 7.62 cm.
Private Collection

It has been suggested by S. C. Welch that this miniature and several other small scale images such as the

Courtesan (NO. 50) were mounted in a royal album compiled by Jahangir at the beginning of the seventeenth century. The couplets at the top and bottom of this page, which have been translated by Annemarie Schimmel, are from Hafiz:

UPPER
We are those whose boat is broken—Oh favorable wind, blow—
Perhaps we may see again that well known [or swimming] friend

LOWER
My crying will destroy the world—
Bring Noah's ark for here is the flood.

The composition of this miniature is closely related to two paintings. One of these, in a manuscript of the *Anvar-i Suhayli* dated 1596, is signed by Miskin, to whom the second page, from an unidentified manuscript has long been attributed (both are published by Beach, *The Imperial Image*, pp. 122-23). While the boats in both pages are more elaborate than the one in this miniature, the figures falling into the water are almost identical.

24. *A Prince Riding an Elephant*   (p. 64)

ca. 1575-80
Opaque watercolor on cotton
Painting: H. 33 cm., W. 39 cm.
Lent by Howard Hodgkin

This painting forms part of a larger image, the second half of which is now in the Calcutta Museum. It has been suggested by Terrence McInerney (*Indian Painting 1525-1825*, London, 1982, pp. 15-17) that originally these paintings may have adorned a tent or other structure and that their execution is extremely close to the work of Abd as-Samad.

25. *Manuscript of the Gulistan of Sadi*

Copied at Fatehpur-Sikri by   (pp. 66, 128)
Muhammad Husayn Zarin Qalam
Dated A. H. 990 (1582-83)
130 folios, 1 miniature
Painting: H. 21 cm., W. 32.3 cm.
Royal Asiatic Society, London (Ms. 258)
Ink, opaque watercolor, and gold on paper
a) Folio 119b-120r (p. 66)
b) Detail, folio 128b (p. 128)

The *Gulistan* is perhaps the best known work of the great Iranian author Muslih ad-Din Sadi (1189-1291). This copy of the manuscript is written on sumptuous, gold-sprinkled, biscuit-colored paper. Folio 128b depicts the manuscript's calligrapher, Muhammad Husayn Zarin Qalam and the artist Manohar, whose father, Basawan, was one of Akbar's most important painters. The artist holds a folio on which is inscribed the words "The work of Manohar, the son of Basawan." A second inscription on a sheaf of paper held by the calligrapher reads "Allah is Great! Portrait of Husayn Zarin Qalam."

26. *Anvari Entertains in a Summer House*   (p. 67)

Attributed to Basawan
From an imperial copy of the *Divan* of Anvari
Completed at Lahore on 1 Dhul-qada, A. H. 996 (September 22, 1588)
Opaque watercolor on paper
Painting: H. 13.97 cm., W. 6.98 cm.
Fogg Art Museum, Harvard University, Cambridge, Massachusetts (1960.117.15, f. 117)

The luxurious copy of the poems of the twelfth-century Iranian panegyrist Anvari, from which this miniature has been removed, contains three hundred and fifty-four folios. The jewel-like quality of this image matches the elegance of the author's poetry. *Anvari Entertains in a Summer House* does not appear to fit readily into the present textual arrangement of the manuscript though it clearly belongs to this copy of the *Divan*. The poem accompanying this miniature begins with the following lines (as translated in Schimmel and S. C. Welch's monograph of the manuscript, *Anvari's Divan: A Pocket Book for Akbar*, New York, 1983, p. 78):

I came, quite drunk, into my house last night
And had with me a loyal and pleasant friend;
And I discovered on the windowsill
A half full bottle of my nightly wine:
Pure as the promises of loving friends
And bitter like the lives of those who love.

27. *It's the Day for the Garden*   (p. 67)

Attributed to Mahesh
From an imperial copy of the *Divan* of Anvari
1588
Opaque watercolor on paper

Page: H. 13.97 cm., W. 7.62 cm.
Fogg Art Museum, Cambridge, Massachusetts
  (1960.117.15, f. 172b and 173a)

Folio 172b, on the right, contains the end of a poem (*qasida*) praising the Seljuq courtier Majd ad-Din Abu al-Hasan al-Imrani (d. ca. 1150), while folio 173a marks the beginning of another. Imrani was a supporter of Anvari who was probably responsible for introducing the poet to Sultan Muizz ad-Din Sanjar (r. 1118-57). Given the Mughals' long love of gardens, it is hardly surprising that Akbar chose to add a miniature illustrating the first two couplets of this second poem, which read (as translated in Schimmel and S. C. Welch, *Anvari's Divan*, p. 86):

> It's the day for the garden, for cheer and for joy;
> It's the day for the market of basil and rose.
> The dust is all mixed with amber and musk;
> The skirt of the zephyr spreads fragrance and scents.

28. *Krishna and Balarama Arrive in Brindaban*   (p. 68)

From an imperial copy of the *Harivamsa*
ca. 1585
Opaque watercolor on paper
Painting: H. 30.14 cm., W. 18.7 cm.
  Page: H. 40.64 cm., W. 29.51 cm.
The Virginia Museum of Fine Arts (68.8.50)

The *Harivamsa* (Genealogy of Hari [Vishnu]) forms an appendix to the *Mahabharata*, one of the two great Hindu epics. In the imperial illustrated copy of the *Mahabharata*, which was translated for Akbar as the *Razmnama* (the Book of Wars) in 1584 (see page 67), the *Harivamsa* was treated as part of the main text. Shortly afterwards Mawlana Shiri was commissioned to make a separate translation, which he completed by the time of his death in 1586. At least twenty-eight miniatures are known from this version (the text of which, along with six illustrations, is now in the Lucknow Museum [57.106]) as compared with just seventeen paintings at the end of the *Razmnama*. The image illustrated here shows Krishna and his fair-skinned brother Balarama accompanying their father Nanda on his return to Brindaban. They are greeted by Yasoda (Nanda's wife), who presents them with a tray of refreshments. The gentle landscape and pastoral setting of this image reflect Krishna's soothing impact on the poor herders, whose conditions are rough but who are made to feel special—indeed

immortal—by his presence. (M. N. Dutt, *A Prose Translation of Harivamsa*, Calcutta, 1897, p. 272).

29. *Krishna and Balarama Fight Jarasandha's Army*   (p. 69)

From an imperial copy of the *Harivamsa*
ca. 1585
Opaque watercolor on paper
Painting: H. 29.2 cm., W. 18.9 cm. Page: H. 34.9 cm., W. 20.6 cm.
The Metropolitan Museum of Art, New York
  (28.63.2)

This scene has been tentatively identified by Beach (*The Imperial Image*, p. 72) as representing the blue-skinned Krishna and his brother Balarama waging war with the army of King Jarasandha (M. N. Dutt, *A Prose Translation of Harivamsa*, Calcutta, 1897, p. 428). Its composition shares a number of similarities with the representation of the same scene in the imperial copy of the *Razmnama* (P. Banerjee, *The Life of Krishna in Art*, New Delhi, 1978, fig. 185). The relationship between the *Harivamsa* and the *Razmnama* is discussed by Robert Skelton in "Mughal Paintings from Harivamsa Manuscript," *Victoria and Albert Museum Yearbook*, 2 (1969), 41-54.

30. *Manuscript of the Jog Bashisht*   (p. 70)

Dated 15 Azar, 47th *Ilahi* year (December , 1602)
323 folios, 41 miniatures
Folio 178b: "Suraghu, the King of the Hunters, Seeks Instruction from the Sage Mandavya"
Opaque watercolor on paper
Painting: H. 27 cm., W. 18.5 cm. Page: H. 43 cm., W. 27 cm.
The Chester Beatty Library, Dublin (Ms. 5)

The *Jog Bashisht* is a Persian translation of the Sanskrit philosophical work *Yogavasishthamaharamayana* (The Great Story of Rama and the Yoga-teaching of Vasishta) completed by the otherwise unknown scholar Farmuli in 1602. Through a series of stories, the sage Vasishta instructs Rama as to the main themes of Vedanta philosphy, in which it is held that the Absolute can be attained without physical separation from wordly affairs. Vedanta, with its rigid notion of the indivisibility of all matter, was as central to Hinduism in Akbar's time as Ibn al-Arabi's similar concept of *wahdat al-wujud* was to contemporary mystical Islam.

The overall feel of the manuscript and its miniatures is one of understated but refined elegance, especially throughout the first one hundred and thirty-two folios where the text pages are sprinkled with small flakes of gold. The names of virtually all the artists who worked on this manuscript were lost when the miniatures were re-mounted at an early period. The binding is of a later date. Numerous notations from the reigns of Jahangir and Shah Jahan are found in the manuscript, and Shah Jahan also inscribed it in his own hand on the day of his accession to the throne. A full list of the miniatures and their subject matter is given by Arnold and Wilkinson in *The Library of A. Chester Beatty: a Catalogue of the Indian Miniatures* (Dublin, 1936, I, 21-25).

31. *Three Events during the Reign of the Caliph al-Mutawakkil* (p. 71)

From an imperial copy of the *Tarikh-i Alfi*
ca. 1592-94
Attributed to Basawan
Opaque watercolor on paper
Painting: H. 42.2 cm., W. 25.8 cm.
The Cleveland Museum of Art, Dudley P. Allen Fund
(32.36 recto)

So great was the scope of the *Tarikh-i Alfi* (The History of One Thousand Years) that new approaches had to be found in order to convey the vast range of historical material that was being collected as Akbar anticipated the Islamic millennium. Unusually large sheets of paper (measuring approximately 45 cm. by 25 cm. or 17 by 10 in.) were chosen for this imperial copy, few of whose pages have survived. The illustrations were relegated to the borders around a large text panel or panels. In this example, the artist has taken the highly unusual step of illustrating three separate scenes on one page. From top to bottom, the three events, all from the reign of the Caliph al-Mutawakkil (847-61), are as follows: a hailstorm in Egypt, the building of a palace in Damascus, and the destruction of Antioch by an earthquake in 850. On the reverse of the folio is a scene showing prayers being offered at the Ka'ba in Mecca during a drought. The book, inscribed with Akbar's name, held by a worshipper at the top left corner of the page, suggests that Akbar, like many other Muslim rulers, made a practice of sending finely calligraphed copies of the Koran to Mecca. In 1576-77 Akbar also sent money with the leader of that year's pilgrimage for the construction of a hospice at Mecca (Badauni, *Muntakhab at-Tavarikh*, Vol. II, p. 246).

32. *Akbar at the Chishti Shrine in Ajmer* (p. 73)

Design by Basawan, painting by Ikhlas,
portraits by Nanha
From an imperial copy of the *Akbarnama*
ca. 1590
Opaque watercolor on paper
Painting: H. 37.5 cm., W. 25 cm.
Victoria and Albert Museum, London
(I.S. 2-1896 23/117)

The event portrayed here occurred in 1562, when Akbar went to Ajmer in the company of Azam Khan and several other members of his court. The text that corresponds to this miniature records that "... the expedition went with all possible speed to Ajmir and arrived at the bliss-conferring city in an auspicious hour. The visit to the illustrious shrine of his holiness the Khwaja [Muin ad-Din Chishti] was performed, and the persons in charge of the sacred city were the recipients of fortune" (*Akbarnama*, Vol. II, p. 243).

33. *Babur Restoring Ulugh Beg's Garden at Istalif* (p. 74)

Design by Miskin, painting by Nand Gwaliori
From an imperial copy of the *Baburnama*
ca. 1589
Opaque watercolor on paper
Painting: H. 25.4 cm., W. 13.7 cm. Page: H. 40.7 cm.,
W. 26.3 cm.
Private Collection

Babur was an inveterate horticulturist. He built eleven gardens in the environs of Kabul alone (in one of which he is buried, according to his final wishes, in a simple grave open to the sky), and one of his very first actions upon the conquest of India was to build a garden in Agra. This miniature from the ca. 1589 copy of the *Baburnama* is the left side of a double-page illustration showing Babur restoring the garden at Istalif (near Kabul) which had formerly been in the possession of Timur's grandson Ulugh Beg (*Baburnama*, p. 216). Both pages were designed by the artist Miskin, this miniature painted by Nand Gwaliori and the right page (now in a private collection) by Sanwala. It was in gardens such as these that the Mughal emperors refined their knowledge of nature. Trees, flowers, birds, beasts, and the landscape itself all came under their loving scrutiny, their pleasures frequently heightened by the use of opium and wine.

34. *Feast at Sultan Jalal ad-Din's House*
at Karrah (p. 74)

From an imperial copy of the *Baburnama*
ca. 1589
Opaque watercolor on paper
Painting: H. 35.56 cm., W. 23.49 cm.
The Art Museum, Princeton University, Gift of
Carl Otto von Kienbusch, for the Carl Otto
von Kienbusch Collection (71-30)

The *Baburnama* was translated from Turki into Persian by Abd ar-Rahim Khan Khanan. According to the *Akbarnama* (Vol. III, p. 862) the Khan Khanan presented his completed work to Akbar on November 24, 1589. Four sixteenth-century illustrated copies of the manuscript exist (see pp. 14, 70, 75). This miniature comes from the earliest of the four copies (twenty-one of whose illustrations are now in the Victoria and Albert Museum), which was probably the actual manuscript presented to Akbar by the Khan Khanan. The manuscript originally had approximately five hundred and ninety folios with fourteen lines to a side and space for one hundred and ninety-three paintings, though only one hundred and twelve are presently known. This miniature, which has not been published before, illustrates a scene that occurred in March 1529 and is described on page 652 of the *Baburnama*: "I dismounted at Sl. Jalalud-Din's house inside Karrah fort where, host-like, he served me a portion of cooked meat and other viands." This event is also illustrated in the other three copies of the *Baburnama* (Tyulayev, *Miniatures of Baburnama*, Samarqand, 1969 pl. 68 has published in color the version in the State Museum of Oriental Culture, Moscow).

35. *Chingiz Khan Dividing His Empire*
between His Sons (p. 75)

Design by Basawan, painting by Bhim Gujarati
From an imperial copy of the *Chingiznama*
ca. 1596
Opaque watercolor on paper
Painting: H. 34.24 cm., W. 21.59 cm. Page: H. 38 cm.,
W. 25.4 cm.
The Metropolitan Museum of Art, New York,
Francis M. Weld Gift Fund, 1948 (48.144, f. 73v)

The main portion of the copy of the *Chingiznama* that this miniature comes from was in the former imperial library in Tehran. The manuscript has three hundred and four folios measuring thirty-three by twenty-four centimeters and ninety-eight illustrations. According

to J. Marek and H. Knizkova, who published the manuscript in part (*The Jenghiz Khan Miniatures From the Court of Akbar the Great,* London, 1963, pp. 29-30). A colophon, now missing, stated that the work was completed on 27 Ramadan, A. H. 1004 (May 25, 1596). The manuscript is often referred to as the *Jami at-Tavarikh,* but all of the known illustrations from the present copy are from the second half of the first section of the *Jami at-Tavarikh,* which is devoted to the life of Chingiz Khan *(Kitab-i Chingiz Khan)* and it is by that name that Abul Fazl refers to this manuscript in the *Ain-i Akbari* (Vol. I, p. 115).

36. *Abaqa Khan Enthroned* (p. 76)

Design and portraits by Farrukh (also known as
Farrukh Chela), painting by Ali Quli
From an imperial copy of the *Chingiznama*
1596
Opaque watercolor on paper
Painting: H. 34.2 cm., W. 21.1 cm. Page: H. 35.8 cm.,
W. 24.4 cm.
Private Collection

The one line of writing in this miniature, executed in red ink, is not from the text of the *Chingiznama* itelf but functions instead as a label for the scene depicted and reads: "representation of the court of Abaqa Khan ibn Hulagu Khan ibn Toluy Khan ibn Chingiz Khan." Abaqa Khan, the Il-Khanid ruler of Iran from 1265 until 1282, was the great-grandson of Chingiz Khan and the grandfather of Ghazan Khan, who commissioned this historical treatise. Akbar must have been fascinated by the religious affiliations and tolerance of his Mongol ancestors: Abaqa Khan was a Buddhist with close ties to Nestorian Christians, but his brother Tagudar (r. 1282-84) converted to Islam and adopted the name Ahmad, and Abaqa's son Arghun Khan (r. 1284-91) remained a Buddhist while governing through a Jewish wazir (Sad ad-Dawla). Although Mughal artists were careful to show that Mongol costumes were a far cry from contemporary Mughal fashions, their depictions of elements such as the magnificent plumed headbands seen in this miniature should not be regarded as entirely historical.

37. *A Fortress under Siege* (p. 77)

Probably from an imperial copy of the *Chingiznama*
ca. 1596
Opaque watercolor on paper
Painting: H. 35.6 cm., W. 23 cm.
Lent by Edwin Binney, 3rd

This miniature has been tentatively assigned to the *Chingiznama* by Beach (*The Imperial Image,* p. 102): its size certainly fits within the range of other known pages and its composition also matches closely that of other miniatures from this manuscript. Its exact subject matter is less certain. An inscription over the gate of the fortress identifies the scene as "the fort of Bhim in the district of Ghazni, the army of Sultan Mahmud," but it is highly unusual for such labels to be added directly within the field of painting rather than in a text panel. More importantly, the fact that the exploits of Sultan Mahmud, who led many raids into India from Ghazni, one hundred and sixty kilometers (one hundred miles) southwest of Kabul, during the first quarter of the eleventh century, are not covered by the *Chingiznama* further suggests that the inscription is a later addition. It is also possible, though less likely, that this miniature originally belonged to the *Tarikh-i Khandan-i Timuriyya* (fig. 8) which measures 39 cm. by 25 cm. and is missing folios 81 through 85 from the section dealing with Timur's campaign in India.

38. *A Cow and Calf* (p. 78)

Attributed to Basawan
Opaque watercolor on paper
ca. 1570
H. 28.57 cm., W. 18.7 cm.
Private Collection

From the early Fatehpur-Sikri years, individual animal studies were commissioned alongside human portraits and miniatures destined for illustrated manuscripts. This tender representation of a cow and calf, one of the earliest known examples of this genre, has been attributed most plausibly by Robert Skelton as an early work of the artist Basawan. The choice of subject matter in this quintessentially Indian image might be interpreted as proof of Akbar's sensitivity towards the special status of the cow among his Hindu subjects. Little is known about the original function of these animal studies, such as whether or not they were placed together in a single album.

39. *Two Mullas* (p. 78)

ca. 1565-70
Opaque watercolor on paper
Painting: H. 24.8 cm., W. 15.7 cm.
Department of Rare Books, McGill University
Libraries, Montreal: 1977.49

The lively expressions and animated gestures of these two figures, with their heavily modelled clothes and well articulated faces, reflect the impact of the formal conventions developed during the production of the *Hamzanama.* The couplets above and below the mullas can be translated as follows:

UPPER
The expectation of spring arises from our narrow-eyed blindness.

LOWER
There are one hundred pleasures in the ash-house which are not found in the rose garden.

40. *Dervish* (p. 78)

ca. 1570-75
Opaque watercolor on paper
Painting: H. 19 cm., W. 12.7 cm.
British Museum, London (13.6.83 lot 44)

This bold figure in a fur-trimmed blue *jama* and flowing red shawl depicted against an unpainted background probably represents a *qalandar,* a dervish on the wilder side of the Islamic mystical fringe. Wandering sufis of this sort were frequent visitors to Akbar's court, where they often made extravagant claims that they were unable to fulfill. The elaborate golden jewelry and other fine possessions worn by this *qalandar* immediately bring to mind figures in Akbar's *Hamzanama,* which was illustrated between 1562 and 1577 (see in particular the bare-chested mystic in a page illustrated by S. C. Welch in *Imperial Mughal Painting,* pl. 3).

Published in color: Christie's sale catalogue, *Islamic, Indian, South-East Asian Manuscripts, Miniatures and Works of Art,* June 13, 1983, p. 18.

41. *A Learned Man* (p. 79)

Attributed to Basawan
From an imperial portrait album
ca. 1575-80
Black line with washes of color on paper
Page: H. 20 cm., W. 13.7 cm.
Private Collection

This figure with his bulging stomach, intent gaze and lively hands, was first attributed to Basawan by S. C. Welch (*Indian Drawings and Painted Sketches;* New York: The Asia Society, 1976, p. 35). The miniature was mounted in 1611/12 in an album made for Prince

Khurram, the future Shah Jahan. On the back of the page is a long inscription in Khurram's hand. Twenty-five leaves from this album were owned, at one time, by the Kevorkian Foundation in New York. (For other pages from this album see Binney, *Indian Miniature Painting from the Collection of Edwin Binney, 3rd,* no. 49 and Ernst Grube, *Islamic Paintings from the 11th to the 18th Century from the Collection of Hans P. Kraus,* New York, n.d., nos. 239-40 and pl. LIII).

42. *A Schoolmaster and Pupil* (p. 79)

ca. 1585
Black line and washes of color on paper
Painting: H. 9.5 cm., W. 7.8 cm.
Private Collection

Education played an important role in the formation of a Muslim prince's character. Akbar began his formal education at the age of four (see p. 14) and was "strongly drawn to the composing of Hindi and Persian poetry and is critical and hair splitting in the niceties of poetic diction" (*Akbarnama,* Vol. 1, p. 520). The emperor at first personally directed the education of his own sons, but eventually thought better of it because "it is an old custom that far-seeing great ones should commit their capable children to the instruction of teachers adorned with outward and inward knowledge so that by seeing and hearing from them...their qualities may be developed." (*Akbarnama,* Vol. 3, p. 105).

43. *A Flowering Pomegranate Tree* (p. 80)

ca. 1570-75
Opaque watercolor on cotton cloth
Painting: H. 27.3 cm., W. 19.68 cm.
Private Collection

While this highly decorative flowering pomegranate tree stands in contrast to the expressionistic exuberance of Basawan's extraordinary tree in his contemporary study of a cow and calf (NO. 38), it nevertheless displays the same keen interest in the natural world. This can also be seen in the numerous examples of Indian flora singled out for illustration in the imperial copies of the *Baburnama* (see for example, Binney, *Indian Painting from the Collection of Edwin Binney, 3rd,* Portland, 1973, p. 37). Here, the unidentified artist has added multicolored birds that appear to have migrated straight from the realm of myth to this amusing conjunction of reality and fantasy.

44. *Landscape Fragment* (p. 80)

ca. 1585-90
Opaque watercolor on paper
Painting: H. 8.6 cm., W. 11.3 cm.
Museum of Art, Rhode Island School of Design, Appropriation (17.457)

Although only a fragment, this image is both detailed and effective. Its receding planes and mountainous background are derived from sixteenth-century European prints brought to the Mughal court during the late 1570s and 80s. Similar landscapes often appear in the upper corners of Mughal miniatures and it is tempting to think that this painting may have been a preparatory study for one of these images.

45. *Two Birds in a Landscape* (p. 80)

ca. 1580-85
From the Berlin Jahangir album (assembled ca. 1608-18)
Opaque watercolor on cotton cloth, with a small extension on paper at the top and bottom
Painting: H. 41 cm., W. 25.5 cm.
Staatsbibliothek Preussischer Kulturbesitz, West Berlin (Libr. Pict. A117 f. 176)

Pairs of birds seated on rocky outcrops were an extremely common artistic device in Persian painting. With the Mughals, however, they took on a whole new life of their own and, even while fleeing India, Humayun found the time to commission painted studies of birds that caught his fancy (Jawhar Aftabchi, *Tazkirat al-Vaqiat,* p. 43). Akbar followed his father's example with even greater zeal and a study of a lone bird in a landscape with a distant cityscape in the ca. 1565-70 Rampur *Tilasm and Zodiac* manuscript (folio 16, illustrated in Karl Khandalavala and Jagdish Mittal, "An Early Akbari Illustrated Manuscript of Tilasm and Zodiac," *Lalit Kala,* 14 (1969), pl. IV, fig. 14) and two roughly contemporary birds painted against a plain green background in the Musée Guimet (3619 Na) can be seen as early predecessors of this pair of birds from the Berlin album. These birds show a wonderful concern for detailed observation of physical form, pose, and character. Ernst Kühnel and Hermann Goetz (*Indische Buchmalereien,* pl. 10) suggest this painting may be by Mansur but this seems to have been based more on the subject matter than a study of that artist's style.

46. *A Family of Cheetahs* (p. 81)

Attributed to Basawan
ca. 1575-80
Opaque watercolor and gold on cotton
Painting: H. 29.5 cm., W. 18.5 cm. Page H. 40.1 cm.,
    W. 27.1 cm.
Lent by Prince Sadruddin Aga Khan

Akbar learnt to hunt with cheetahs as a child in Kabul in 1555 (*Akbarnama*, Vol. II, p. 630), when a captured animal was presented to Humayun by Wali Beg. The cheetah was named Fatehbaz (Player of Victory) and its keeper, Dunhu, was given the title of Fateh Khan. The emperor remained extremely fond of these animals throughout most of his life and on the eve of the birth of his daughter Khanam, in 1569, he rode from Agra to Gwalior in order to personally oversee the capture of another trapped animal (*Akbarnama*, Vol. II, p. 506). The powerful limbs and lively gestures of the cheetahs portrayed in this painting reveal the animals' beauty, and suggest the fascination they must have had for Akbar.

Published in color: A. Welch, *Arts of the Islamic Book*, No. 50.

47. *Raja Rai Singh of Bikaner* (p. 81)

Attributed to Basawan
From an imperial portrait album
ca. 1590
Opaque watercolor on paper
Painting: H. 11.8 cm., W. 6.6 cm.
Private Collection

Rai Singh was the son of Kalyan Mal of Bikaner. He belonged to the Rathor tribe and entered Akbar's service at Ajmer during the fifteenth year of his reign. Rai Singh, who is mentioned often in the *Akbarnama*, became the ruler of Bikaner in 1571. He served Akbar loyally for many years and played an important part in the emperor's Gujarat campaigns. His daughter was married to Prince Salim on June 26th, 1586. Like Raisal Darbari (NO. 54) he often was put in charge of guarding the imperial harem by the emperor. By the end of Akbar's reign, he attained the impressive rank of leader of 4,000 and was promoted to the rank of leader of 5,000 by Jahangir shortly after the latter's accession to the throne. Rai Singh died in 1612. The identification of this courtier as Rai Singh of Bikaner was first made by S. C. Welch (*Art of Mughal India*, New York, 1963, p. 164).

48. *Wandering Ascetic* (p. 82)

From an imperial portrait album
ca. 1585
Opaque watercolor on paper
Painting: H. 14.6 cm., W. 9.5 cm. Page: H. 38.88 cm.,
    W. 26.18 cm.
The Cleveland Museum of Art, Gift of Mr. and Mrs.
    Severance A. Millikin (67.244)

This figure, like the dervish (NO. 40) is typical of the strange assortment of visitors that frequented Akbar's court. The emperor's interest in ascetics and holy men, which went beyond mere curiosity, is reflected in a statement of his recorded by Abul Fazl, "Although I am the master of so vast a kingdom, and all the appliances of government are to my hand, yet since true greatness consists in doing the will of God, my mind is not at ease in this diversity of sects and creeds, and my heart is oppressed by this outward pomp of circumstance; with what satisfaction can I undertake the conquest of empire? How I wish for the coming of some pious man, who will resolve the distractions of my heart" (*Ain-i Akbari*, Vol. III, p. 433).

49. *Self-Portrait* (p. 82)

By Kesu Das (also known as Kesu the Elder)
ca. 1570
Opaque watercolor on paper
Painting: H. 15.6 cm., W. 8.25 cm. Page: H. 25.4 cm.,
    W. 15.2 cm.
Williams College Art Museum, Williamstown,
    Karl E. Weston Fund (81.44)

Kesu Das, seen here with his drawing board under his left arm and a coconut held between his hands, was one of Akbar's leading artists. In this painting, as in another self-portrait dated 1589, now in an album made for Jahangir in the Staatsbibliothek für Preussischer Kulturbesitz (Kühnel and Goetz, *Indische Buchmalereien*, p. 39), the artist has chosen to present himself as a rather humble, almost timid, man. His work figures prominently in the *Razmnama, Tarikh-i Khandan Timuriyya, Chingiznama*, and the ca. 1590 *Akbarnama*, as well as several other major Mughal manuscripts. Kesu Das was particularly interested in European prints and engravings and made numerous copies of them. He has been extensively studied by Beach ("The Mughal Painter Kesu Das," *Archives of Asian Art*, Vol. XXX, 1976-77, pp. 34-52).

50. *Courtesan* (p. 82)

ca. 1590
Opaque watercolor on paper
Page: H. 9.4 cm., W. 5 cm.
Private Collection

This figure of a courtesan with a vibrant orange and red skirt and mustard-yellow bodice profiled against a light green background gives us a rare glimpse into the life of women at Akbar's court. The lively diva, perhaps a dancer or singer of renown, is captured in an initmate moment as she applies collyrium to her eyes with the help of a small hand-mirror. The unidentified couplets on this page, which might be later additions, are well matched to the subject of the painting:

UPPER
Since your form defies description after just
    one glance,
What can I say in praise of your beauty but,
    "see yourself in the mirror."

LOWER
Such a tree does not grow in the gardens of Iram;
Such an idol is not found in the picture house
    of China.

51. *A Chaghatay Noblewoman* (p. 82)

From an imperial album
ca. 1595
Opaque watercolor and gold on paper
Painting: H. 22.6 cm., W. 13.1 cm. Page: H. 45.9 cm.,
    W. 30.2 cm.
Private Collection

Inscribed beneath the noblewoman is a false attribution to the artist Nadir as-Zaman (Colnaghi, *Indian Painting*, 1978, p. 25.). While the identity of this corpulent and rather daunting figure remains a mystery, her headdress reveals her ancestry. Chaghatay noblemen and women were an important part of Akbar's court as the emperor was related to many of them. Moreover, it was through this side of his family that he was able to trace his lineage back to Chingiz Khan. In 1575-76 Akbar even revived several old Chaghatay customs including the spreading of royal tables full of food in the audience hall at Fatehpur-Sikri, during Mirza Sulayman's stay there. Badauni (*Muntakhab at-Tavarikh*, Vol. II, p. 220) noted, however, with a certain amount of disdain, that after the Mirza's departure the revived customs also departed.

52. *A Muslim Courtier* (p. 83)

From an imperial portrait album
ca. 1585
Opaque watercolor on paper
Painting: H. 10.3 cm., W. 7.8 cm.
Private Collection

Muslims from India, Iran and Turan formed the largest part of Akbar's court. Feelings between these various groups were often tense, possibly because the Indian Muslims and the Turanis were Sunni while many of the Iranians were Shias (see page 46). Although the identity of this figure remains unknown, his religious affiliation is indicated by the fact that his coat is tied under his right arm (as opposed to his left which was the Rajput practice).

53. *A Rajput Soldier* (p. 83)

ca. 1575
Opaque watercolor on paper
Painting: H. 12.36 cm., W. 7.6 cm.
Lent by Catherine and Ralph Benkaim

The slight but wily-looking soldier of (presumably) high rank shown in this portrait against an unpainted background personifies one of the great benefits Akbar derived from his victories over the Rajputs, and the treaties they subsequently concluded. On the one hand peace was brought to large areas of the volatile "western front," and on the other hand large numbers of able-bodied Rajput soldiers (along with their brilliant generals) were acquired for the ever-active Mughal army. In an economy whose sole means of expansion was the conquest of new territories and treasuries, the worth of this soldier with his frightening array of finely crafted weapons cannot be overestimated. The fact that he was selected to sit for a portrait perhaps indicates that he had served Akbar particularly bravely in one of the emperor's triumphs of the 1570s.

54. *Portrait of Raisal Darbari* (p. 83)

From an imperial portrait album
ca. 1580-85
Opaque watercolor on paper
Painting: H. 24 cm., W. 17 cm.
The Chester Beatty Library, Dublin (Ms. 44, No. 2)

Raisal Darbari, the keeper of the imperial harem, was the son of Raja Soja of the Shaykhawat Rajputs. He lived a long life and had twenty-one sons. In 1602 Akbar elevated him to the rank of leader of 2,500 men and 1,250 horses. During Jahangir's reign he was promoted to the rank of commander of 3,000 and served in the Deccan. The date of his death is not recorded in any of the imperial histories.

55. *Portrait of Tansen* (p. 83)

ca. 1580
Opaque watercolor on paper
Painting: H. 24.76 cm., W. 16.19 cm.
The Chrysler Museum, Norfolk, Virginia; purchased
    with funds from the Grandy Art Trust Fund
    (58.27.20)

An inscription (reading "*shabih-i tansen*") across the bottom of this figure's long white *jama* identifies him as Tansen, Akbar's brilliant chief musician. Though shown against the standard flat green background, he has been anchored in space on a flower-strewn field. Tansen came to Akbar's court in 1562 and rose to great prominence in its atmosphere of artistic freedom. His fame was so great at Fatehpur-Sikri that, according to Jahangir (*Tuzuk-i Jahangiri,* Vol. II, p. 71), Shaykh Salim ad-Din Chishti requested that Akbar send Tansen to sing for him as he approached death in 1572. Tansen himself died in 1589. The National Museum of India possesses another portrait of Tansen (50.14/28), showing the musican with the same aquiline nose and dark complexion, and wearing the same long white *jama* with two bells tied around his waist. The issue is discussed further in an editorial note entitled "A Contemporary Portrait of Tansen" in *Lalit Kala,* 1-2 (1955-56), pp. 11-21 (in which the National Museum of India portrait is reproduced in color as pl. A) and by Hiren Mukherjee in a note entitled "Portraits of Tansen," *Lalit Kala,* 14 (1969), p. 57.

56. *Manuscript of the Kitab-i Saat* (p. 85)

Copied at Hajipur by Muhammad Yusuf
    for Mirza Aziz Koka
Dated 21 Shawwal, 991 (7 November 1583)
51 folios plus 4 flyleaves, 12 miniatures
Page: H. 27.4 cm., W. 19.8 cm.
Private Collection

Folio 26a: "Mercury in Gemini"
Ink and opaque watercolor on paper

In addition to the miniatures this manuscript also has four zodiac diagrams. The miniatures depict the planets as personified by figures or animals set within landscapes, beginning with Mars in Aries on folio 24b and ending with Jupiter in Pisces on folio 35a. The importance of this manuscipt lies both in its subject matter (only one other late-sixteenth-century Mughal illustrated astrological treatise exists) and its patron Mirza Aziz Koka (ca. 1542-1624) who was Akbar's foster brother. The Mirza's interest in the arts extended beyond the commissioning of manuscripts: he also built gardens and wrote poetry. One of his gardens, in Agra, was singled out by Badauni for its "garden house adorned with paintings" (*Muntakhab at-Tavarikh,* Vol. III, p. 389).

CHAPTER IV
The *Kitabkhana* as a Center of Collection

57. *Manuscript of the Zafarnama* (p. 89)
(not in exhibition)

Copied by Shir Ali for Sultan Husayn Mirza
Dated A. H. 872 (1467-68)
539 folios
6 double-page miniatures
H. 23.5 cm., W. 15.2 cm.
John Work Garrett Library, Johns Hopkins
    University, Baltimore

Folio 82v & 83r "Timur Granting an Audience in a
    Garden at Balkh on the Occasion of His Succession
    to the Line of the Chaghatay Khans."
Ink, opaque watercolor and gold on paper

Sharaf ad-Din Yazdi's *Zafarnama,* an extensive account of Timur's life from his twenty-fifth year until his death, was completed in 1424-25. The six miniatures of this manuscript, though relatively few compared to the numerous illustrations of other copies of the *Zafarnama* are remarkable for their quality. Sir Thomas Arnold (*Bihzad and his Paintings in the Zafar-nama MS.,* London, 1930), among others, has attributed them to the renowned Timurid master Bihzad and suggests that they were executed at Herat and added to the manuscript around 1490. On the sumptuously decorated flyleaf of the manuscript is a series of seals and autograph inscriptions of Mughal emperors, including Akbar, Jahangir, and Shah Jahan (see p. 17), who recorded that "This noble *Zafarnama,* which is one of the marvels of the age, has been deposited in the private library of this suppliant at the court of God, on the 25th day of the month Bahman, corresponding to the 6th day of the month Jumada II, in the year 1037 of the Hijra (February 12, 1628), which is the date of my blessed accession; and because of its exceedingly fine character it shall always remain in my presence and shall frequently be read." Both the subject matter and brilliant compositions of such miniatures as "Timur Granting an Audience in a Garden at Balkh" must have appealed greatly to the Mughals, who prized their relationship to Timur and saw themselves as the legitimate inheritors of his empire.

58. *Two Camels Fighting* (p. 93)

By Abd as-Samad
ca. 1580-90
Opaque watercolor on paper
Painting: H. 18.8 cm., W. 20.4 cm.
Private Collection

Signed by Abd as-Samad in tiny writing at the bottom of the left text panel, this painting is a reversed copy after an original by the famous Persian master Bihzad datable to ca. 1525 (Binyon, Wilkinson, and Gray, *Persian Miniature Painting,* 1933; rpt. New York: 1971, pl. LXXXVII A). The touching message written by Abd as-Samad in two panels at the top of the painting recalls the personal plea left by the seventy-year-old Bihzad on his original version (*Ibid.,* p. 131). Addressed to his son Muhammad Sharif Khan, who was also a painter but later became one of Jahangir's leading ministers, it reads:

> This master and *shaykh* [Abd as-Samad], whose faculties have stopped working, whose pen has stopped moving, and whose perfect sight has grown weak, prepared this with a broken pen and sent it off as a souvenir for his knowledgeable, witty, and astute son Sharif Khan, who is happy, fortunate, prosperous, and chosen by the mercy of the Merciful.

This same fighting camel motif was also used on a contemporary Mughal carpet (see NO. 73).

59. *Manuscript of the Gulistan of Sadi* (p. 95)

Copied at Bukhara in A. H. 947 (1567-68)
128 folios, 13 miniatures

H. 34 cm., W. 22 cm.
The British Library, London (Or. 5302)

Folio 30a: "The Old Wrestler Who Withheld One of His Secrets to Overthrow an Arrogant Pupil" by Shahm Muzahhib
Ink, opaque watercolor and gold on paper

Six of the paintings in this copy of the *Gulistan* (Rose Garden) of Sadi are contemporary with the manuscript, the remaining seven were added at the Mughal court during the early 1600s. The colophon, which appears to be genuine, states that the manuscript was calligraphed by the great Mir Ali al-Husayni *(wuffiqa bi-kitubatiha al-abd al-mudhhib),* who is generally thought to have died in 1556. Two of the miniatures (folios 30a and 91a) have identical inscriptions stating, "It was ordered in the days of the prosperity of the great king Jalal ad-Din Muhammad Akbar, may Allah perpetuate his kingship and sovereignty." Shahm, the artist of the miniature illustrated here and three other paintings in the manuscript, according to Losty, (*The Art of the Book in India,* p. 86) worked for Sultan Abd al-Aziz (r.1539-49) in Bukhara.

60. *The Head of Saint John the Baptist* (p. 97)

ca. 1580
Stone
H. 6.1 cm., W. 5.2 cm. Depth: 4.1 cm.
Private Collection

This unique sandstone plaque is probably connected with the 1575-77 artistic mission to Portuguese Goa. Although the European image from which it is derived remains unknown, its shape, material and size suggest that it once was set into a wall, possibly in an area such as the emperor's Hall of Public Audience. Similar kinds of objects can be seen in several Mughal paintings (albeit of a slightly later date) such as the *Darbar of Jahangir* now in the Museum of Fine Arts, Boston (see S. C. Welch, *Imperial Mughal Painting,* pl. 17).

61. *Polyglot Bible* (p. 99)

1568-72
Volume I
Page: H. 39.37 cm., W. 28.12 cm.
Houghton Library, Harvard University, Cambridge (f Bible A. 569)

When the first Jesuit mission arrived at Fatehpur-Sikri in 1580, it brought with it seven of the eight volumes of the *Polyglot Bible,* which had been printed between 1568 and 1572 by Christophe Plantin in Antwerp under the sponsorship of King Philip II of Spain. This volume is from the same edition, but not part of the actual set taken to India and presented to Akbar in the first week of March, 1580 amidst lavish ceremonies in which the emperor kissed each volume as a sign of great reverence. Vol. I contains the beginning of the Old Testament in the Hebrew, Latin Vulgate, and Greek Septuagint versions, along with a literal Latin version of the Septuagint, with a Chaldean paraphrase at the foot of the left page and a Latin translation at the foot of the right page – the variety of scripts must have instantly aroused Akbar's interest. The title pages in Vol. I were conceived by the Lord High Almoner of Spain (Don Luis Manrique) and designed by Pieter van der Borcht before being engraved by the Flemish artist Pieter van der Heyden (Ebba Koch, "The Influence of the Jesuit Mission on Symbolic Representations of the Mughal Emperors," *Islam in India,* I (1982), p. 16). Title pages in other volumes were also engraved by the Flemish artists Jan Wierix, Philipp Galle, and Gerard van Kampen.

62. *Joseph Telling His Dream to His Father*

After Georg Pencz   (p. 100)
Germany, 1544
Engraving on paper
Engraving: H. 10.9 cm., W. 7.3 cm.
Museum of Fine Art, Boston, Harvey D. Parker
     Collection (P2354)

63. *Joseph Telling His Dream to His Father*

(p. 100)
By Kesu Das (also known as Kesu the Elder)
ca. 1590
Detached page from the *Muraqqa-i Gulshan*
     (Gulshan Album)
Opaque watercolor and gold on paper
Painting: H. 21.4 cm., W. 10.8 cm. Page: H. 42.2 cm.,
     W. 26.5 cm.
St. Louis Art Museum, Gift of J. Lionburger Davis
     (403.52)

European prints and engravings were a great source of technical and compositional inspiration for Mughal artists. Often individual figures or elements of European engravings, by such artists as Dürer, Pencz and Cort, were incorporated into Mughal paintings. This painting is an example of an entire composition being copied. Kesu Das, in particular, seems to have been fascinated by European images and this miniature is the second version of *Joseph Telling His Dream to His Father* that he painted. The earlier one is in the Chester Beatty Library. Both have been carefully studied by Beach in "The Mughal Painter Kesu Das," *Archives of Asian Art* XXX and "An Early European Scene in Mughal Painting," *Oriental Art* vol. 22 no. 2. On the reverse of this page is a calligraphy by the celebrated Mir Ali (see pages 60, 87).

64. *Three Angels in a Landscape*   (p. 101)

ca. 1585
Opaque watercolor on paper
Page: H. 46 cm., W. 31 cm.
The Chester Beatty Library, Dublin (Ms. 62, No. 2)

Although they have been set into a standard Mughal landscape with rocky outcrops and a distant cityscape, these angels with their billowing robes appear to have been copied from a European print. However, it has not been possible to identify the subject of this curious scene showing an angel presenting a fish to another angel, who is seated on a European throne by the banks of a river or lake, while attended by a third angel. Nor has it been possible to identify the European print from which some or all these figures were taken. Such problems highlight the fact that by the 1580s Mughal artists were able to successfully integrate local and extraneous elements into a unified whole.

65. *Four Europeans*   (p. 101)

ca. 1590
Opaque watercolor on paper
Painting: H. 26.4 cm., W. 17.5 cm.
India Office Library, London (I.O.L.J. 16.6)

Although the figures in this scene are clearly European, their source is not immediately identifiable. It is also possible, indeed likely, that the artist conjured up one or two of the figures from his imagination, which might account for some of their awkard gestures, strangely skewed clothing and the pseudo-European writing on the book held by one of the attendants. On the reverse of this painting is a Persian quatrain written in *nastaliq* by the Mughal calligrapher Abd ar-Rahim al-Haravi and dated 1597-98.

66. *Madonna and Child* (p. 102)

Attributed to Basawan
ca. 1590-1600
Opaque watercolor and gold on paper
Page: H. 40.37 cm., W. 24.37 cm.
Lent by Edwin Binney, 3rd

Akbar's fascination with representations of the Madonna and Child, included among the paintings, prints, and objects brought to Fatehpur-Sikri by a Jesuit mission in 1580, is vividly described in letters sent by the Jesuit fathers to their superiors in Goa (see pp. 98, 99, 101). This fresh influx of European material left a telling mark on Mughal painting throughout the rest of the century, in terms of both subject matter and technique. This supremely elegant miniature showing the Madonna and Child placed within a wholly Mughal setting has been attributed to Basawan by S. C. Welch (*A Flower from Every Meadow*, p. 99), who also noted that its borders are identical with those of the Berlin Jahangir album. The unidentified couplets set into gold floral arabesques at the top and bottom of the page read as follows:

UPPER
A moon in beauty has been born from the sun,
The moon has given him milk from the breasts
    of her beauty.

LOWER
A rose has grown from the garden canal of beauty,
The garden has washed its face with the water
    of beauty.

67. *A Scholar with His Pupil* (p. 103)

ca. 1570-80
Opaque watercolor on paper
Painting: H. 21.3 cm., W. 14.9 cm. Page: H. 25 cm.,
    W. 17.3 cm.
Lent by Edwin Binney, 3rd

The striking bearded figure in his green coat and white *jama* has yet to be identified, but the two handsomely bound books in his possession, as well as the fine

inkpot (compare with NO. 75), suggest that he could well be one of the many scholars and theologians who gathered at Akbar's court. It is equally plausible that the rather worried figure on the left in an orange-red coat and fur hat could be his pupil or secretarial assistant. It has been suggested by S. C. Welch that this painting might be a late work of Mir Sayyid Ali, who left India in 1572.

68. *A Prince and a Hermit* (p. 104)

Attributed to Abd as-Samad
ca. 1580-85
Opaque watercolor on paper
Painting: H. 34.5 cm., W. 22.8 cm. Page: H. 39.6 cm.,
    W. 37.3 cm.
Lent by Prince Sadruddin Aga Khan

The iconography of this painting, as A. Welch (*Arts of the Islamic Book*, p. 160) has noted, derives from Iranian prototypes of aristocrats or rulers meeting poor dervishes. The contrast of these two aspects of society symbolize the juxtaposition of spiritual and temporal authority, a theme of great interest to Akbar.

Published in full: A. Welch and S. C. Welch, *Arts of the Islamic Book*, p. 161.

69. *A Prince Hunting with Falcons* (p. 105)

Attributed to Abd as-Samad (but inscribed with
    the name Mir Sayyid Ali)
ca. 1585
Opaque watercolor on paper
Painting: H. 21.59 cm., W. 13 cm.
Lent by Ralph and Catherine Benkaim

Although this painting bears an inscription in the top right corner that reads "the work of Mir Sayyid Ali the artist," it can be attributed on stylistic grounds to Abd as-Samad, another Safavid master Akbar inherited from his father. Furthermore, Mir Sayyid Ali left India in 1572 while this representation of the traditional royal hunt exhibits the hallmarks of Akbari painting from the mid-1580s. In contrast to his unhappy colleague, Abd as-Samad stayed on in India and received a number of commissions outside the *kitabkhana*, including that of supervisor of the mint at Fatehpur-Sikri in 1577.

CHAPTER V

The *Karkhanas:*
The Imperial Workshops

70. *A Courtier with a Winecup* (p. 108)

ca. 1570
Embroidered silk
Textile: H. 195.58 cm., W. 121.28 cm.
Los Angeles County Museum of Art, The Nasli
   Heeramaneck Collection, Gift of Joan Palevsky
   M73.5.702

This young courtier, standing in an arched doorway holding an elegant winecup in one hand and the hilt of a sword in the other, is embroidered on a fine piece of silk with a satin ground that was probably hung in a palace doorway. Similiar hangings are shown in an illustration from the *Jahangirnama* now in the collection of the Raza Library in Rampur (Karl Khandalavala (ed.), *An Age of Splendour – Islamic Art in India,* Bombay, 1983, p. 41). The courtier's archaic Safavid costume and demeanor suggest that Akbar's textile designers lagged behind his artists in the search for new Mughal forms of expression. Most of the figure's clothing, except for his cloak, has been rewoven, and his eyes have also been altered. Large areas of the background have been reinforced with coarse red vertical threads. We are grateful to S. C. Welch for bringing this important object to our attention.

71. *Fragment from an Animal Carpet* (p. 109)

3rd quarter of the 16th century
Cotton warp, wool weft 60,000 knots
   per square meter
H. 139 cm., W. 98.1 cm.
Private Collection

With its forceful rhythm of beasts and birds emerging from each other's mouths and clusters of equally two-dimensional flowers, the "red-ground carpet," of which this is a fragment, is generally considered to be one of the two earliest extant Mughal carpets. While this carpet is characterized more by recurring motifs than an overall pattern, the other carpet, a fragment of which belongs to the Musée des Arts Décoratifs in Paris (Inv. 5212), shows animal heads subsumed within a more conventional scrolling arabesque pattern (see Skelton et al, *The Indian Heritage,* p. 74). The significance of the grotesque animal heads is uncertain although they might be distantly related to the legend of Alexander the Great and the Talking Tree *(waq-waq).* A textile with a similar pattern is seen covering a yurt behind an enthroned figure of Timur in the 1467-68 *Zafarnama* manuscript that later entered Akbar's collection (NO.57). It has been suggested (Martin Dickson and S. C. Welch, *The Houghton Shahnameh,* Cambridge, Massachusetts, 1981, p. 109) that this carpet was at least partially designed by the painter Mir Sayyid Ali which would place its date of manufacture before his departure from India in 1572.

72. *Pictorial Carpet* (p. 110)

ca. 1580-90
Cotton warp and weft, woolen pile
639,100 knots per square meter
H. 2.43 m., W. 1.54 m.
Museum of Fine Arts, Boston
   Gift of Mrs. Frederick L. Ames in the name of
   Frederick L. Ames (93.1480)

This is one of the uniquely Mughal "pictorial carpets." While its imagery is clearly related to contemporary paintings, the carpet's composition lacks the visual cohesiveness of a miniature. Instead it is divided into a series of vignettes with a genre scene of figures in a palace at the top, a hunting scene with a cheetah on a cart in the middle, and a phoenix attacking a composite beast that in turn is attacking seven elephants at the bottom. Although the origin of this strange beast is not known, an almost identical one, also attacking seven elephants, decorates the Delhi Gate at the Red Fort in Agra. Interspersed between these images are a series of animals that link the various part of the carpet to each other. The peculiarities of this rug's composition and the fact that this kind of imagery rarely appears in other Mughal rugs suggest that weavers and designers found it easier, ultimately, to work with more traditional approaches towards the fields of their carpets.

73. *The Widener Animal Carpet* (p. 111)

Late 16th century
L. 403.5cm, W. 191.2cm
Cotton warp and weft, woolen pile
368,500 knots per square meter

Though traditionally dated to ca. 1625 during the reign of Jahangir (see, for example, *The Arts of Islam,* London, 1976, p. 117 and Skelton et al, *The Indian Heritage,* London, 1982, p. 75) the basis for such an attribution is tenuous, and the lively animals that swerve across the red ground of this carpet actually seem closer to the mood of painting during Akbar's reign. With the recent discovery of Abd as-Samad's earlier copy of Bihzad's fighting camels (NO. 58), Nanha's copy dated 1608-09 (see p. 113) also becomes less significant for the dating of this carpet which features this same motif. The intrusion of an elephant and rider within its own two-dimensional picture plane in the very center of the carpet and the inclusion of animals such as the galloping rhinoceros at the top are typically Mughal.

74. *Pair of Lion Heads* (p. 114)

Second half of the 16th century
Bronze with gilding
H. 37 cm., W. 31 cm.
Museum für Ostasiatische Kunst, Cologne (42.5 A,B)

These heads were purchased by Adolf Fischer in Japan at the turn of the century and were thought to have come from the Summer Palace in Beijing (*Vortrag, Gehalten auf dem 15 ten Internationalen Orientalisten-Kongress in Kopenhagen,* Brill, 1908, pp. 584-87). Their attribution to Mughal India was originally made by S. C. Welch (in the forthcoming *Festschrift for Pupul Jayakar*), who argues that they may have functioned as ornamental capitals. Based on the heads' shape, construction and design (see pp. 114-115), it seems more likely that they decorated the prow or stern of a boat. Their extraordinary weight rules out other possibilities for their use such as on the top of a standard.

75. *Small Fluted Vessel* (p. 116)

Last quarter of the 16th century
Dark green jade
H. 9.5 cm., Diam. Base 5.3 cm.
The Brooklyn Museum, Lent by Robin Martin (L79.19)

This small dark green jar with fluted sides was first attributed to Mughal India in an unpublished article by Amy Poster, who also pointed out similar examples in paintings from Akbar's reign, such as the ca. 1570-80 miniature of scholar and pupil (NO. 67), that allow it to be tentatively dated to the sixteenth century. Probably used as an inkpot, it is one of the earliest known Mughal jades, a material especially fancied by Jahangir, who was particularly keen on collecting original Timurid jade objects.

76. *Throne Panel* (p. 117)

Second half of the 16th century
Wood
H. 6.1 cm., W. 49.7 cm.
Lent by Howard Hodgkin

This panel is one of the few carved wooden objects that can be confidently dated to Akbar's reign. Its figures with heavy swords and small shields are as lively as they are entertaining. Originally the panel formed part of a wooden throne such as the one depicted in folio 201 of the ca. 1604 Chester Beatty *Akbarnama.* Similar thrones, with carved figural decorations, of slightly later date can be seen in the miniatures made for Jahangir and Shah Jahan (see, for instance, the painting of Shah Jahan enthroned by Abul Hasan in Beach, *The Grand Mogul,* pl. 27).

77. *Gold Coins* (p. 119)

a) Round *mohur*
Minted at Fatehpur-Sikri in A. H. 986 (1578-79)
Weight: 10.902 gm., Diameter: 22 mm.
The American Numismatic Society, New York:
0000.999.7070
b) Square *mohur*
Minted at Fatehpur-Sikri in A. H. 987? (1579-80)
Weight: 11.804 gm., 18 x 18 mm.
The American Numismatic Society, New York:
1973.56.130

Since 1441-42 no gold coins had been struck in northern India until Akbar reversed this trend in 1562-63; two years later he had four gold mints in operation (Deyell, "Development of Akbar's Currency System," p. 10). The *mohur,* the standard Akbari gold coin, had a basic weight of 11 grams (.38 ounce) and bore the *khalima* (the Islamic protestation of faith) on its obverse and Akbar's name, the name of the mint, and the hijra date on the reverse. In 1577 Akbar completely revised the operation of his mints and also introduced square coins (*Akbarnama,* Vol. III, pp. 320-21), which have a long history in India but had not been used before by the Mughals (*ibid.,* p. 18). It was in this same year that the mint at Fatehpur-Sikri started to produce gold and silver coins in great quantities under the direction of the famous artist and calligrapher Abd as-Samad, but production ceased again after only four years. In A. H. 986 (1578-79) both round and square *mohurs* were minted at Fatehpur-Sikri but after that only the square coins were produced.

78. *Silver Coins* (p. 119)

a) Square *rupee*
Minted at Fatehpur-Sikri in A. H. 985 (1577-78)
Weight: 11.371 gm., 21 x 21 mm.
American Numismatic Society, New York:
  1917.216.352
b) Square *rupee*
Minted at Fatehpur-Sikri in A. H. 986 (1578-79)
Weight: 11.022 gm., 18 x 19 mm.
American Numismatic Society, New York:
  1917.215.623

Square silver coins are among the oldest types of money to survive in India. Akbar's use of these coins which were minted as early 1556-57 and were struck at Fatehpur-Sikri from 1577-78 to 1581-82 reflect his efforts of adopt local monetary traditions (Deyell, "Development of Akbar's Currency System," p. 18). *Rupees* are relatively large (25 mm.) coins with a standard weight of approximately 11.5 grams (.40 ounce). Prior to the promulgation of the Din-i Illahi in 1582 all of Akbar's *rupees* were inscribed on the obverse with the *khalima* surrounded by the names of the four Companions of the Prophet and on the reverse with the emperor's full name, Jalal ad-Din Muhammad Akbar Badshah Ghazi, and the mint and date. According to Abul Fazl the emperor minted nine different types of silver coins, of which the *rupee* was the most important (*Ain-i Akbari* Vol. I, p. 32).

79. *Copper Coins* (p. 119)

a) Round *dam*
Minted at Fatehpur-Sikri in A. H. 986 (1578-79)

Weight: 20.755 gm., Diameter: 23 mm.
The American Numismatic Society, New York:
  1927.179.16
b) Round *dam*
Minted at Fatehpur-Sikri in A. H. 987 (1579-80)
Weight: 20.460 gm., Diameter: 22 mm.
The American Numismatic Society, New York:
  1927.179.17

The thick copper *dam,* based on the older Suri *paisa,* was the least valuable Akbari coin and also the simplest in terms of design. Its standard weight was 21 grams (.73 ounce) and it was usually about 7 mm. thick. Unlike the Akbari gold *mohur* and the silver *rupee,* the copper *dam* carried neither a religious reference nor the emperor's name, listing only the mint in which it was manufactured and the hijra date. Based on surviving catalogued coins, the mint at Fatehpur-Sikri produced copper *dams* from A. H. 981 (1573-74) until A. H. 989 (1581-82).

80. *Farman* (p. 120)

ca. 1598
Ink, with red, blue and gold highlights on paper
Archives of the Catholic Archdiocese of Agra, India.

Few Akbari *farmans* (official documents) have survived. This one, issued by Akbar to the Jesuit Fathers in Surat (see p. 121), with its background of floral and animal designs, is one of the finest. It can be attributed to the late 1590s on the basis of both its formal characteristics and subject matter. In the upper right hand corner of the document is a seal composed of a central circle bearing Akbar's name and eight smaller circles inscribed with the names of Akbar's Timurid ancestors. We are grateful to Dr. Shakebi for providing us with the following translation:

  When it was sumitted to
  the emperor that the fathers *(pedariyan)* of
  ... wanted to build a House of Worship
    (ibadatkhana)
  in the city of Cambay (Khambayat)
  this august *farman* was
  issued enjoining the ruler *(hakim)* of
  the city of Cambay not to stand
  in their way and allow them to
  lay the foundation of it and keep
  themselves busy in worshipping.
  Issued on the seventh day of the
  month of Farwardi of the year...

CHAPTER VI
Akbar and the Power of Images

81. *Shah Abu al-Maali* (p. 125)

By Dust Muhammad
ca. 1556-60
Opaque watercolor on paper
Painting: H. 17.5 cm., W. 14.5 cm. Page: H. 33.7 cm.,
   W. 24.6 cm.
Lent by Prince Sadruddin Aga Khan (Ms. 126)

Dust Muhammad was one of the talented Safavid artists who joined the Mughal court at Kabul in the 1550s. According to Bayazid Biyat (as quoted by Dickson and S. C. Welch, *The Houghton Shahnameh,* Vol. I, p. 119), he entered the service of Humayun's brother, Kamran, because "he could not get by without the wine the Shah (Tahmasp) had forbidden." After Kamran's death in 1550, he went to work for Humayun. He was a pupil of the great Timurid master Bihzad, and was as accomplished a calligrapher as

he was a painter. His stay in India, however, was brief, for he appears to have been back in Iran by the first years of the 1560s where he worked on a number of projects, including the copying of Korans (ibid., p. 118).

This intensely observed, though slightly awkward, portrait of Shah Abu al-Maali, one of Humayun's closest friends, was probably executed shortly after the emperor's death in 1556. Inscribed on the folio that Abu al-Maali is holding are the words, "God is Great. Jannat Ashiani [a posthumous title for Humayun]. This portrait is the likeness of Shah Abu al-Maali of Kashgar, whom his Majesty keeps close to him in royal service. The work of Master Dust the Painter." Despite Abu al-Maali's friendship with Humayun, he rebelled against Akbar in 1564. His demise, at the hands of Mirza Sulayman, is recorded by Abul Fazl (*Akbarnama,* Vol. II, pp. 320-21), whose dislike of the Shah is obvious, "At the time of his being strangled, his impure character displayed itself, and he made entreaties and lamentations in order that he might, perhaps, by a thousand humiliations, gain a few more days of life...But the result was only to show his worthless character...The world was cleansed of his hateful existence, and he by his own acts hastened to the pit of destruction."

CHRONOLOGY of Important Historical and Artistic Events

[Events with approximate date only are marked*]

1526 Babur defeats Sultan Ibrahim Lodi at Panipat and captures the throne of India

1527 Babur commissions a Garden of Victory at Sikri, near Khanva, where he has just defeated Rana Sangram Singh of Mewar.

1530 Babur dies and is succeeded by his son Humayun.

1531 Income from the district of Sikri granted as a *waqf* (religious endowment) for Babur's tomb.

1540 Sher Shah Sur defeats Humayun and forces him to abandon Agra and Delhi. On his way to temporary exile in Iran, Humayun rests in the Garden of Victory at Sikri.

1542 Akbar born in Umarkot.

1545 Humayun retakes Qandahar and Kabul.

1549 Safavid artists Abd as-Samad and Mir Sayyid Ali enter service of Humayun in Kabul.

1555 Humayun reconquers India.

1556 Humayun dies and is succeeded by his son Akbar, who shortly afterwards defeats Hemu at Panipat.

1557 Akbar defeats Sikandar Shah Sur.

1560 Akbar dismisses his former regent Bayram Khan from the post of Chief Minister.

*Illustrated manuscripts of the *Tutinama* produced ca. 1560-65 (Nos. 8-10).

1561 Akbar annexes Malwa in central India.

Bayram Khan assassinated.

1562 Akbar makes his first pilgrimage to the tomb of Khwaja Muin ad-Din Chishti in Ajmer.

Akbar marries the daughter of the Raja of Amber.

The musician Tansen arrives at Akbar's court.

*Work begins on an illustrated version of the *Hamzanama* (Nos. 11-12).

1562 -63 Construction of Humayun's tomb begins in Delhi.

1564 -65 Work begins on a new palace at Nagarchin near Agra.

1565 Akbar orders the reconstruction of the fort at Agra. Work continues for at least five years.

*Illustrated *Tilasm* and *Zodiac* manuscript produced ca. 1565-70 (fig. 1).

1567 -68 Illustrated manuscript of Sadi's *Gulistan* completed (No. 59).

1568 Akbar conquers Chittorgarh in Mewar.

Illustrated manuscript of Amir Khusrau's *Ashiqa* completed.

1568 -69 Commemorative statues of Jaimal and Patta, Rajput enemies who fell at Chittorgarh, completed at the Elephant Gate of Agra Fort.

1569 Akbar captures the strategic fortress of Ranthambhor in northeastern Rajasthan.

Akbar's first son, Prince Salim, born at the monastery of Shaykh Salim ad-Din Chishti in Sikri.

1570 Akbar's second son, Prince Murad, born.

Illustrated manuscript of the *Anvar-i Suhayli* completed (fig. 5).

Akbar repairs and enlarges the fort at Ajmer.

1570 -71 Humayun's tomb completed.

1571 Akbar issues an order to start work on the construction of Fatehpur-Sikri.

1572 Akbar's third son, Prince Daniyal, born.

Shaykh Salim ad-Din Chishti dies.

Mir Sayyid Ali departs for Mecca.

1573 Akbar conquers Gujarat.

Akbar encounters Europeans for the first time during the siege of Surat.

Celebrations staged in Fatehpur-Sikri to mark the circumcision of the three princes.

1573 -74 Mileposts and caravanserais constructed along the route from Agra to Ajmer via Fatehpur-Sikri.

Koran copied for Akbar in Lahore by Hibatullah al-Husayni (No. 21).

1574 Translation Bureau established at Fatehpur-Sikri.

1574 -75 Imperial Record Office established at Fatehpur-Sikri.

1575 Haji Habibullah leads a cultural mission from Fatehpur-Sikri to Goa.

Akbar orders the construction of the House of Worship at Fatehpur-Sikri for the staging of religious debates.

1576 Bengal added to the Mughal dominions.

1576 -77 Akbar commissions a new Chahar Suq (bazaar) in Fatehpur-Sikri.

1577 Haji Habibullah's mission returns from Goa.

**Hamzanama* project completed.

1577 -78	Akbar orders a reorganization of the imperial mints.
	Abd as-Samad placed in charge of the Fatehpur-Sikri mint.
1578	Father Pereira, the Jesuit Vicar-General of Bengal, arrives in Fatehpur-Sikri at Akbar's invitation.
	Akbar has a mystical experience while hunting.
	Shaykh Ibrahim, a nephew of Shaykh Salim ad-Din Chishti, is appointed governor of Fatehpur-Sikri.
1579	Akbar reads the Friday sermon in the Jami Masjid at Fatehpur-Sikri.
	The Decree of Infallibility is promulgated in favor of Akbar.
	Akbar makes his last pilgrimage to Ajmer.
	Akbar sends an embassy to Goa to invite a Jesuit mission to Fatehpur-Sikri.
	Fire ravages the Imperial Storehouse at Fatehpur-Sikri.
1579 -80	Akbar establishes an experimental House of the Dumb outside Fatehpur-Sikri.
1580	Rebellion breaks out in the eastern provinces of Bihar and Bengal.
	The first Jesuit mission from Goa reaches Fatehpur-Sikri.
	*Illustrated manuscript of the *Darabnama* produced ca. 1580-85 (fig. 6).
1581	Akbar marches on Kabul with Prince Salim, and defeats his half-brother Mirza Hakim Muhammad.
1582	The *Din-i Ilahi*, a new code of religious behavior, is formulated.
	Akbar orders the translation of the *Mahabharata* into Persian as the *Razmnama* (fig. 7).
	Akbar commissions a copy of the *Shahnama* to be transcribed and illustrated.
1582 -83	Mir Fathullah, a leading mathematician and inventor, enters Akbar's service at Fatehpur-Sikri.
	Sadi's *Gulistan* is copied by Muhammad Husayn Zarin Qalam in Fatehpur-Sikri (No. 25).
1583	Akbar reorganizes the administration of his empire, with the three princes placed in control of the main branches of government.
	The first Jesuit mission departs from Fatehpur-Sikri.
	Akbar orders the construction of a fort in Allahabad at the confluence of the Ganges and Jumna rivers.
	Illustrated manuscript of the *Kitab-i Saat* completed for Akbar's foster-brother Mirza Aziz Koka in Hajipur (No. 56).
1584	*Initial work in progress on an illustrated manuscript of the *Tarikh-i Khandan-i Timuriyya* (fig. 8).

1585	Prince Salim marries a daughter of Raja Bhagvan Das of Amber amid extensive celebrations in Fatehpur-Sikri.
	Akbar leaves Fatehpur-Sikri for the Panjab in the wake of Mirza Hakim Muhammad's death in Kabul.
	*"Keir" *Khamsa* of Nizami illustrated for Akbar.
	*Illustrated manuscript of Nasir ad-Din Tusi's *Akhaq-i Nasiri* produced ca. 1585-90 (No. 19).
1586	Lahore becomes the new Mughal capital.
	Akbar captures Kashmir.
1587 -88	Translation of the *Ramayana* commenced.
	Abul Fazl begins work on the *Akbarnama*, the official history of Akbar's reign.
1588	Illustrated manuscript of the *Divan* of Anvari completed (Nos. 26-27).
1589	Tansen dies.
	Abd ar-Rahim Khan Khanan's translation of the *Baburnama* presented to Akbar (Nos. 33-34).
1590	Akbar conquers Orissa in eastern India.
	*First illustrated version of the *Akbarnama* produced (Nos. 4, 13-17, 32).
	*Illustrated translation of the *Harivamsa* produced (Nos. 28-29).
1592	*Illustrated manuscript of the *Tarikh-i Alfi* produced ca. 1592-94 (No. 31).
1595	Fayzi, the poet-laureate, dies.
1596	Akbar conquers Berar in the Deccan.
	Illustrated manuscript of the *Chingiznama* completed (Nos. 2, 35-37).
1597 -98	"Dyson-Perrins" *Khamsa* of Nizami illustrated for Akbar.
1598	Agra reinstated as the Mughal capital.
1599	Prince Murad dies.
1601	Prince Salim rebels against Akbar while he is absent in the Deccan.
	Akbar captures Khandesh.
1602	Illustrated manuscript of the *Jog Bashisht*, Farmuli's translation of the *Yogavasishtamaharamayana*, is completed (No. 30).
1604	Prince Daniyal dies.
	Work in progress on a second illustrated version of the *Akbarnama* (Nos. 1, 18).
1605	Akbar dies, and is succeeded by Prince Salim as the Emperor Jahangir.

BIBLIOGRAPHY

Abul Fazl, *Akbarnama*, tr. H. Beveridge. 3 vols. Delhi: Ess Ess Publications, 1973.
——————, *Ain-i Akbari*, tr. H. Blochmann et al. 3 vols. New Delhi: Munshiram Manoharlal, 1977.
Affifi, A. E., *The Mystical Philosophy of Muhyid Din-Ibnul Arabi*. Cambridge: Cambridge University Press, 1939.
Aftabchi, Jawhar, *Tazkirat al-Vaqiat*, tr. Charles Stewart, Delhi: Idarah-i Adabiyat-i Delli, 1972.
Ali, M. Athar, *The Mughal Nobility under Aurangzeb*. Bombay: Asia Publishing House, 1968.
Arnold, Sir Thomas W., *Bihzad and His Paintings in the Zafarnamah MS*. London: Bernard Quaritch, 1930.
——————and J. V. S. Wilkinson, *Painting in Islam*. Oxford: Clarendon Press, 1928.
——————. and J. V. S. Wilkinson, *The Library of A. Chester Beatty: A Catalogue of the Indian Miniatures*, London: Emery Walker, 1936.
The Arts of Islam. London: The Arts Council of Great Britain, 1976.
Asiatic Art in the Museum of Fine Arts. Boston: Museum of Fine Arts, 1982.
Aziz, Abdul, *The Imperial Library of the Mughals*. Delhi: Idarah-i Adabiyat-i Delli, 1974.

Babur, Zahir ad-Din Muhammad, *Baburnama*, tr. A. S. Beveridge, New Delhi: Oriental Book Reprint Corporation, 1970.
Badauni, Abd al-Qadir, *Muntakhab at-Tavarikh*. tr. G. S. A. Ranking, W. H. Lowe and T. W. Haig. 3 vols. Delhi: Idarah-i Adabiyat-i Delli, 1973.
Banerjee, P. *The Life of Krishna in Art*. New Delhi: National Museum of India, 1978.
Beach, Milo C., *The Grand Mogul: Imperial Painting in India 1600-1660*. Williamstown, Mass: Sterling and Francine Clark Institute, 1978.
——————, "The Gulshan Album and Its European Sources," *Bulletin of the Museum of Fine Arts, Boston*. Vol. 63, No. 332 (1965).
——————, *The Imperial Image: Paintings for the Mughal Court*. Washington: The Freer Gallery of Art, 1973.
——————, "The Mughal Painter Kesu Das," *Archives of Asian Art*, Vol. 30, (1976-77).
Begam, Gulbadan, *Humayunnama*, tr. A. H. Beveridge. Delhi: Idarah-i Adabiyat-i Delli, 1972.
Bernier, François, *Travels in the Mogul Empire A. D. 1656-1668*, tr. A. Constable. New Delhi: S. Chand and Co., 1979.
Binney, Edwin, 3rd, *Indian Miniature Painting from the Collection of Edwin Binney, 3rd*, Portland, 1973.
Binyon, Laurence, J. V. S. Wilkinson and Basil Gray, *Persian Miniature Painting*. New York: Dover Publications, 1971.
Brand, Michael and Glenn D. Lowry, *Fatehpur-Sikri: A Sourcebook*. Cambridge, Mass.: Aga Khan Program for Islamic Architecture, 1985.
Bussagli, Mario, *Indian Miniatures*. tr. R. Rudorff. New Delhi: The Macmillan Company of India, 1976.

Chandra, Pramod, *The Tuti-Nama of the Cleveland Museum of Art*. Graz: Akademische Druck-u. Verlagsantalt, 1976.

——————, "Ustad Salivahana and the Development of Popular Mughal Art," *Lalit Kala*, Vol. VIII, 1976.
Clavijo, Ruy Gonzalez, *Embassy to Tamerlane 1403-1406*, tr. Guy Le Strange. London: George Routledge and Sons, 1928.
Correia-Afonso, John, ed., *Letters from the Mughal Court: The First Jesuit Mission to Akbar. (1580-1583)*. Bombay: Heras Institute of Indian Culture, 1980.

Das, Ashok Kumar, *Mughal Painting during Jahangir's Time*. Calcutta: The Asiatic Society, 1978.
De Laet, Joannes, *The Empire of the Great Mogol*, tr. J. S. Hoyland. Delhi: Idarah-i Adabiyat-i Delli, 1975.
Deyell, John S., "Development of Akbar's Currency System and Monetary Integration of the Conquered Kingdoms," unpub. paper delivered at the Conference on the Monetary System of Mughal India, National Humanities Center, Research Triangle Park, North Carolina, June 1981.
Dickson, Martin and Stuart Cary Welch, *The Houghton Shahnameh*. 2 vols. Cambridge, Mass: Harvard University Press, 1981.
Dimand, M., *Indian Miniature Painting*. Milan: The Uffici Press, 1959.
Du Jarric, Pierre, *Akbar and the Jesuits*, tr. C. H. Payne. London: George Routledge and Sons, 1926.
Dutt, M. N., *A Prose Translation of Harivamsha*, Calcutta, 1897.
The Eastern Carpet in the Western World: From the 15th to the 17th Century. London: Arts Council of Great Britain, 1983.

Egger, Gerhart, *Der Hamza Roman*. Vienna: Osterreichisches Museum für angewandte Kunst, 1969.
Encyclopedia of Islam. 1st ed., 4 vols., Leyden: E. J. Brill, 1913-38.

Falk, Toby, *Persian and Mughal Art*. London: Colnaghi, 1976.
Fitch, Ralph, in *Early Travels in India, 1583-1619*, ed. W. Foster. London: Humphrey Milford and Oxford University Press, 1921.

Gans-Ruedin, Erwin, *The Indian Carpet*. London: Thames and Hudson, 1984.
Gascoigne, Bamber, *The Great Mughals*. Delhi: B. I. Publications, 1971.
Gluck, Heinrich, *Die Indischen Miniaturen des Hamza-Romanes im Osterreichisches Museum für Kunst und Industrie in Wien und in anderen Sammlungen*. Leipzig: Amalthea-Verlag, 1925.
Grabar, Oleg, tr. in his review of A. A. Semenov, "Inscriptions on the Tombs of Timur and His Descendants in the Gur-e Amir," *Epigrafika Vostoka*, 2, 44-62, published in *Ars Orientalis*, Vol. II, 1957.
Gray, Basil, *The Arts of the Book in Central Asia; 14th-16th Centuries*. Boulder, Colorado: Shambala/UNESCO, 1979.
——————, *Persian Painting*. New York: Skira/Rizzoli, 1977.
Grube, Ernst, *Islamic Paintings from the 11th to the 18th Century from the Collection of Hans P. Kraus*. New York: H. P. Kraus, n.d.

Hamzanama, Vollständige Wiedergabe der Bekannten Blätter der Handschrift aus den Beständen aller Erreichbaren Sammlungen. Vol. I, Graz, 1974.

Haq, M. Mahfuzul, "The Khan Khanan and His Painters, Illuminators and Calligraphists," Islamic Culture, Vol. 5, No. 4, 1931.

Haravi, Nizam ad-Din Ahmad, Tabaqat-i Akbari, tr. B. De. 3 vols Calcutta: Asiatic Society of Bengal, 1927-1939.

Hodgson, Marshall. The Venture of Islam. 3 vols. Chicago: University of Chicago Press, 1974.

Islamic, Indian and South-East Asian Manuscripts, Miniatures and Works of Art. Christie's sale catalogue, June 13, 1983.

Jahangir, Nur ad-Din Muhammad, Tuzuk-i Jahangiri. tr. A. Rogers, ed. A. Beveridge. New Delhi: Munshiram Manorharlal, 1968.

Kambu, Muhammad Salih, Amal-i Salih. 3 vols. ed. G. Yazdani. Calcutta: Royal Asiatic Society of Bengal, 1912-39.

Keene, H. G. A Handbook for Visitors to Delhi and Its Neighbourhood. Calcutta: Thacker Spink & Co., 1882.

Khan, Iqtidar Alam, "The Nobility under Akbar and the Development of His Religious Policy," Journal of the Royal Asiatic Society, parts 1 and 2, 1968.

Khan, Shah Nawaz, Maathir al-Umara, tr. H. Beveridge. 3 vols. Patna: Janaki Prakashan, 1979.

Khan, Zayn, Tabaqat-i Baburi tr. Sayed Hasan Askari. Delhi: Idarah-i Adabiyat-i Delli, 1982.

Khandalavala, K., ed. An Age of Splendour – Islamic Art in India. Bombay: Marg Publications, 1983.

_____ and Jagdish Mittal, "An Early Akbari Illustrated Manuscript of Tilasm and Zodiac," Lalit Kala 14 (1969).

Khandamir, Qanun-i Humayuni, tr. B. Prashad. Calcutta: Royal Asiatic Society of Bengal, 1940.

Koch, Ebba, "The Influence of the Jesuit Mission on Symbolic Representations of the Mughal Emperors," Islam in India: Studies and Commentaries; ed., C. W. Troll, Vol. 1, 1982.

_____, "Jahangir and the Angels: Recently Discovered Wall Paintings under European Influence in the Fort of Lahore," in India and the West, ed. Joachim Deppert. New Delhi: Manohar Publications, 1983.

Kühnel, Ernst and Hermann Goetz, Indische Buchmalereien aus dem Jahangir-Album der Staatsbibliothek zu Berlin. Berlin: Scarabaeus Verlag, 1924.

Lahawri, Abd al-Hamid, Padshahnama, ed. K. Ahmad and M. A. Rahim. 3 vols. Calcutta: Asiatic society of Bengal, 1867-68.

Losty, Jeremiah P., The Art of the Book in India. London: British Library, 1982.

McCall, John E., "Early Jesuit Art in the Far East, IV," Artibus Asiae, II, 1948.

McInerney, Terrence, Indian Painting: 1525-1585. London: David Carrit Limited, 1982.

Maclagan, Sir Edward. The Jesuits and the Great Mogul. London: Burns, Oates, and Washbourne, 1932.

Marek, J. and H. Knizkova, The Jenghiz Khan Miniatures from the Court of Akbar the Great. London: Spring Books, 1963.

Monserrate, A., The Commentary of Father Monserrate, S. J., tr. J. S. Hoyland. London: Oxford University Press, 1922.

Mukherjee, Haren, "Portraits of Tansen," Lalit Kala, 14 (1969).

Petruccioli, Attilio, "The Process Evolved by the Control-Systems of Urban Design in the Moghul Epoch in India: the Case of Fathpur-Sikri," Environmental Design, I, 1984.

Pinder-Wilson, Ralph, Painting from the Muslim Courts of India. London: World of Islam Festival, 1976.

Pope, A. U., ed. Survey of Persian Art. 6 vols. London: Oxford University Press, 1938-58.

Qandahari, Muhammad Arif, Tarikh-i Akbari, ed. Muin ud-Din Nadwi, Azhar Ali Dihlavi, and Imtiyaz Ali Arshi. Rampur: Raza Library. 1962.

Qazi, Ahmad, Calligraphers and Painters, tr. V. Minorsky. Washington: The Smithsonian Institution, 1959.

Rizvi, S. A. A., Religious and Intellectual History of the Muslims in Akbar's Reign. New Delhi: Munshiram Manoharlal, 1975.

_____ and V. J. Flynn, Fathpur-Sikri. Bombay: Taraporevala, 1975.

Robinson, B. W. et al., Islamic Painting and the Arts of the Book. London: Faber and Faber, 1976.

Roy, S., "Akbar" in The History and Culture of the Indian People, Vol. VII. Bombay: Bharatiya Vidya Bhavan, 1980.

Schimmel, Annemarie, Calligraphy and Islamic Culture. New York: New York University Press, 1984.

_____ and Stuart Cary Welch, Anvari's Divan: A Pocket Book for Akbar. New York: The Metropolitan Museum of Art, 1983.

Simsar, Mehmed, tr. The Tutinama. Graz: 1976.

Simpson, Marianna Shreve, "The Production and Patronage of the Haft Aurang by Jami in the Freer Gallery of Art." Ars Orientalis, XIII, 1982.

Skelton, Robert, The Indian Heritage: Court Life and Arts under Mughal Rule. London: Victoria and Albert Museum, 1982.

_____, "Mughal Paintings from Harivamsa Manuscript," Victoria and Albert Museum Yearbook, 2 (1969, 41-54).

_____, "The Shah Jahan Cup," Victoria and Albert Museum Bulletin, Vol. II, No. 3, 1966.

Slohmann, Vilhelm, "The Indian Period of European Furniture," Vol. LXV, No. I, Burlington Magazine, 1934.

Smart, Ellen, "Six Folios from a Dispersed Manuscript of the Baburnama," in Indian Painting. London: Colnaghi, 1978.

Smith, Vincent A., A History of Fine Art in India and Ceylon. Oxford: Clarendon Press, 1930.

Soucek, Priscilla, "Comments on Persian Painting," Iranian Studies, vol. 7, Nos. 1-2, 1974.

Storey, C. A., Persian Literature: A Bio-Bibliographic Survey. 2 vols. London: Luzacs and Co., 1953.

Swietochowski, Marie Lukens, "The Development of Traditions of Book Illustrating in Pre-Safavid Iran," Iranian Studies, Vol. 7, Nos. 1-2, 1974.

The Textile Gallery. London: The Textile Gallery, 1984.

Titley, Norah M., Miniatures from Persian Manuscripts. London: British Library, 1977.

Tusi, Nasir ad-Din, The Nasirean Ethics, tr. G. M. Wickens. London: George Allen and Unwin, 1964.

Tyulyayev, S., Miniatures of Baburnama. Moscow: State Fine Arts Publishing House, 1960.

Walker, Daniel, "Classical Indian Carpets," *Hali,* Vol. IV, No. 3, 1982.

Welch, Anthony, *Calligraphy in the Arts of the Muslim World.* Austin: University of Texas Press, 1979.

_____ and Stuart Cary Welch, *Arts of the Islamic Book: the Collection of Prince Sadruddin Aga Khan.* Ithaca and London: Cornell University Press, 1982.

Welch, Stuart Cary, *A Flower from Every Meadow.* The Asia Society, New York, 1973.

_____, *The Art of Mughal India.* The Asia Society, New York, 1963.

_____, *Imperial Mughal Painting.* New York: George Braziller, 1978.

_____, *Indian Drawings and Painted Sketches.* The Asia Society, New York, 1976.

_____, *Room for Wonder: Indian Painting during the British Period 1760-1880.* New York: The American Federation of the Arts, 1978.

_____, *Wonders of the Age: Masterpieces of Safavid Painting,* Cambridge, Massachusetts: Fogg Art Museum, Harvard University, 1979.

Wilkinson, J. V. S., *The Lights of Canopus.* London: The Studio Limited, 1929.

_____ and Laurence Binyon, *The Shah-Namah of Firdausi: The Book of the Persian Kings.* London: Oxford University Press, 1931.

INDEX

Type set by Finn Typographic Service, Inc., Stamford, Connecticut
Printed and bound by Toppan Printing Company Ltd., Tokyo, Japan
Designed by Peter Oldenburg
Map drawn by Joseph Ascherl